Legacy of Trust

Life After the Sudbury Valley School Experience

Daniel Greenberg
Mimsy Sadofsky

For further information, contact:
Cedarwood Sudbury School
Santa Clara • (408) 296-2072
http://www.webpage.com/scvs

Sudbury Valley School Press
Framingham, MA 01701

CONTENTS

PART V STUDENTS WHO FINISHED THEIR SCHOOLING ELSEWHERE

PART VI CONCLUDING REMARKS

APPENDICES

Foreword

Sudbury Valley School was founded in 1968. From the beginning it was the school's intention to follow as closely as possible the lives of its students after they left the school, especially since such studies have been rare for non-traditional schools.

In 1972 the Trustees authorized the first follow-up study[1], a copy of which can be found in Appendix E. A commentary on this study was published the following year[2] and is reproduced in Appendix F. A second study, contained in Appendix G, was conducted in 1975[3]. Subsequently, in 1981-1982, two members of the school community — both parents of enrolled students, one a Professor of Psychology at Boston College, and the other a staff member at the school — designed and carried out their own survey of Sudbury Valley alumni independently of the school or its

---

1 "Former Students — What Are They Doing Now? (A Trustees' Study)", compiled by Hanna Greenberg, *Sudbury Valley School Newsletter*, Volume 1, Number 9 (June 1972) (Sudbury Valley School Press; Framingham, MA), pp.4-17.

2 "Reflections on the Trustees' Study of Former Students", by Phyllis Toback, *Sudbury Valley School Newsletter*, Volume 3, Number 1 (October 1973) (Sudbury Valley School Press; Framingham, MA), pp.4-11.

3 *A Study of Former Students at Sudbury Valley, Done in 1975*, by Barbara Chase (Sponsored by the Board of Trustees) (Sudbury Valley School Press; Framingham, MA, 1975) 52pp.

sponsorship. The results were published in 1986[4]. Because that survey had been made, the school did not sponsor its own study of alumni during the 1980's. An article derived from that survey was written by one of the authors in 1982[5] and can be found in Appendix H.

In June of 1990, the Sudbury Valley School Assembly authorized the School Meeting to carry out the present study during 1991. The responsibility for the execution of the study and the presentation of its results devolved upon the authors.

---

[4] "Democratic Schooling: What Happens to Young People Who Have Charge of Their Own Education?", by Peter Gray and David Chanoff, *The American Journal of Education*, Volume 94, Number 2 (February 1986) (University of Chicago Press; Chicago), pp.182-213.

[5] "Going to College: Six Former Students", by David Chanoff, *Sudbury Valley School Newsletter*, Volume 11, Number 6 (April 1982) (Sudbury Valley School Press; Framingham, MA), pp.3-12.

Part I

Aims and Methods

1

"An Unfaltering Trust"

This book is about adults who participated, while students, in a remarkable experiment in education.

Sudbury Valley School was founded in 1968 as a place where each student could be trusted fully to make every decision about how to grow from a child into an adult, seeking such advice as he or she wished. In this book we try to determine what the legacy of such trust might be.

The idea of the school starts from Aristotle's observation that human beings are naturally curious. The central tenet of the school's educational philosophy is the belief that if people are allowed to follow their innate instinct to increase their understanding of their environment, the outcome will be a life of intense exploration and growth. At Sudbury Valley it is assumed that each student constantly alters, renews, and adds to his or her model of the world, and each student is trusted to construct a unique world view through the interplay of inborn curiosity and experience. The school maintains that this will lead to minds that are developed as fully as possible, to human beings who function in harmony with their own selves and the world around them. The gift of complete trust is expected to create adults who feel in control of their own lives; adults who have a high level of trust in themselves.

At Sudbury Valley, trust implies responsibility. Each student entering the school becomes totally responsible for all decisions relating to their own education, their own expenditure of time and effort, and also for all decisions that have community impact. The school is a functioning participatory democracy, similar to many towns in New England, where it is located. Thus, the trust placed in each student includes the conviction that the group of people composing the school community can, and will, assume the full responsibility for managing and governing itself.

What does all this mean in practice? It means a school with a student body that has grown from about 60 in 1968 to 125 students in 1991. These students attend school in a large nineteenth century granite house set on nine beautiful wooded acres, in suburban Framingham, twenty miles from Boston. Included in the school community are staff members, whose main function is to serve as role models for the students by pursuing various interests, and to make themselves available to everyone in the school.

Students range in age from as young as four to over twenty. They freely choose where to be, who to be with, and what to do, and are completely free to change their choices as many times as it occurs to them to do so during a day, a week, a month, or a year. Movement is free in the school, both outdoors and indoors, and groups form and reform spontaneously many times each day. The rooms are furnished much like family rooms in houses, and the activities range from playing with building blocks to exploring architectural design, from trading secrets to trading baseball cards, from reading the classic philosophers to building chain mail armor. Few activities that one might expect to see in a school are absent, but these represent only a small number of the myriad activities that are engaged in each day. Sometimes students are outdoors building snowmen — six year olds learning from sixteen years olds. Sometimes they are learning to climb the enormous beech tree — sixteen year olds learning from ten year olds. Sometimes several are fishing peacefully. Sometimes they are in the School Meeting — people from four to sixty making decisions relating to the management of the school, people of all ages struggling together to solve problems. No one ever stops to ask them if they are spending their time wisely. It is exciting to talk to any child in the school, seven or seventeen years old, and find that they are grappling with substantial issues, well and happily, in an atmosphere steeped in support, trust and tolerance. Tolerance for 125 different world views; 125 individual ways of thinking about everything.

We invite you to enter this book and discover what has become of people who have gone to school at Sudbury Valley.[1]

---

[1] Appendix J contains an extensive list of publications and other materials describing in detail the various aspects of the school's educational philosophy and daily operation.

2

Why This Study Was Made

It would seem perfectly natural for a school to investigate the fate of its former students, to find out what has been going on in the lives of people who were acquaintances or friends for several years. Indeed, many schools, especially those incorporating students in their teens or older, make some attempt — usually through an alumni office — to keep track of their graduates. Sudbury Valley School too sends out questionnaires every year to keep updated on its former students. There are usually fifty to seventy-five responses of varying length. The answers are circulated in a newsletter issued annually, which serves the purpose of generally keeping in touch.

There is, however, more than curiosity at work in launching an organized investigation into the lives of former students. The school — or any other person launching such a survey — is looking for something specific that makes the enormous expense and effort worthwhile. What this "something" is turns out to be more difficult to define than one might expect at first glance.

The obvious question any person interested in education would like to have answered is simply this: Is Sudbury Valley School a good school? Implicit in this question are several others: Is it as good as, better than, or worse than other schools today? Is it good for some people and not for others? Does it have serious handicaps? Do its benefits outweigh its handicaps? Any school would like to know the answers to these questions for itself. A school like Sudbury Valley, based on principles that are radical departures from those that underlie the prevailing educational models, is more motivated than most schools to have answers available.

The problem is that in the current state of development of social theory, it is quite impossible for *any* school to come up with convincing replies to these questions. The chief obstacle is the existence of a huge multiplicity of factors that affect the lives of every individual as he/she grows up, and contributes to the unfolding of his/her life. Genetic factors, economic class factors, parental influences, family influences, community influences (in the broadest sense of the term), personal character traits determined by individual mental and psychological variations, political and socio-economic factors in the external environment — these and other factors all affect the growing child, in addition to the influence of the school.

Moreover, there is no general agreement on how to assess, characterize, or measure the traits of an adult, at any given time in his/her life. There is no universally accepted catalog of human character traits, and there is certainly no consensus on how to determine whether or not a person has this or that defined trait. Furthermore, people change as they grow older; there is no time at which a person becomes a "finished product" as an adult.

It is therefore clear that any study, of any school, must perforce consist of a series of impressions, based on tentative hypotheses that can never be verified or disproved, but only be given varying degrees of support. This study is no exception.

What, then, was the point of this investigation?

There were, in fact, several levels on which we operated. The first, and simplest, was the following. We are constantly besieged by people seeking, for their own reasons, to know what becomes of our students. For example, many parents who consider enrolling their children feel somehow that seeing the school in operation, and understanding (and even approving of) its underlying philosophy, is not quite enough. They want to be reassured that others who have taken the plunge before them have not paid dearly for that decision. Somehow, seeing what has become of others who attended Sudbury Valley reassures them (or, in some cases, helps them decide to stay away), even though there are no real grounds for relating the life outcomes of former students to the anticipated life outcomes of present or future students. So this study answers questions like, "I am thinking of sending my four year old child, and I realize that once I start, I am basically making a commitment for the child's entire schooling. What has become of former students who went to Sudbury Valley for all of their schooling?" And questions like, "My child is fifteen. For her/him, the Sudbury Valley environment is a radical departure from every form of schooling that came before. What has happened to others who came to Sudbury Valley at the age of fifteen in the past?" These, and similar questions, can now be answered with some confidence, based on a fair-sized sample; whereas, prior to this study, the school could provide at best only anecdotal responses.

Another goal of this study is to provide a starting point for examining some expectations we have had about the influence a Sudbury Valley education may have on students who experience it for varying lengths of time, at different parts of their lives. For despite all the disclaimers about the impossibilities of drawing any firm conclusions about a school's influence on a person's future life, we feel that the very strong messages we seek to convey in our school have some likelihood of affecting the students at whom the messages have been directed.

By examining the lives of our former students — especially if we are careful to distinguish among groups of students who spent different amounts of time at the school, and experienced it at different ages — we expect that some patterns will emerge, however faintly, to suggest that the Sudbury Valley School experience does indeed make a difference. We realized from the outset that we would have to be cautious and circumspect about drawing conclusions from the limited data available, and from the virtually nonexistent theoretical framework to analyze the data; but we felt that nevertheless a few trends would become noticeable above the "background noise". As it turned out, we were not disappointed in this expectation. We think that dispassionate readers of this study will, by the time they have finished looking at it carefully, concur that something worthy of note goes on in the school that does indeed make a difference in the way students go out into the world.[1]

The limited goals of this study, as just enumerated, defined in turn some limitations on our selection of former students to be the subjects of the study. Most importantly, we decided from the outset not to include students

---

[1] The earlier studies reached similar conclusions; see Appendices E - H. Compare also the remarks of Gray and Chanoff (*loc. cit.*, p. 208) a decade earlier than this study: "In [our] report we have outlined the experiences of a group of young adults who graduated from a school where no school work was required and little (at least of the traditional sort) was done and where curricula, academic requirements, tests, and grades did not exist. Our principal conclusion is that these people, including both those who started the school early in their primary years and those who started in their secondary years, have not suffered as a result of attending such a school. They have gone on to good colleges and good jobs. They have become, or are clearly en route to becoming, productive members of our society, contributing to the economy in nearly the entire range of ways that people can contribute. They are taking responsible positions in business, music and art, science and technology, social services, skilled crafts and academia. . . . The implications regarding our ability to structure effective educational institutions that accord with our society's socio-political ideals are too significant to dismiss. . . ."

who attended school for less than one year, or whose attendance was so sporadic that they never really experienced the school. Nor did we expend much energy in tracking down students who attended for one year, although we did include those we could readily find. This is not to intimate that the school had no value for such students, or exerted no influence on their future lives. In fact, over the years we have encountered repeated instances where students who have had even the briefest encounter with the school have declared that it affected them profoundly and changed the course of their lives. But we nevertheless felt that it was beyond the normally accepted bounds of credibility to assert, as a matter of course, that a brief period of enrollment could have long-lasting effects.

Other persons who had attended the school were also excluded from the study, for similar reasons. Thus, people who enrolled as adults — and we have had more than a few over the years — were not made part of the study, because we felt we could not justify any claims with regard to a group of people who spent all their formative years in traditional schools; this, again, despite much anecdotal evidence that adults exposed to the school frequently came away transformed. Nor did we include people who left school before the age of nine, no matter how many years they attended, because it seemed to us to require more evidence than we could muster to support the thesis that people who had spent virtually their entire mature school lives in traditional schools had received something of lasting value from Sudbury Valley during their early childhood here — something that all their later school experiences did not undo or, more important, did not actually produce, no thanks to Sudbury Valley.

Finally, in order to limit ourselves to former students who had at least some significant life experience after leaving Sudbury Valley, we left for future studies those who were under the age of twenty at the time we began our survey (January 1, 1991) or those who had left school during the two years before that date.

We thus embarked on this study in order, hopefully, to assuage some of the anxieties of educators, observers, and prospective parents, about expected outcomes for children who enroll in Sudbury Valley School; and also to see if we could uncover for ourselves some evidence for the types of outcomes we had anticipated when we first set up a school based on our peculiar combination of principles.

3

A Description of the Study

Our questionnaire was designed with the intention of focussing on the specific areas that were of concern to us. In addition to the usual demographic data, we were looking for information on the work engaged in by our former students after they left Sudbury Valley School, their further formal education, and other information that might give insight into the way the respondents conducted their lives. In all of our questions we sought factual information which could not be colored by the attitudes of the interviewers. In designing this study, we carefully avoided questions that dealt with the opinions, character traits or beliefs of the respondents. Such material, undoubtedly of interest, will have to be left to studies conducted by persons not associated in any way with the school community.

Because of this carefully delimited scope, we feel that the compiled data presented in this book gives, in those areas which were investigated, a valid picture of the lives of our former students who are respondents, a picture in no way dependent on the fact that this study was sponsored by the school.

In the course of the interviews, the respondents frequently offered comments about their lives or about the school, and the interviewers at times recorded these comments. As it happens, the overwhelming majority of these spontaneous comments were positive. We have no way of knowing how much this had to do with the fact that they were talking to a representative of the school. Perhaps the respondents simply chose to be upbeat, out of politeness or out of a desire to present themselves as favorably as possible. On the other hand, perhaps they had very little negative to say. We have interspersed samplings of these comments throughout the chapters in Parts II through V.

Appendix A contains a copy of the questionnaire, and the cover letter giving specific instructions to the interviewers in addition to the oral instructions given.

The interviews were conducted mostly by telephone, though a few were done in person and a few through written responses.[1] It was not possible to generate uniformly complete answers to all of the questions. Partly this was due to the large number and uneven preparation of the interviewers, which made it impossible to have each interview conducted in the same manner, and partly it was due to the enormous variation in the willingness and the availability of the interviewees to spend the time and take the pains to provide detailed answers to all the questions. As a result, in many instances some questions were not answered at all, others were answered partially, and often the answers were not fully recorded. Despite these limitations, we felt the material available was rich enough in detail to present a textured picture of the answers to the study's fundamental questions.

In developing a database for this study, we started with a complete list of every person now alive who had ever enrolled at Sudbury Valley School from its inception.

In order for the study to fulfill its declared aims, as discussed in Chapter 2, we introduced a succession of filters to remove the following sets of students from the complete list:

— All those who were enrolled for less than one school year, or who attended so sporadically during their period of enrollment that they never achieved a continuous experience of the school.

— All those whose enrollments ended before they were nine years old.

— All those who were under the age of twenty on January 1, 1991.

— All those who left school after December 31, 1988.

— All those who were over the age of twenty-one when they first enrolled at the school.

In addition, we had to remove a total of twenty-seven people who, because of their personal situation or because of their former relationship with

---

[1] The people who conducted these interviews were: Jeannine Bouffard, Barbara Chase, Katy Doherty, Carol Draper, Denise Geddes, Susan Gilmartin, Daniel Greenberg, Hanna Greenberg, Jeremiah Griswold, Martha Hurwitz, Debra McDonald, Antoinette Matisoo, Melissa Ponte, Jennifer Purves, Joan Rubin, and Mimsy Sadofsky.

the school, were inaccessible to anybody conducting a survey from within the school community, sponsored by the school.

> *The study was thus limited to former students who were accessible to us and who met the following criteria: they left school after the age of nine; they first enrolled under the age of twenty-one; they were, while enrolled, in continuous contact with the school for at least one year; they were over the age of twenty on January 1, 1991; and they had been out of school at least two years on January 1, 1991.*

We began with a total of 237 people who fell within the parameters of the study and constituted the database for the study. Of these, 188 (79%) provided the responses that were used in this study. Appendix B provides a listing of some key information about the respondents.

The total database was then divided into three major groups. The first group consisted of students who attended Sudbury Valley for virtually their entire school lives. The members of this group were defined as those who entered the school before they were ten years old and stayed until they had reached a level of maturity that made them feel ready to move on to a post high school environment. This group is focussed on in Part II of this book.

The second group consisted of students who left school at an age when they were ready to move on to a post high school environment, but had not spent virtually their entire school lives at Sudbury Valley. Because of the way we defined the first group, all members of this group must have entered SVS at age ten or later. This group is focussed on in Part III and Part IV of this book.

This second group was divided into four sub-groups defined according to the length of their stay at the school. The defined sub-groups were:

(1) students who attended for five or more years;
(2) students who attended for three or four years;
(3) students who attended for two years;
(4) students who attended for only one year.

The third group consisted of students who left school before they were ready to move on to a post high school environment, and continued their schooling at some public or private elementary school, middle school, or high school, or the equivalent. This group is focussed on in Part V of this book.

In the third group, two sub-groups were defined:

(1) students who attended Sudbury Valley more than one year;
(2) students who attended Sudbury Valley for only one year.

In assigning students to sub-groups, we had to exercise a certain degree of judgment. Variations in enrollment of a few months in duration were often ignored. For example, a student who enrolled in November of one year, reenrolled the next November, and stayed through June was considered to have spent two years in school; while a student who enrolled in April and stayed through the following June was considered to have spent one year at school.

It was also necessary to exercise some degree of judgment in the amount of effort to be expended to reach people in various sub-groups. We were willing to extend ourselves to a greater degree to reach students who had spent several years here than we were to obtain responses from students who spent only one year at school.

Table 3.1 summarizes the sizes and response rates for the various groups and sub-groups defined.

We would like to mention the possibility that there is a slight skewing of all the material collected in the study. It is theoretically conceivable that the twenty-seven people who are inaccessible to internally conducted studies, and/or the forty-nine people whom we were unable to contact, constitute a group whose demographic profile differs from that of the respondents included in the study. From our personal knowledge of the people involved, we do not believe this to be the case; but until these people can be included in a future study, we cannot be sure. This cautionary remark notwithstanding, we are comfortable in presenting as valid the data collected from a large group of former students who represent such a large proportion of the total pool.

The raw data gathered from the interviews was entered into a computer database designed to include as much of the information as possible. The conversational comments were entered into a separate database. The structures of both databases are presented in Appendix C.

The analysis of these databases constitutes the heart of this study and is the basis for the material which is presented in the following chapters.

Table 3.1

Sizes and Response Rates for Data Sub-Divisions

Group	Sub-Group	No. in Group	No. in Sub-Gp	Number Responses in Group	Number Responses in Sub-Gp	Percent Response
Entire school lives at Sudbury Valley		27		27		100%
Left SVS at end of high school age years		162		136		84%
	Attended five years or more		22		21	95%
	Attended three or four years		53		50	94%
	Attended two years		48		41	85%
	Attended one year		39		24	62%
Left SVS before end of high school age years		48		25		52%
	Attended two or more years		22		17	77%
	Attended one year		26		8	31%
TOTALS		237		188		79%

Part II

"SVS Kids"

4

Students Who Spent Virtually All Their School Years at Sudbury Valley

There is a group of students who can be said to be uniquely products of the Sudbury Valley School experience. For them Sudbury Valley was essentially the only school they attended during the typical school age years. This group contains all those who enrolled at Sudbury Valley before they were ten years old and who attended continuously until they had reached a level of maturity consonant with moving on to a post high school environment. Their histories can be expected to reflect the effect that exposure to the Sudbury Valley environment might have on students who spend virtually all of their formative years at the school. There are twenty seven people in this group, of whom fifteen are males, and twelve are females. All responded to our survey.

All but one of this group received SVS diplomas. The only one not to receive a diploma left before he was 15 years of age to pursue a career as a professional ballet dancer, and continued his general education by taking college courses.

Basic Demographics

— How old are they now?

The distribution of this group by age on January 1, 1991 is shown in Figure 4.1. At the time of the study this was still a very young group, as makes sense for an institution that was begun in 1968. The oldest members of this group were almost thirty-two years old, the youngest just over twenty; the average was twenty-seven; and the median age was twenty-six.

Figure 4.1

Distribution by Age, January 1, 1991

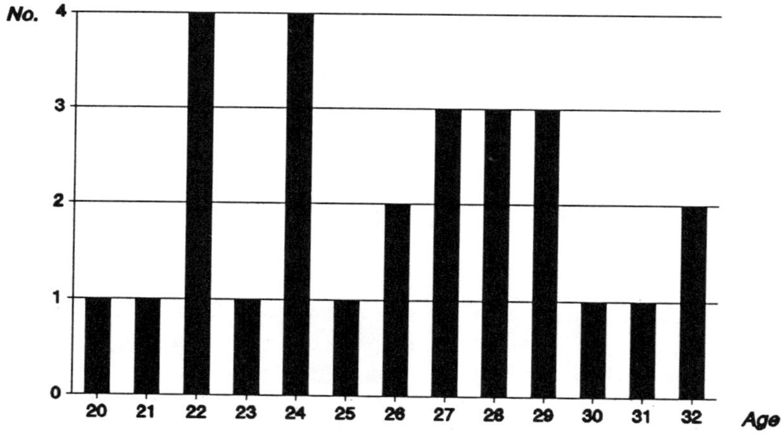

— Their marital status

Seventeen (63%) of the twenty-seven people were single, six (22%) were married, and four (15%) were living with significant others. Only six (22%) members of the group were either married or cohabiting for more than three years. Only one person has children, a single child aged two. This data is consistent with the general tendency of the educated population in this country to marry at an increasingly older age and to postpone childbearing.

—— Where do they live?

Table 4.1 shows where these people live. Fifteen of these former students reside in Massachusetts, thirteen (48%) in the Greater Boston area from which the school draws its population. Two live outside the United States, and the others are scattered around the country.

Table 4.1

Current Geographical Distribution of the Group

No.	*Town*	*State*
1	San Francisco	California
1	Chicago	Illinois
1	Boston	Massachusetts
1	Cambridge	Massachusetts
3	Framingham	Massachusetts
3	Marlboro	Massachusetts
1	Natick	Massachusetts
1	Southboro	Massachusetts
1	Southwick	Massachusetts
1	Sudbury	Massachusetts
1	West Springfield	Massachusetts
1	Waltham	Massachusetts
1	West Newton	Massachusetts
1	Baltimore	Maryland
1	Duluth	Minnesota
1	St. Paul	Minnesota
1	Annan-Hudson	New York
1	New York	New York
1	Pittsburgh	Pennsylvania
1	Eatonville	Washington
1	Seattle	Washington
1	Vancouver, BC	Canada
1	London	England

— How old were they when they enrolled?

Figure 4.2 shows the ages at which these people entered the school. Members of this group came to Sudbury Valley between the ages of four and nine, at an average age of six.

Figure 4.2

Distribution by Age of Entry

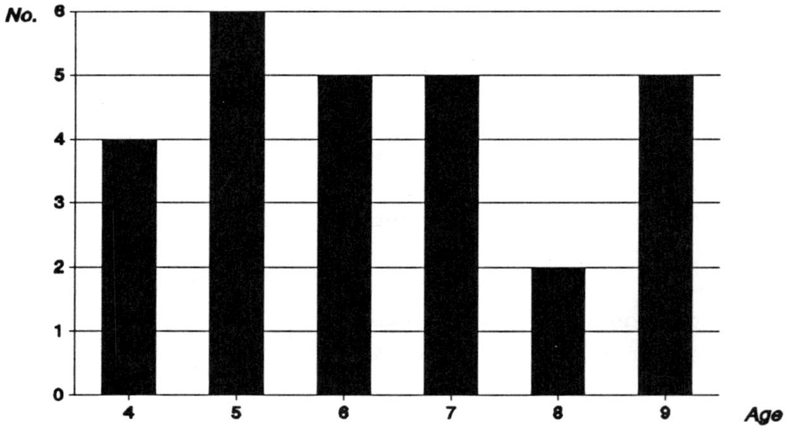

— What was their prior schooling?

Ten of the twelve students who entered Sudbury Valley later than the age of six-and-a-half had previously attended an elementary school elsewhere — eight public, two private. One other member of the group came to SVS for a short period, attended public school, and then returned at the age of seven. *The other sixteen (59%) had no school experience other than SVS.* Even a short exposure to a more traditional school has some impact on a child's subsequent educational development; still, data about this group can nevertheless be seen as fairly representing the result of a long term commitment solely to Sudbury Valley.

— How long did they remain at Sudbury Valley?

Figure 4.3 shows the number of years that people in this group spent at the school.[1] The bulk of the group remained at SVS from nine to fourteen years with an average enrollment period of twelve years. One person stayed only seven years (the one who entered at the oldest age, nine and a half, and graduated at the earliest age, sixteen); and one stayed for fifteen years.

Figure 4.3

Distribution of Length of Stay at the School

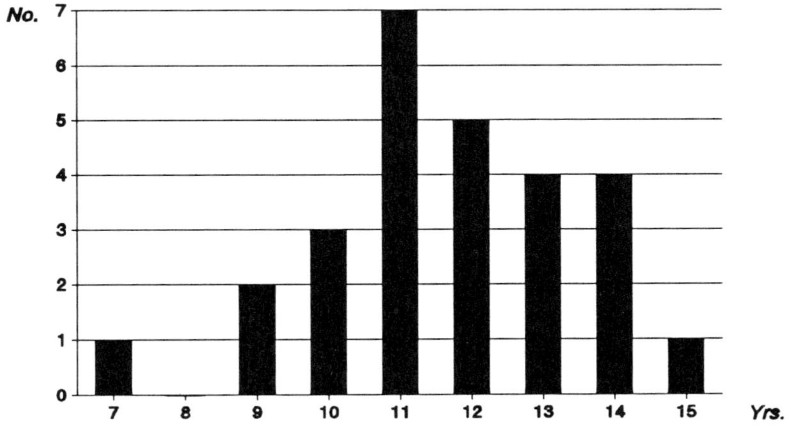

— How old were they when they left school?

Figure 4.4 shows the ages at which the members of this group left the school. The one person who left without a diploma left at about fifteen,

---

[1] We count only years actually enrolled in the school. For students who left Sudbury Valley for a time and subsequently returned, the time spent away from Sudbury Valley is not included in the calculation of the length of stay at school.

while all the others left between sixteen and twenty. Eighteen was the average age of leaving. In general, these students were not in a hurry to leave school, as can be seen from the significant number who remained until age nineteen or twenty. Altogether Figures 4.2, 4.3, and 4.4 reveal a profile of a group of people who started young, stayed a long time, and left on the brink of adulthood.

Figure 4.4

Distribution by Age at Leaving

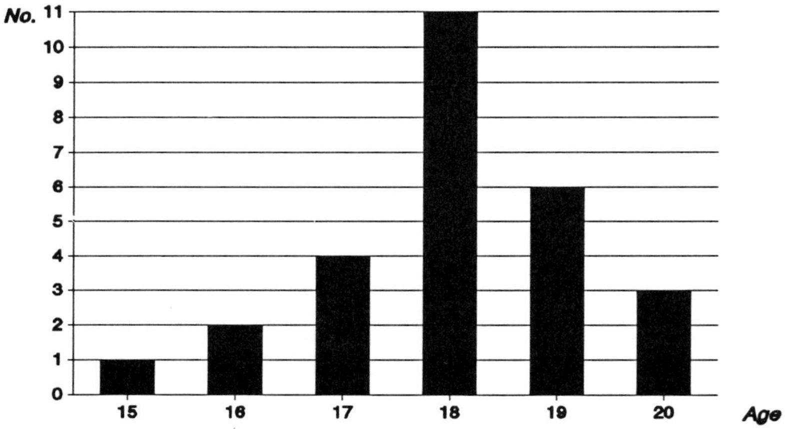

—— Where did they live?

Table 4.2 shows the geographical distribution of this population at the time that they became students here. While most of the families that made long term commitments to the school came from towns in the immediate vicinity of the school, several came from farther afield, in particular two from Chelmsford and one from Randolph, both of which are about an hour's commute each way. Southboro, Marlboro, and Sudbury border on Framingham, and Holliston and Newton are about one-half hour away.

Table 4.2

Geographical Distribution While in School

No.	*Town*
2	Chelmsford
6	Framingham
3	Holliston
3	Marlboro
4	Newton
1	Randolph
2	Southboro
6	Sudbury

Occupations

—— What are they doing now?

Because these are still young adults, it is obviously not yet possible to know what their long term careers will be. However, when we examine the range of occupations that this group is presently engaged in, we find an extraordinarily rich variety of pursuits. These are summarized by general categories in Table 4.3. Note that the number of people in the various categories in Table 4.3 add up to a number greater than twenty-seven. This is because several people have more than one occupation and fall into more than one category.

Occupations marked with an asterisk in Table 4.3 denote either entrepreneurial or self-employed situations. All the people who are in business for themselves are, by definition, business-people. Their "Business Management" role is noted only by the asterisk.

Table 4.3

Present Occupations (Arranged by Categories of Occupation)

Category	*Number in Category*	*Specific Occupations*
Business Management	5	supermarket department manager (2) retail manager (2) technical supervisor, copy machine co.
Office Manager/ Executive Assistant	3	hospital unit clerk program coordinator, art theater museum archive worker
High Tech	2	computer software tester *volumetric equipment calibration and reconditioning
Professional	3	accountant, Big Six firm social worker, rehabilitation clinic treatment social worker with families of abused children
Research & Development	1	advanced technology laboratory manager
Education	4	professor of mathematics home schooling assistant aerobics teacher resident assistant in college dormitory
Law Enforcement	1	probation officer
Trades	2	*house renovator *custom color photograph processor
Design	2	*clothing designer *commercial graphic artist
Creative Arts	5	*art photographer glass blower *artist screenplay writer *quilter songwriter (2)

Category	*Number in Category*	*Specific Occupations*
Performing Arts	4	*musician in group (3) ballet dancer
Unskilled Labor	3	art museum guard office clerk waitperson
Student	8	art history choreography fashion design art criminal justice international studies environmental studies English literature

Table 4.4 lists the occupations in which each member of this group is currently engaged. The list is in ascending order of age. There is no predominance of any category of work in either the younger or the older part of the group. No one over twenty-five is engaged in an unskilled job. On the other hand, four people over the age of twenty-five are continuing with formal studies in their fields of interest.

Table 4.4

Present Occupations (Arranged in Order of Age)

Age	*Present Occupation*
20	supermarket department manager
21	English literature student
22	art museum guard
22	home schooling assistant
22	international studies student; college resident assistant
22	supermarket department manager
23	accountant, Big Six firm
24	aerobics teacher; waitperson

Age	Present Occupation
24	computer software tester
24	criminal justice student; probation officer
24	environmental studies student
25	musician; clerk in legal services company
26	ballet dancer
26	fashion design student; chain clothing store manager
27	technical supervisor, copy machine service company
27	social worker in a rehabilitation clinic
27	program coordinator in an art theater
28	hospital unit clerk; glass blower
28	choreography student; clothing designer; screenplay writer
28	art history student; museum archive worker
29	musician; songwriter; music store manager
29	advanced technology laboratory manager; volumetric equipment calibration and reconditioning
29	custom color photolab; musician; art photographer; songwriter
30	professor of mathematics
31	quilter; artist; house renovator
32	art student; commercial graphic artist
32	treatment social worker with families of abused children

—— Range of Occupations

The current occupations are only a part of the total panoply of occupations engaged in by these students after they left the school. In Table 4.5 we present as complete a list as we have available of what these pursuits have been. (Note that the occupations listed in Table 4.3 are included in the more extensive Table 4.5.)

Occupations marked with an asterisk in Table 4.5 denote either entrepreneurial or self-employed situations. Again, the number of people in the various categories in Table 4.5 add up to a number greater than twenty-seven. This is because several people have more than one occupation and fall into more than one category. The category of "student" shown in Table 4.3 has been dropped in Table 4.5 since a subsequent section will take up in greater detail the education pursued by the members of this group.

Table 4.5

Occupations Engaged in Since Leaving Sudbury Valley (Arranged by Categories of Occupation)

Category	Number in Category	Specific Occupations
Business Management	8	supermarket department manager (3) retail manager (5) technical supervisor, copy machine co.
Office Manager/ Executive Assistant	8	hospital unit clerk program coordinator, art theater museum archive worker legal secretary theater manager (2) research assistant administrative assistant office manager (2)
High Tech	8	computer software tester *volumetric equipment calibration and reconditioning computer technician a.v. technician computer lab assistant computer programmer (3)
Professional	3	accountant, Big Six firm social worker, rehabilitation clinic treatment social worker with families of abused children
Research & Development	2	advanced technology laboratory manager biology lab assistant mathematical topology research
Education	6	professor of mathematics home schooling assistant aerobics teacher resident assistant in college dorm (2) ESL teacher college math teaching assistant
Law Enforcement	1	probation officer

Category	Number in Category	Specific Occupations
Trades	10	*house renovator *custom color photograph processor book restorer copier technician auto stereo installer professional pastry chef professional chef desktop publisher truck driver photographic technician vending machine maintenance bartender (2) assistant trainer, dressage construction worker
Design	4	*clothing designer *commercial graphic artist window display costume assistant
Creative Arts	5	*art photographer glass blower *artist screenplay writer *quilter songwriter (2)
Performing Arts	5	*musician in group (3) ballet dancer (2)
Unskilled Labor	20	art museum guard waitperson (4) housepainter (2) grocery clerk (3) retail cerk (7) office clerk (3) camp counselor research analyst (2) bank teller library clerk (2) telephone moderator intern with state rep

Category	Number in Category	Specific Occupations
Unskilled Labor *(cont'd)*		environmental research intern
		marine research intern
		telephone canvasser
		shipping clerk
		data entry (2)
		factory worker
		warehouse worker
		cleaning crew supervisor
		messenger (2)

It might be interesting to note that twenty-five out of the twenty-seven members of this group (93%) held jobs while they were students at Sudbury Valley. One had an internship as a photographer's assistant. The others had the normal types of jobs that high school students hold: nine worked in grocery stores, ten were retail clerks, four were office workers, four were waitpersons, two were veterinary assistants, one was a factory worker, one was a handyman, one was a security guard, one was a janitor, and one worked in a library.

— Where have they worked?

Table 4.6 lists some of the companies and institutions where the former students in this group have been employed or are currently employed. The Table is arranged by job category. We have included it to give some idea of the variety of work environments these people have chosen. The list is not comprehensive nor does it list companies where people were employed at unskilled labor.

Table 4.6

Places of Work
(Arranged by Categories of Occupation)

Category	*Company or Institution*
Business Management	Boston Copy Co.
	Pennsylvania Company
	Sudbury Farms
	East Coast Music
	LaSalle Music
	Benetton
Office Manager/ Executive Assistant	Ronald Lauder Foundation
	Maynard Fine Arts Theater
	San Francisco Cinematheque
	Gemini
	Peabody Museum
High Tech	Kodak
	MITRE
	Hampshire College Academic Computer Center
Professional	Coopers & Lybrand
	New York City Educational Alliance
	Mt. Sinai Hospital
	Rusk Institute for Rehabilitation
	Massachusetts Department of Social Services
Research & Development	Integrated Genetics
	A.R.E.S.
Education	Johns Hopkins University
	Northwestern University
	Sudbury Fitness Center
	Anita Roberts
	Massachusetts Institute of Technology
	University of Rochester
	Clonlara West
Law Enforcement	Metropolitan Day Reporting Center

Category	*Company or Institution*
Trades	Darkstar Laboratories Chase Vending Machines Avalon Data Systems Auto Stereo Place Framingham Copy Dunn Copy
Design	Smith College Light Opera Ingals, Quinn, Johnson Ad Agency
Performing Arts	Dancers Stage of San Francisco San Francisco Ballet Pacific Northwest Ballet Berkshire Ballet Pittsburgh Ballet Rain Maestro Subgum and the Whole

— Personal comments on employment

In the course of the interviews some people made casual remarks that offered glimpses into their relationship to their work. A recurring theme was the fulfillment that their work gave them. Here are some of their comments:

> *Working as a veterinary assistant, and dancing professionally, have both been very satisfying. In the first case, because I love animals, and in the second case because the physical demands are great, and the people in the creative arts are mavericks who enjoy creative input.*
>
> *Counseling people in crisis gives me satisfaction.*
>
> *I enjoy work that is important to the environment.*
>
> *I enjoy the flexibility and freedom of working for myself, as well as the discipline and focus required by creative endeavors.*
>
> *In all my work, the situations that have given me satisfaction are those in which there has been an opportunity to*

learn and to have freedom to pursue projects which allow me to express my personal relationship with the material I am working with at the time.

I am very happy with my job.

I love teaching aerobics because I like performing, being healthy, having energy, and being with people.

I am very happy with my work and family.

I like being self-employed for the flexibility and control it gives me.

Doing research is incredibly rewarding. It is collegial, and there is often a lot of excitement among the people involved.

Other aspects of work were also commented on. One person noted that "I define myself by my work; I am a craftsman and personally committed to the quality of my product." In the same vein, another remarked: "I like to be looked upon as knowledgeable in my field." One person noted, wryly, "I accomplished my goal of getting into the business world, but now I wonder if I really want it"; to which he immediately added, "I am generally happy with what I am doing."

Further Formal Education

— Where did they continue their schooling?

Out of the twenty-seven members of this group, twenty-five (93%) have, at some time or another, attended formal classes in order to further their education. Fourteen (52%) of the twenty-seven completed the requirements for one or more degrees. Table 4.7 lists the schools attended after Sudbury Valley for which we have information; however our list of these institutions is incomplete. Schools marked with an asterisk are those from which degrees were received.

Table 4.7

Schools Attended After S.V.S.

Type of School	*Number Attending*	*Number Completing Degrees*	*Names of Schools*
art schools	4	n/a	San Francisco Ballet School Royal Winnipeg Ballet School Andrighetti Glass Works Boston Museum School
trade schools	3	n/a	Aerobic Fitness of America Keefe Tech Executive Secretarial College
community college	1	0	Mass Bay Community College
college	24	AA (1) BS (2) BA (11)	*American College in London Amherst College *Babson College *Bard College Bemidji College *Boston College *Boston University Brandeis University City of London Polytechnic Institute Clark University *Colorado Institute of Art Eastman School of Music Framingham State College *Hampshire College Harvard University Extension Holyoke College Institute of European Studies *Macalester College Marist College Mass College of Art New England Conservatory *Northeastern University

Type of School	*Number Attending*	*Number Completing Degrees*	*Names of Schools*
college *(cont'd)*			Oberlin College Roger Williams College Rutgers University San Francisco Art Institute *Smith College Sorbonne University Southeastern Mass University University of Lowell University of Massachusetts, Amherst *University of Rochester *University of Victoria, British Columbia University of Washington *University of Wisconsin Vassar College *Wesleyan University
graduate school	3	MSW (2) PhD (1)	*Columbia University *University of Connecticutt *Massachusetts Institute of Technology Cambridge University

— Education vs. occupation

Next we examine the relationship between what the members of this group chose to study in their further formal education, and what they chose to do as occupations. Again we were hampered by the overall youthfulness of the group. Many of them had not fully completed their education, or were planning further education, and many of them were still developing and evolving in their chosen occupations. Nevertheless we thought it would be interesting to study the connection between formal study and work with the data now available. We did not include in the Table the nine members who either were primarily students or had not pursued any further formal education in a serious manner. Table 4.8 summarizes the material available for the eighteen former students remaining in the sample. The table is arranged by ascending order of age.

One phenomenon that becomes apparent from Table 4.8 is that formal education seems to play two very separate roles in the lives of these people. First, as might be expected, they use school as a vocational training institution to prepare them for a career, usually one in which some certification is needed. In addition, many of them seem to delight in pursuing some academic interest totally unrelated to their occupations simply for the pleasure of indulging their curiosity.

Table 4.8

Relationship of Formal Education to Occupation

Age	*Type of School*	*Degrees*	*Area of Study Concentration*	*Most Recent Occupation*
22	college		English literature, American history	art museum guard
22	college, art school		fine arts	home schooling assistant
23	college	BS	accounting	accountant, Big Six firm
24	college, trade school, adult ed		voice, aerobics	aerobics teacher, waitress
24	college		electronic music, computer science	computer software tester
25	college	BA	American history, music	musician, clerk in legal office
26	college, art school		dance	ballet dancer
27	community college, trade school		liberal arts, electronics	technical supervisor in a copy machine service co.
27	college, graduate school	BA, MSW	religion, social work	social worker in a rehabilitation clinic
27	college		reproductive media (film, tape, photo)	program coordinator in an art theater

Age	*Type of School*	*Degrees*	*Area of Study Concentration*	*Most Recent Occupation*
28	college, trade school, art school	BA	Japanese, anthropology	hospital unit clerk, glass blower
28	college, art school		dance	clothing design, screenplay writer, choreography student
29	college		biology, business	advanced technology lab manager
29	college		music	entrepreneur of custom photo lab, jazz musician, photographer, song writer
30	college, graduate school	BA, PhD	music, mathematics	professor of mathematics
31	college	BA	art	quilter, artist, house renovator
32	college, adult ed.	AA	art, advertising design	commercial graphic artist, art student
32	college, graduate school	BA, MSW	psychology, social work	treatment social worker with families of abused children

— Personal comments on education

Some of the remarks offered by the interviewees bore on their education. One person said, "I had a hard time parroting back what the professors wanted me to learn, but I usually learned what I thought was important in my courses." Another said, of her college education, "I was interested in learning, not grade oriented" — although she was on the Dean's List for most of her college career! A frequent theme was reflected in this comment: "Sudbury Valley taught me to be independent and helped me understand how much I love learning."

A common observation was: "I found myself academically more serious than most freshmen when I entered college. I had a focus and could apply myself more easily." Another person said: "I discovered in college that other students had a much harder time adjusting. I had initiative and discipline." And a third said, "I did well in college because I was not burned out like other students. My enthusiasm helped me through my difficulties."

None of the students expressed any difficulty getting into college. One "got into art school via my portfolio." Another summed up her attitude towards college this way: "Sudbury Valley allowed me to approach college with a fresh outlook. I brought a 'consumer attitude' to college, and I expected to get a high level of academic experience."

When asked whether they had any future plans for continuing additional formal education, seven out of the ten people who hold bachelor's degrees reported that they were planning to seek graduate degrees. One of those who had obtained a Master's Degree indicated plans to study for a PhD. In addition, three people who had taken college courses planned to complete work for a college degree. Six other members in this group indicated a more general interest in continuing higher education in areas of their special interest. Thus, a total of seventeen people (63%), were planning to continue their formal education in some manner.

Travel

One of the things that seems to stand out in this group of former students is an extraordinary interest in travel. For a great many of them, regardless of their incomes, travel has been an important way to stretch their horizons, and they have become a remarkably cosmopolitan group. As one person put it, "Travel provided me with the bulk of my educational experiences outside of Sudbury Valley. It gave me a 'classical education.' I spent a lot of time exploring museums, looking at great art, and doing freelance photography." Another commented, "Travel has changed my life, and I intend to continue to keep traveling. Seeing and experiencing foreign cultures sparked an interest in me to study foreign languages and cultures, which I continue to be interested in as a hobby."

Table 4.9 lists some of the areas visited by these students. It is organized by age, and is based on incomplete information. Those who have not traveled, or for whom no information is available (a total of four) are not included.

Table 4.9

Travel Experiences

Age	*Places Visited*
20	Greece
21	England
22	Ireland, Scotland, England, France, Netherlands, Germany, Austria, Italy, Luxembourg
22	Finland, European continent, cross-country USA
22	Spain, Morocco, Italy, Germany, Canada, Mexico, extensively in the USA
22	Greece
23	England, Netherlands, Scotland, Switzerland, USA
24	Extensively in USA, Canada
24	Korea, France, Italy, Germany, England, Belgium
24	Australia, Brazil, Argentina, Thailand, England, Continental Europe
26	South America, Continental Europe, Canada, throughout USA
26	France, England, Italy, Germany, Switzerland, Belgium, Florida
27	Continental Europe, Israel, Caribbean, extensively in USA
27	Australia, Great Britain, Continental Europe
28	Israel, Western USA, France, Finland, Canada, Continental Europe
28	England, France, Spain, extensively in USA
28	Australia, Italy
29	Korea, Japan, Hawaii, Continental Europe, Australia, New Zealand
29	Scotland, Continental Europe, Caribbean
30	Great Britain, France, Germany, Italy, Austria, Hungary
31	Continental Europe, extensively in USA
32	Throughout USA — hiking, biking and canoeing

This young group has obviously traveled extensively. With few exceptions they have managed this with limited budgets. We wonder whether their long years of involvement with a democratic school, which had to be managed on a shoestring by carefully setting priorities, has helped them do the things they want to do in life with limited funds.

Personal Perspectives

Several members of this group made a point of mentioning their community-oriented activities. "Religious affiliation with the Jewish community is important to me," said one. "I worked in an alternative sentencing center, established through the Crime and Justice Foundation through college," said another. Other typical comments were: "I enjoy work that is important to the environment"; "I MUST work in environmental protection"; "I am politically active in the radical left, including demonstrations and rallies."

Some of the people interviewed remarked on the influence that their long experience at SVS had on shaping their lives. Since the oldest member of this group is only thirty-two, none of them can view their school experience from a long term perspective. Nevertheless, some of their comments are interesting.

> *Sudbury Valley taught me how to relate to people — to be a person; to be myself, instead of being concerned with the system. Sometimes refusing to be a part of the system makes it harder to accomplish things, but maintaining personal integrity is most important.*

> *Sudbury Valley taught me the importance of commitment and persistence in working toward my goals.*

> *Sudbury Valley provided me with the background necessary face up to my artistic gifts and pursue my work with the self-discipline required.*

> *Schooling at Sudbury Valley made it easy to think and work independently. However the social environment was too limited, and as a result there was some initial discomfort involved in peer interactions outside SVS.*

> *The leadership skills I learned at Sudbury Valley were most helpful to me.*

Many of the respondents talked about the importance of relationships with other people. Comments such as, "Relationships past and present are important to me," recurred often. One person remarked ruefully, "I regret I didn't spend more time socializing at Sudbury Valley, instead of doing so much academic work"!

But perhaps the comment that sums it up best is this simple one: "Sudbury Valley gave me a wonderful childhood."

5

Reflections of "SVS Kids"

For several years now, Sudbury Valley has been engaged in an ongoing oral history project. The object is to record and preserve recollections of life at the school through the eyes of former students and staff members. These reminiscences are gathered in the course of long, relaxed interviews, during which the questioner and the former student have ample time to converse at leisure and examine all sorts of issues in depth.

During these interviews, the subjects also have a chance to talk about their experiences after leaving Sudbury Valley, and to reflect about the affect the school has had on their lives. Of the twenty-seven people in our study who attended Sudbury Valley as virtually their only school, seven have been interviewed as part of the oral history project.

We have included some of what these people said. We believe this material will give the reader insight into the nature of these former students, their character, and the way they look at the world, all in their own words. These reminiscences do not prove any particular point, or generalize about all members of the group. Rather, these more extensive quotations may convey a slightly richer picture of some of our former students, and what they take with them from their experiences at the school as they go out into the world.

Here are some of the things said by a young woman who was twenty-four years old, just graduating with honors as a student of criminal justice, when this study was made. She was twenty-one, and had just finished her freshman year, at the time her oral history interview was recorded:

I used to think I was shy. I think I was trying to talk myself into being shy but I'm not; I'm not any more if I was.

It's funny though, I don't say anything in class but the kids in my classes think I know everything that's talked about. I asked a kid, "What makes you think I know what I'm doing here?" and he said, "I don't know, just the way you are in class, you look like you're getting into it." I don't ask questions too much. Can't think of anything to ask, or I figure it out as he goes on with his lecture.

Sudbury Valley prepared me to be independent, to set out what I want to do and do it. A few things have been hard for me, like not having expertise in grammar, not knowing what exams were about or how to write a good exam. Well, the mistakes I made in the first quarter, I figured out in the second one; and the ones I made then, I learned from later. I'm constantly learning what my mistakes are. At Sudbury Valley I learned how to take criticism. When a teacher makes a comment, if its a negative comment I don't say, "Oh, that's absurd. Why did he write that?" I go, "Yeah, yeah, he's right. I didn't do that." It doesn't hurt my feelings.

At first I felt that the people I met who went to public school had it over me, but I thought of the things that I had over them — like being in college not because my parents wanted me to be there but because it was something I wanted to do. If I want to better educate myself it's up to me.

Take math. When I first started school, the very first class I ever had to take was math. What really aggravated me was having to do something that I didn't want to do. At Sudbury Valley if you didn't want to take math, you didn't take math. So getting used to going from no set curriculum to all this that you have to do was hard. But even though I may not always believe in the philosophy of the way the college is run, I have to change, I have to adapt to different things. As long as I feel I'm getting something out of it, it doesn't really bother me how it's set up: if I personally feel that I'm getting something then I'm satisfied. I don't necessarily agree with a grade system. I think it's foolish. But if I feel like doing something, I say, "I don't care."

My English and my math SAT scores weren't anything to put on a piece of paper. I didn't study for them at all. I took them as a big curiosity thing because it was the first test I ever took that had a grade. "Wow, a grade! This is going to be neat." But those were the biggest strikes against me because those were my two weakest subjects. I just had no interest in them. But I learned from Sudbury Valley how to voice my opinion and how to say what I want and that's what got me into college. I said to myself, "I'm going to get myself in there one way or the other." I was persistent and I did it.

They took me because I talked, I showed that I wanted to be there and that I wasn't being forced to be there, that it was something I felt I had to do. I walked right in and talked to the Dean. I was really nervous about my interview; it was something I never did before. He said, "What can I tell you about the University?" and that was an instant shock. I was kind of blank for a second, then I said "Well, to tell you the honest truth, I've already made my decision to enter this school, so I think I know as much as I possibly should know about being a student here. What I think you should know is about me and why I want to be here." And he moved around in his chair, looked back at me and said "OK, go for it." And I went on and on and on and he said, "OK, why Criminal Justice?" And I told him about the Judicial Committee. I told him about the staff. I told him about everything. He said, "You know something? I'm going to call my office and I'm going to tell them." He told me right then and there, "You'll see your acceptance letter," and "I'll see you in the Fall." I said, "Thank you very much."

He mentioned the SAT's. He said, "You seem to be a very intelligent girl but you have really bad scores." And I said "Look, its because I don't have any interest in those two subjects, and I never concentrated on them very much. But I'm here now and I know I'm going to come across courses that I have to take that I have no interest in. I have the desire to do it now and I promise you I'll do it." He said "OK."

I had confidence. I was scared, but I looked at it this way: I said, "OK, try it. I'm never going to know what's going to happen unless I try it. So if I try it and I screw up, I chalk it up and say 'OK, I can't do it right now.' But eventually I will."

I was confident that I could do the work because I always had encouragement from people saying that I could do anything I wanted to do. Even a staff member who I never really talked to much would say, "Look, you can do it if you want to do it and you will do it." And other people, friends and everything. I think if you have a desire to do something and an interest in it you do it. You take the extra step to work a little harder or find out how to do it. I have to work harder than other kids because they know the tricks of the trade of cramming for an exam or taking a test. So I have to put in an extra couple of hours compared to what they do.

I didn't start college for two years after I graduated from Sudbury Valley. I did a lot of other things first. I worked. I travelled. I worked for a little over a year because I had planned on going to Europe. I worked about sixty hours a week at two jobs; full time at Filene's, and then in a fruit and nut stand as part-time assistant manager. I saved all my money, and went to France. I was in Europe about six months altogether. Then I came home. I made the decision to come home before I spent all my money, because I had seen what I wanted to see, met people, done the things I wanted to do. I went to France, England, Germany, Switzerland, Italy. I bought a EuRail pass and just went to different countries. I learned a lot about being able to relate to people, being able to deal with hairy situations when you have to, being totally away from everything you're used to. I think that was one of the best things I ever did. Then I could come back here when I decided to, settle down and start studying.

I came back in October of that year and I started applying to schools and deciding what I wanted to do.

Another rather different perspective emerges from the laconic remarks of the twenty seven year old who is now the technical supervisor of a large copy machine service company; he was interviewed three years earlier.

My work is satisfying because I'm on my own. I go to the office once or twice a week at the most. Dispatch straight from my last call at night to my first call the next day. Every day is different, it's always a different angry secretary that I get to meet. A very big part of my job is psychology, and calming people. "Why does this machine suck?" "Oh, it doesn't suck." You just have to know how.

And also the work. It's a puzzle. Every time I go to a machine to fix it, this machine is supposed to be doing something, and it's not doing it, and I have to figure out why. It's like you're driving, you're going down this road and you have a decision to make: Do I follow this road or do I follow that one to try to find the problem? If I follow this one, how long am I going to go down it, trying different things before I have to turn around and try a different one, or go back and start over again? It's a lot of problem solving, mechanical and electrical problem solving, and it's interesting and it pays well and you feel like a hot shit when you get this machine that's not doing anything, and you figure out the problem. But then there are days when you come back to earth and you can't figure out something easy.

I think that Sudbury Valley helped me to deal with people, and not be condescending to them, or lie to them. I've got a good relationship with the customers, I think.

I want to be comfortable, you know. I'd love to be rich, but if I have to do it at the expense of being aggravated, or unhappy, or get ulcers by the time I'm 30, I'm not going to do it. I'm not worried about it. I'll be financially comfortable. I am now.

This interview was done with a twenty-seven year old, female, social worker.

One thing that strikes me is that I know people who say to me, "Oh, I wouldn't know what to do with my time if I had a month off." And I think "What are you talking about? Just use your time." I never feel that if the structure in my life was lost, what am I going to do? I don't feel lost. My ego doesn't fall apart in chaos if I don't have a schedule. I just live. I make my time what I want it to be. I never feel like, "Oh, my God, what would I do without structure imposed upon me from the outside?" So many people I work with talk like that. Even about my job: in my job, we're alone most of the day, most of the time. I'm a social worker in a hospital setting and we're on our own to make our own schedules and get our work done. A lot of people come here and don't know how to do that. They say, "Well, I don't know how to structure. This day is too unstructured for me. I won't get my work done because I don't know how to balance my day to get it done." And that I can't fathom. That never happens to me. I wonder how I'm going to get my work done, but I appreciate having the freedom to organize my day the way I want to.

I don't think going to Sudbury Valley gives you a problem with authority. If anything, you just have more understanding that the person in authority is the only one taking responsibility in many instances, but you have an idea of responsibility, so you can look at what they're looking at. If you've been to Sudbury Valley, you realize that this stuff has to get done, and you chose to work there and get it done. So even if you can't stand your boss, you realize you have to get it done. You're not at a disadvantage because you never had a boss in school.

I'll just explain one thing about work. Just because you go to Sudbury Valley and you choose your own profession doesn't mean you're going to like your job. Just because you go to Sudbury Valley doesn't mean you're going to have a harder time with authority or getting to work every day because you have to. Or taking tests because you have to. You're not at a disadvantage. First of all, you're at an advantage because you're not fed up with it when you're faced with it for the first time. People who are dealing with it their whole life are fed up with it. By the time they get to college, they don't want to see another test.

I looked for a college that had a heterogeneous population, as much as possible. They called it "diverse" in my day. I looked for a place that sort of promoted a certain amount of freedom for the students. The school that I went to had expectations but it didn't have a tremendous number of requirements, although I did apply to schools that had more requirements. I looked for places that had good departments in what I was interested in, in dance and in religion. I also looked for schools with good reputations. I visited them and felt the atmosphere and that kind of thing. I took out books from the library, read about the colleges, looked at how many stars they had, read what students had written about them, and visited. I was pretty careful. The interviews were the best feature of my applications I think, because kids from Sudbury Valley are used to talking. They talk a lot. Coming from that school and having to explain it, gives you sort of a leg up. You present as responsible, as articulate, as thinking. You're used to talking to adults. One thing about college is that you're used to having classes not meet all day every day, so that when you get to college and classes meet twice a week for an hour and you have free time, you know what to do with it, you know how to handle that, it's not a shock. And you're not shocked that, "Oh, my God, how am I going to learn this material if I don't sit every day in class?" You're used to intensity in classes. You're used to designing your own schedule. You're used to setting aside time to study because no one's going to do it for you. You have a lot of free time. You learn how to balance that. That comes very easy. What's a little bit hard at first is tests. It takes about one semester and that's it. You're fine.

I think at Sudbury Valley you learn to respect how other people live because you live with them for half the day. You eat maybe two meals a day with them, you spend most of the waking day with a person. So you learn to respect how other people live and you wonder about how they live and that sort of translates, later, into the need to travel to do that. You learn respect for different types of people at Sudbury Valley School and now, travelling, I like to see how other people live. I like to see how people do their laundry in Venice.

The following effusive, enthusiastic and extensive comments were made by the twenty nine year old musician and songwriter and who is now also the manager of a music store.

I became a musician just by doing it. Just by playing. I guess I've always been a musician in some sense. I started writing my own songs when I was about eleven or twelve years old, as soon as I could play chords. I'd make up my own songs. And I've been doing it ever since. So it's been a good long time that I've been doing it, writing words and music.

Obviously when I was younger I didn't really have an idea of where it was leading to. When I got older, I honed it more, but I didn't really have a niche where I was, where my place was in music, where my songs were. Not until maybe 1984 or 1986, when I really started writing substantial songs, where I could feel that this is a song. You know, this is a real song.

When I left the school I got involved with a band, guys who were older than me. These guys were the first guys I was ever involved with who knew how to do harmonies. So I learned. Everybody in this band sang, so they let me lead sing a few songs. Then I started bringing in my own songs, and we'd learn them together. We played them. They liked them. And they were supportive of them.

We'd play gigs. We had a guy managing us. We played a lot of schools and a lot of colleges. We were booked through a big booking agency in Boston, and we made enough money to pay back our expenses. A lot of times we'd have to rent power amplifiers or lights or a truck, so the expenses would be several hundred dollars.

Our band evolved into another band which became very successful. We were in the WBCN Rock and Rumble in 1987 and went to the finals, played the Orpheum which was a lifelong dream of mine, and which was pretty great. Got a lot of air play. Got a lot of record label interest. Made a lot of contacts, did very well and then one of the members left because he said that he wanted to pursue his own thing which, to this day, he hasn't done.

I moved on. Within the last three or four years, I got involved in playing a lot of acoustic shows. Just myself on an acoustic guitar and singing. Sometimes one of the other guys from the band plays as well. In the beginning I had some other people from other bands play with me, percussion, bass. And then I started moving it more towards a band format. Now I have a group of about eight different musicians — two backup singers, a bass player, a percussion player, a guitar player, and me and a keyboard player. I get gigs, but I'm not playing out as much because today the music scene in Boston is a lot different and you don't have people going out as much to clubs to see bands, where in 1987 people were flocking to clubs. The more you played, in 1987, the more people would come to see you. Now, it's the total opposite. We saw it starting to happen then, realizing that you can't play all the time, in Boston. So we started playing outside of Boston a little bit. Still, it was a very small circle.

Now I have a very close friend, who I've known since 1982, managing me, someone who worked on the road with well-known artists. We went to L.A. and spoke with some different people and some different record labels. So I'm working towards getting a record deal. My manager believes in me, sees my vision, and knows that I'm going to make a record and we're going to get a record deal. We're going to make a hit.

I find, when we're on, when the band is on and we have a great night, we captivate people. Now I'm living at home, I'm not working forty hours a week anymore. I have a brand new 8-track setup in my home studio, and I'm out here in the woods, away from everything that goes on in the city, although I'm very involved in the industry. And I find that now that I have such a low profile in the city, every time I'm out, people want to know where I'm playing next, what's going on, am I recording? I find that we get more and more people out to see us and people seem more excited about us.

I love performing. I'd like to tour. What my manager and I are talking about doing is getting in a camper, putting the gear on a trailer, and going out across the country and playing clubs. I want to get out to the people. I really feel that the music that I'm writing, is different than a lot of other bands, because it has so many different aspects of music involved in it; it's an energy thing, it's a feel thing, and, as people say, it's a groove thing. I think it's different enough that people will be intrigued because it's like no other band. And I think it's accessible enough that people will understand it, that they'll get it, that the average working guy in Indiana or in Louisiana or in Wyoming or in Nebraska, will know what we're doing. It's not foreign to them. It's also a very visual thing. We have a gret backdrop, a really cool, almost psychedelic looking backdrop and every show we try and do something a little different.

What my manager and I are trying to do right now is shop a deal. I feel frustrated at times. I wish I was a little further. Now that I don't have a job, I am free to be where my heart feels I need to be, which is writing songs. However long it takes for me to get a record deal, that's how long it will take. When I get itchy, my manager always brings me back down to reality because that's really his job. I know that once somebody has the same vision, and sees what I'm doing and believes in it, I will have the opportunity to prove myself. All I'm looking for is an opportunity to prove to people that I'm a legitimate song writer and that I can write hits and make records that people will want to hear.

I have my parents who love what I do and are totally supportive of it. The main reason for moving back home was that I felt that I had worked forty hours a week for so long — for ten, twelve years — that if I was really going to make it in this field, if I was truly going to be successful, I had to center my career around my career, instead of centering my career around my work. When I was working, it was forty hours a week, forty five hours a week and then I could do my music. There wasn't a lot of time to write. My thoughts were blurred. Now I realize that if I'm going to be serious about it, then whatever I do has to come after my music. Nobody else's store, nobody else's business can come before that.

The thirty year old professor of mathematics, interviewed as a graduate student at the age of twenty-six, although far less talkative about his inner thoughts, nevertheless revealed a clear notion of where he was going with his life at each of its stages:

I left school at about seventeen and I worked at the Natural Grocer [an innovative natural foods store] for a year and a half. I was interested in the Natural Grocer and I wanted to work there, and I wasn't at all interested in going to college at that point. I thought about it, but it was clearly something that I didn't particularly want to do right then. I didn't have any good reason to go to college.

I decided to go to college because I wanted to do more music with other people who were interested in classical music. That was the primary motivation. The secondary motivation was that I wanted to see what it was like to be around a university and to be around other people who were interested in academic things, and to have a rich amount of academic things going on around me that I could participate in if I wanted to or talk to people about if I wanted to. I felt it was something that would be really different from Sudbury Valley in the sense that instead of being one person interested in something, if I was interested in something in college, I figured that there would be lots of other people around who were interested in it too. There would be lots of people to talk to. It turned out that as I got more interested in math, there weren't very many people I could talk to, because where I was there just weren't many people who were that good at math.

I wanted to go to graduate school at MIT and I got in there. They looked at my college transcript, and they looked at recommendations, which was probably the most helpful thing. I had good recommendations, some of them from people who faculty at MIT knew. I went to England in between college and graduate school. I got a scholarship: applying for it was like applying to another graduate school. They award ten a year to Americans.

Cambridge, England was fun. It wasn't so useful mathematically, but it was a lot of fun. The students there were really advanced. They were much more advanced than I was and so I was always scrambling to understand anything that a lecturer was talking about when I went to classes. I was getting sort of worried there, but after a while, being back here, I realized that I wasn't really any stupider than them. I just didn't know nearly as much. The undergraduate math program at Cambridge is really good. It's probably better than any undergraduate math program in this country and is certainly a lot better than mine was.

My wife and I got to Cambridge a month early and we travelled in England and then when I finished in June, we travelled for a couple of months. We travelled for most of June and all of July and a little bit of August. That was really nice. Travelling in France was the best, because France is really cheap and you get good food all the time. And it's also really *pretty. We travelled in England and in Germany and we'd stay in youth hostels and try to live really cheaply and then we went to France and, at the exchange rates then, for under $10 we could both stay in a hotel and for under $10, we could both have a good meal, with wine, at a restaurant. So it was really amazing.*

In her interview, the sister of the graduate just quoted saw the world from a quite different point of view, yet shared with her brother many of the same perspectives on life:

When I went to college, the biggest gap in my knowledge was not knowing how to write a research paper. I mastered the tools that I needed to do it, and it didn't take me long. But to learn to write an essay took me longer. Not an essay on what I thought. That I can do easily. But an essay on what you're supposed to feed back to the teacher. Each teacher wants you to feed back something else, and what you need to know is not so much how to write, but what it is that teacher wants. It's a matter of learning what the teacher wants and not learning for the sake of learning. You're supposed to figure out what they think is important. I didn't know that when I went to college; I learned that there. To me, it's more valuable to learn what I *think is important.*

I learn a lot from other people — from those who offer me knowledge, or those I can extract knowledge from. The people I don't learn from are people who stand up there and read from a textbook that I could also read from, and don't actually say what they think is important. They expect you to extrapolate, from something that they haven't said, what they might think is important. That's not learning. That's memorizing what somebody else thinks is important without having any reason to see why that person even thinks it's important.

I wasn't that happy in that atmosphere. It's not that I didn't learn. But I didn't feel I got the kind of guidance in terms of the kinds of things I should be studying or things that might be significant later on. So you go on and you learn for yourself. But I could have done that without them.

I work part time right now because I want to blow glass. I have to earn enough money doing something else to pay to blow glass, because it costs a lot of money both to take courses and to rent the studio (which costs $30 an hour). I also volunteer my time to assist other people and learn that way.

I love blowing glass, but I'm not sure if I'll ever be good. You can make a piece that's pretty, but that doesn't mean you're going to be good. I have an eye for beauty, but I don't always know where the starting point is to get to that. I'm not sure yet if I can ever make a career out of it. It might just always be a hobby.

I used to feel that I had to give, give, give and I had to teach people because I knew more about life and I had to somehow contribute. But now I don't have that. Something changed and that's gone. I don't feel I have to change the world or I have to convert people or show them my way. I just have to live. I just have to be happy in my life. My contribution to the world doesn't have to be some great change.

It's not selfish, it's just not selfless. You don't have to be selfless all the time. Go enjoy life.

I'm not saying I won't do things in the world. I still contribute. I still work on the kinds of things that I feel change the world that I can maybe affect. But I don't have to be doing something twenty-four hours a day to change the world. I can help people some of the time. Or maybe I can help them in another way that's not so giving of myself all the time.

I think I'm a better person now. I think I'm more whole. There are a lot of people in the world who have to control everything, or have to always be serving, or have to somehow make everybody see things their way. I don't need that. I'm more self-sufficient in my emotional needs. If I become a physiotherapist, as I'm considering doing, I'm sure I'll be able to contribute to that field. I'll be able to help people get better and treat people the way that I've been treated by physiotherapists. But I also know that I can do something else and get satisfaction from that too. I don't have to give my whole self to be satisfied; I can just give a part.

I have total confidence that I can do what I set out to do. That comes mostly from my track record. At Sudbury Valley you get a track record. Even as a young person, at Sudbury Valley you do things and you get things done by yourself or with others — with other children or with other adults. It's a self-confidence that you establish: you see how things work and you can go after something and get it done. One of the big things about Sudbury Valley is that it gives you that.

There are some areas in my life where I don't have that track record, and where I don't have self-confidence. When I first started blowing glass, I was devastated when the first piece that I dropped on the floor smashed into a hundred little pieces. I was ruined for the whole day. I thought, "This is my piece. This is my dream piece. This is a concept that I had and it was so beautiful and now it's in pieces." Once it shatters, it gets cold and you can see the color and you know how it was going to turn out. And you're devastated. Everybody else goes about their business and gets on with it and says, "You know, you have to get used to this. This happens." But last week I was making a beautiful white plate. I really loved it. It was a new thing; I had seen somebody else's work that was white and I was inspired and tried it, and here was this gorgeous thing — and then it smashed into a hundred pieces. The person I was working with said, "How come you're not upset?" I said, "Well, I am upset a little bit, but I've broken pieces before. It's going to happen. It happens to the masters all the time, too." Not as often, but it still happens to them. You just have to say, "Well, ok, that one broke, but I'm going to make another one right now and it's not going to break." So you have to reestablish your track record. When you have things that are failures, you have to go and try it again, learn from what happened, learn from the mistake.

Finally, we have the thoughts of the twenty nine year old musician, songwriter, art photographer, and entrepreneur owner of his own custom color photolab. Here is what he had to say:

There are two big things I learned about democracy in the School Meeting, which I think apply equally well to life in America at large. To me they've always explained the incredibly low voter turnout that happens in this country. The biggest rule is, that everything's going to run itself fairly reasonably with or without your presence. Once you have a fundamental trust in the reasonableness of the society you're in, you don't have to attend to every detail, and not attending to every detail is not a sign of not caring about it. It's a sign of basic faith that the system will more or less run along reasonable lines with or without your attention and that you can devote your attention other places. That's certainly how I felt about a lot of political things in my later life. I have a certain faith in the government, in the country, in the overall will of the American people. I can pretty much sleep easy knowing that America as a whole is going in a certain direction. There may be variants, there may be scoundrels, there may be scandals, but the basic overall thrust is going to be fairly reasonable, and I don't have to lose too much sleep over it. So I don't find myself super politically involved. I find myself the opposite. I find myself realizing that democracy guarantees me a certain reasonableness in society and that I don't have to worry about that aspect of my life. And I think that's one of the best things about democracy, that you're not constantly looking over your shoulder wondering what's going to happen.

The other thing was the cold hard fact of majority rule. There's a lot of times in the School Meeting — and this is a good example for life, where it's just as true — when your own particular interests and the majority's are not the same and you just have to bite it. It's just a fact of life. The larger group's will is the will that is usually gone with, and when your personal individual thing comes in conflict with this larger, greater, good of the community, a lot of times you just have to swallow that fact. For example, you can't expect the government of the United States to hand you money to do your particular project. There's a larger interest at stake. It's not just what you want to do with your life. So that was another big thing. A lot of people have to learn that lesson. When the majority feel a certain thing and you feel another thing, you just have to live with that and come back the next day happy with that instead of being permanently upset about it.

The musical group that I'm working with now runs by the "one lone nut" theory. What we say is that if one person disagrees with the entire group, they basically have to eat their disagreement. If one person has a problem with something and it's not shared by any other person in the group, then it's their personal problem. Whereas if two people from different perspectives feel something strongly, we tend to take that as a sign that we should try to figure out another way to do things. That's the way the group runs.

I felt more and more fortunate as I was out in the world at having had the school experience. I felt fortunate specifically at having been born at the time I was because the early years of the school were amazing years. I feel much more a child of the sixties even though I was only six years old then, than I feel a child of the seventies, when I was in my teens, which most people think of as their formative years. I think in many ways the sixties were a much more interesting time in our culture. There was a lot more up for grabs, a lot more questions being asked and I feel very excited to have been part of all that. That still informs a lot of my life, that experience. I've grown more and more to appreciate over time the lucky confluence of events that happened in my early childhood.

I feel like I'm in an accelerated development in many ways. I was able to enjoy a period when a lot of people are just waiting for their life to begin. They hate their school or they hate their whole childhood or something, and they really start being themselves when they become adults. I haven't really fundamentally changed my behavior with the exception of paying bills. I'm doing the exact same thing I was doing when I was six years old except that I now allot a certain chunk of my time for paying my bills and for making money. That's the only difference. You can say that's a major thing but I'm not sure that is such a major thing. I mean, I think that's something you do, but the rest of my life is fundamentally like what it was when I was a kid. I do what I want to do every day. And that's a very unusual lifestyle. I feel like I have the inborn right, because I grew up this way, to stop what I'm doing in the middle of the day and play the piano for half an hour. Because I run my own business and I can set my own hours and I don't see why I should work eight continuous hours when I feel like playing the piano in the middle of the day. That drives my partner crazy, because I'll say, "I didn't have any time today to do grocery shopping." And she'll say, "Well, you played the piano." And I'm like, "Yeah, that's not grocery shopping. That's what I want to do." I took time off from work to do something I wanted to do. I didn't take time off from work to do grocery shopping. I'll do grocery shopping after my work hours. I've set aside certain hours in my life every day for work and, if I can work faster and have some of those hours free for leisure, I take them. So in a sense, it's just the same except when I was younger I didn't worry about my bills.

Travel has played a pretty big role in my early years. After I left the school for about five or six years I took every possible opportunity to travel and I lived for a year in Europe. I think that living for a year in Europe was probably for me in my life what a lot of people go to university for. It was being exposed to a very divergent bunch of cultural things that I wouldn't have been exposed to if I had just sat here in America. I was seeing a lot of different perspectives about the world at once. And it was also being very, very far away from home, in every sense of the word — physically, culturally, mentally, everything.

I think a lot of people maybe go to university because it exposes them to life. They'll take a philosophy course. They'll start reading philosophers that maybe they wouldn't have read otherwise. Now, I don't go with that. If I want to read philosophers and I'm too lazy to get a book off the shelf, I'm not that interested in philosophy. If I really want to do something, it's all available to me at any time at any place. But the thing about going to Europe was that it gave me that totally outside perspective on my culture, on American culture and on my life. When I came back I was more determined than ever to do exactly the things I'm doing now. I realized a lot of good things about the kind of life I could lead in America. I also realized I had options. I realized, hey, if I didn't like the American option, I had a European option. I had other options. I could live anywhere I wanted to. It made me realize that the ultimate vote is the vote you take with your feet. If you choose to live somewhere, do it for the reasons that help your life. I'm where I am because this is one of the few big-sized cities where you can still get a lot of space cheap. When you're an artist and you need space for your band to rehearse and space for your theater company, that's a primary consideration. So being in a city where space is cheap feeds a lot of other artistic endeavors. I don't think I'd be here if rents were what New York's rents are. I would have found another place to be. I would have kept looking until I found some place first rate, wherever it would have been.

Travel in that sense, too, has definitely played a big role in my life because it made me realize that places are important. You exist on your own to a certain degree but the place where you do something affects you and affects your options. You have to choose the place you're in like you choose everything else in your life or it will be chosen for you and you'll just have to live with the consequences. And I think that in a way that's true of the school. I definitely think the sense of place, the building, the physical surroundings, being in New England and specifically in Massachusetts with its tendencies of thought, those are all factors. You can't really separate them from being at Sudbury Valley School. The school would be a very different place if it was located in the hills of Greece. It might be the same place philosophically, but it would not be the same place in any other way.

Seven sets of reflections, seven very different perspectives on life. Yet, common threads run through them, as we might expect from students long immersed in the philosophy and practice of Sudbury Valley.

Part III

Long Term Students

6

Students Who Spent a Major Portion of Their School Lives, Including Their High School Age Years, at Sudbury Valley

We now turn to those students who entered Sudbury Valley School at ten years of age or older, attended at least five years, and left feeling that they had completed their basic schooling. These students are of particular interest because although Sudbury Valley can certainly be said to have played a significant role in their development, they were also subjected to considerable influence from their prior schooling. There were twenty-two people in this group, and we were able to reach twenty-one of them. All of the data presented in this chapter will refer to the twenty one respondents only, of whom twelve were male, and nine female.

Nineteen of these twenty one students received diplomas before leaving. One of the other two left school just short of her sixteenth birthday to pursue studies and a career in ballet. (It is a piquant coincidence that the only person in the group of people who spent basically their *entire* school lives at SVS and left without a diploma also left for a career in ballet; see Chapter 4.) The other non-diplomate in this group left SVS to attend college as a matriculated student just before she turned seventeen — the youngest student in her freshman class!

Basic Demographics

—— How old are they now?

Figure 6.1 shows the distribution of this group by age on January 1, 1991. This too is still a very young group, as was the group discussed in Chapter 4. The oldest members of this group are only three years older than the oldest members of the former group, and the average and median ages of both groups are identical.

Figure 6.1

Distribution by Age, January 1, 1991

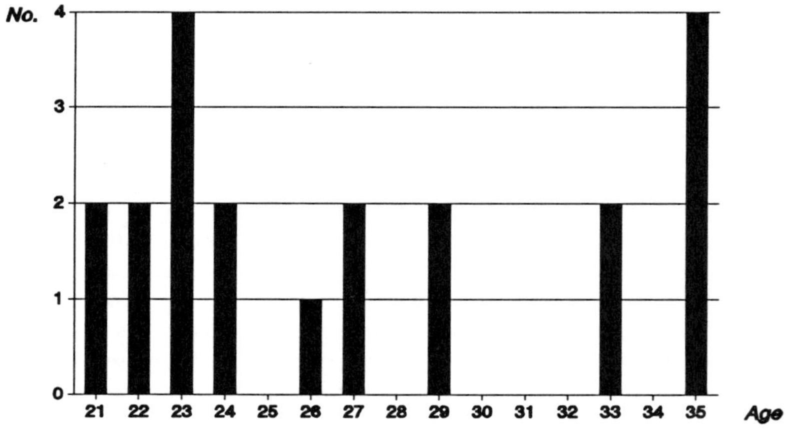

—— Their marital status

The family situation in this group is also remarkably similar to that of the group in Chapter 4. Of the twenty one people, twelve were single (57%); five were married (24%); four were living with significant others (19%). (Of the five who had been married, one was divorced at the time of the survey.) Only three of the group had been either married or cohabiting for more than three years, and two of these were married to each other, for thirteen years. They had been childhood sweethearts at SVS. The third had been living with one significant other (also someone met at SVS) for sixteen years.

There are four children born to members of this group, two of them to the couple who have been married to each other for thirteen years, one each to two others. The oldest child is five, one is four, and the other two are infants. All in all, both this group and the group in Chapter 4 seem to be postponing child rearing as well as long term relationships and marriage.

Where do they live?

Table 6.1 shows where these people live. Thirteen (62%) live in Massachusetts, all of them in the area from which the school draws its students.

Table 6.1

Current Geographical Distribution of the Group

No.	*Town*	*State*
1	Los Angeles	California
1	San Francisco	California
1	Indianapolis	Indiana
1	Ashland	Massachusetts
1	Cambridge	Massachusetts
1	Canton	Massachusetts
1	Charlestown	Massachusetts
1	Chelmsford	Massachusetts
4	Framingham	Massachusetts
2	Natick	Massachusetts
1	North Grafton	Massachusetts
1	Watertown	Massachusetts
1	East Livermore	Maine
1	New York	New York
1	Vida	Oregon
2	Bristol	Tennessee

— How old were they when they enrolled?

Figure 6.2 shows the ages at which this group entered the school. Their starting ages begin at ten (by definition — those starting earlier fell into the group analyzed in Chapter 4) and range to fifteen. The average age of entry is twelve, double that of the group in Chapter 4, a fact which, alone, highlights the difference between the two groups.

Figure 6.2

Distribution by Age of Entry

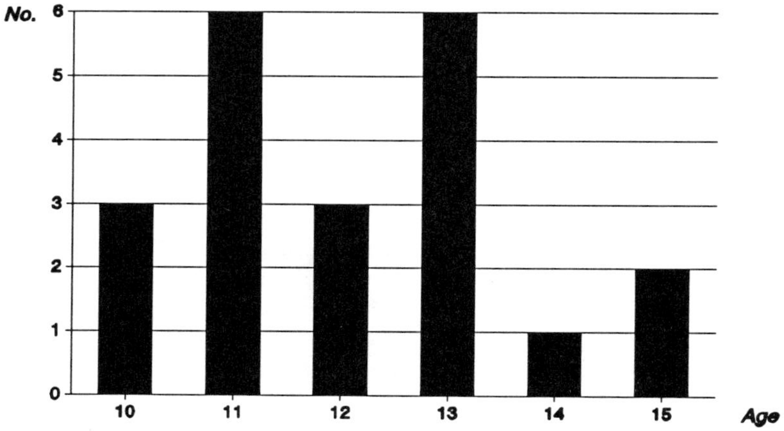

— What was their prior schooling?

Every one in this group had extensive prior exposure to more traditional schools before entering Sudbury Valley. Every one had a record of prior attendance at an elementary school. One went to a private elementary school and three went to both private and public elementary schools; the other seventeen went to public elementary school only. Ten of them (48%) went to middle schools, all public, before Sudbury Valley; one of the ten also went to a private middle school. One student started public high school before entering SVS. It is interesting to note that not a single member of this group or of the group in Chapter 4 had been homeschooled before entering Sudbury Valley (a reflection of the embryonic state of home schooling in the Sixties and Seventies).

—— How long did they remain at Sudbury Valley?

Figure 6.3 shows the number of years the people in this group spent at the school.[1] The average length of stay is six years, exactly half that of the group in Chapter 4. This is consistent with the average age of entry being double that of Chapter 4.

Figure 6.3

Distribution of Length of Stay at the School

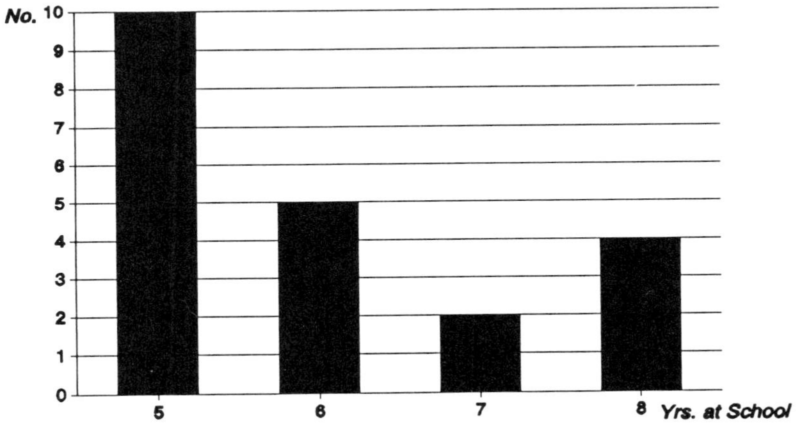

[1] We count only years actually enrolled in the school. For students who left Sudbury Valley for a time and subsequently returned, the time spent away from Sudbury Valley is not included in the calculation of the length of stay at school.

— How old were they when they left school?

Figure 6.4 shows the ages at which members of this group left the school. The average age of leaving is eighteen and a half, which means that a considerable number of students chose to continue to attend Sudbury Valley beyond the age at which they would have been comfortable as students in a more traditional school. In this respect, the sample is similar to that in Chapter 4.

Figure 6.4

Distribution by Age at Leaving

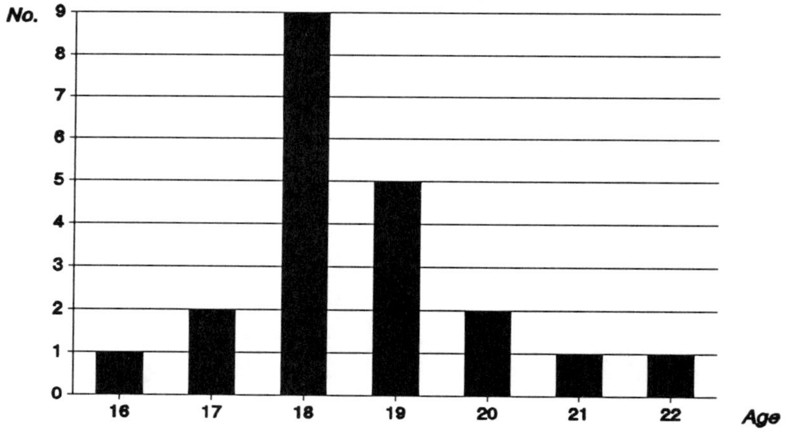

— Where did they live?

Table 6.2 shows the geographical distribution of this population at the time that they were students here. One student came from Randolph, a considerable distance from the school, while most of the others had a commute of thirty minutes or less each way.

Table 6.2

Geographical Distribution While in School

No.	*Town*
1	Acton
2	Ashland
6	Framingham
1	Harvard
1	Holliston
1	Hopkinton
1	Hudson
2	Lincoln
2	Natick
1	Randolph
1	Southboro
2	Sudbury

Occupations

— What are they doing now?

As was the case with the sample in Chapter 4, this group's generally young age precludes an analysis of long term careers. However, we are able to examine their range of occupations. Here too we find an extraordinarily rich variety of pursuits, which are summarized by general categories in Table 6.3. Occupations marked with an asterisk denote entrepreneurial or self-employed situations. Note that several individuals have more than one occupation and fall into more than one category.

Table 6.3

Present Occupations
(Arranged by Categories of Occupation)

Category	*Number in Category*	*Specific Occupations*
Business Management	6	supermarket department manager screen printing company manager music store manager *owner, game store *owner, crafts cafe *owner, homemade ice cream company
Office Manager/ Executive Assistant	1	office manager
High Tech	3	*custom computerized machine shop software documentation for advanced music programs assistant director of administrative computing in a college
Professional	2	senior behavior specialist and department manager, rehab facility land surveyor
Research & Development	1	R&D contract administrator
Education	2	health club trainer English teacher in Europe
Marketing	3	health club sales public relations *homemade ice cream wholesaler and vendor
Trades	5	*operator of recording studio *caterer *saw mill owner and operator baker technical photographer

Category	*Number in Category*	*Specific Occupations*
Design	2	*dressmaker *technical illustrator, including computer graphics
Creative Arts	1	*artist
Performing Arts	4	*musician in group (3) dancer
Unskilled Labor	2	waitperson (2)
Student	6	sociology journalism fashion design jazz dance pastry arts hairdressing

Table 6.4 shows the age of each of the people in this group and lists the occupations in which each of them are currently engaged. There is no predominance of any category of work in either the younger or the older part of the group. No one over twenty three is engaged in an unskilled job.

Table 6.4

Present Occupations (Arranged in Order of Age)

Age	*Present Occupation*
21	health club sales and trainer
21	caterer, hair dressing student
22	*owner, games store
22	dancer, jazz dance student
23	English teacher in Europe
23	waitperson, baker, pastry arts student
23	fashion design student, *dressmaker
23	waitperson, journalism student

Age	*Present Occupation*
24	public relations, office manager
24	senior behavior specialist and department manager, rehab facility
26	sociology student, assistant director of administrative computing in a college
27	*owner, crafts cafe; technical photographer
27	music store manager, *musician, *operator of recording studio
29	screen printing company manager, *musician
29	*homemade ice cream producer, wholesaler, vendor
33	*artist, technical illustrator including computer graphics
33	*R&D contract administrator
35	*musician, software documentation for advanced music programs
35	*custom computerized machine shop, *saw mill owner and operator
35	supermarket department manager
35	land surveyor

— Range of occupations

Table 6.5 presents as complete a list as we have available of all the occupations engaged in by members of this group after they left the school (including those in the above Table of present occupations). As in Table 6.3, occupations marked with an asterisk denote either entrepreneurial or self-employed situations. The totals of the number of people in each category in Table 6.5 adds up to a number much greater than the twenty one in the sample. This is because many people have had more than one occupation and fall into more than one category. The category of "student" shown in Table 6.3 has been dropped, since a subsequent section will take up in greater detail the education pursued by the members of this group.

Table 6.5

Occupations Engaged in Since Leaving Sudbury Valley (Arranged by Categories of Occupation)

Category	*Number in Category*	*Specific Occupations*
Business Management	11	supermarket department manager screen printing company manager music store manager *owner, game store *owner, crafts cafe *owner, homemade ice cream company newspaper manager catering service manager clothing store manager restaurant manager video store manager *partner in natural foods business (2) buyer in a chain food store
Office Manager/ Executive Assistant	2	office manager bookkeeper
High Tech	4	*custom computerized machine shop software documentation for advanced music programs assistant director of administrative computing in a college programmer (2)
Professional	2	senior behavior specialist and department manager, rehab facility nurse fire fighter reforestation planner and worker land surveyor
Research & Development	2	R&D contract administrator research in psychology
Education	3	health club trainer English teacher in Europe Sudbury Valley School staff member

Category	*Number in Category*	*Specific Occupations*
Marketing	4	health club sales public relations *homemade ice cream wholesaler and vendor real estate marketing and sales
Trades	10	*operator of recording studio *caterer *saw mill owner and operator baker technical photographer new supermarket setup seamstress newspaper reporter typesetter chef carpenter (2) lens maker trucker (2) heavy equipment repair
Design	6	*dressmaker *technical illustrator, including computer graphics *hand painted clothing designer and producer (2) graphic artist display designer
Creative Arts	1	*artist
Performing Arts	4	*musician in group (3) dancer

Category	*Number in Category*	*Specific Occupations*
Unskilled Labor	16	waitperson (5) retail clerk (8) warehouseman (3) grocery clerk (2) chambermaid ranch hand zoo keeper cruise crew survey researcher house cleaner delivery person

While they were attending school at Sudbury Valley, sixteen of these twenty-one (76%) held jobs. Some of the jobs were relatively advanced, such as apprentice potter, mechanic, clerk typist, legislative aide to a State Representative, computer repairman, and computer consultant to a college department. The others were more routine jobs, typical of those held by high school students: nine were retail or grocery clerks, two were waitpersons, two worked in childcare, one worked in a mailroom, one was a shipping clerk, one worked in a gas station, one was a stablehand, one worked in catering, and another as a cake decorator. The significant number of relatively advanced positions held by members of this group may be meaningful; it probably says something about children who have the nerve to walk away from traditional educational settings in their middle years and come to Sudbury Valley. These people seem to develop, or maybe already have, an extraordinary degree of independence, focus and responsibility.

— Where have they worked?

Table 6.6 lists some of the places where members of this group have worked or currently work. The table is arranged by job category and contains only a sampling; we have included it to give an idea of the nature of the work environments this group has chosen.

Table 6.6

Places of Work
(Arranged by Categories of Occupation)

Category	*Company or Institution*
Business Management	E.U. Wurlitzer Amherst Collegian Natural Grocer Mad Martha's Great American Hero Sage's Supermarket Wayside Caterers Gameworld
High Tech	Curry College Honeywell-Bull
Professional	New Medico Hahnemann Hospital Willamette National Forest
Research & Development	Raytheon
Education	Sudbury Valley School World Gym
Marketing	Holiday Magic Beacon Management
Trades	Vineyard Gazette Graham's Restaurant PFS Framing
Design	Aspen Design Co. Raytheon
Performing Arts	Adventure Set Band

— Personal comments on employment

Comments made by members of this group in the course of the interviews were often revealing. The egalitarian atmosphere of the school clearly affected one person's ideal work environment: "I want to be a composer with a band where all the members have equal interests in composing, arranging, and playing."

Life at the school, an environment in which the entrepreneurial spirit thrives, seemed to be a factor in the unfolding of the careers of several people:

> *I see my work experience as the plasticene projects at SVS [a series of intricate self-initiated crafts and role-playing projects, involving a mixed-age group of students and extending over a period of years] translated into real life. Work incorporates my daydreams about how mechanical things work and how separate mechanical components work together. Running a machine shop is a novel experience because a machine shop contains all of the equipment necessary to reproduce itself.*

> *Working on [my university newspaper], I started lower than entry level — paste up, with the worst hours. I stuck with it, working with fifty-five other students. I was promoted to production manager and head type-setter. Finally I made it to the top. I changed the whole style and format of the paper. I wrote all the computer programs for the paper. It was one of the best times of my life.*

> *I am always learning. One of the most interesting educations has been running my own businesses. Work has to be fun. I have many businesses: pretzel factory, ice cream factory, picture posing business on the street, and others.*

Repeatedly, these people indicated that their work gave them pleasure and an outlet for their creativity:

> *Programming work gives me satisfaction. I see the impact I make and the results of my labor.*

> *Computer programming gives me a sense of accomplishment that the work that I did was mine, and I created it.*

> *All my work has given me satisfaction. I want to be the best I can be. I know my creativity combined with my business sense will help me succeed.*

I enjoy catering, especially managing catering. Doing all jobs well is satisfying.

Even pizza delivery was satisfying because I got very healthy and had fun driving around in the snow.

I love my current job doing rehab as a supervisor of a staff of twelve behavior specialists because of the progress I see in clients. I enjoy watching and helping people recover.

My job seems to be the perfect mix of outdoors activity and challenging work involving mapping and computers.

Further Formal Education

— Where did they continue their schooling?

Out of the twenty-one members of this group, nineteen (90%) have, at some time or another, attended formal classes in order to further their education. Seven (33%) of these completed the requirements for one or more degrees. Table 6.7 lists the schools attended after Sudbury Valley; however, our list of these institutions is incomplete. Schools marked with an asterisk are those from which degrees were received.

Table 6.7

Schools Attended After S.V.S.

Type of School	*Number Attending*	*Number Completing Degrees*	*Names of Schools*
art schools	2	n/a	American School of Ballet Perry Dance School DeCordova Museum School Worcester Museum School
trade schools	2	n/a	Blaire Hairdressing School Walt Disney World Coop Program
community college	2	0	Mass Bay Community College

Type of School	*Number Attending*	*Number Completing Degrees*	*Names of Schools*
college	16	AA (2) BS (1) BA (4)	Berklee College of Music *Boston College Center for Early Education Central New England College Curry College Fordham University *Framingham State College (3) Hampshire College Indianapolis University *Johnson & Wales Univ. (2) Los Angeles City College Lowell University Mass. College of Art *Mt.Ida College Northeastern University (3) Santa Barbara City College Schiller International Univ. *Univ. California (Santa Barbara) *Univ. Maine (Machias) Univ. Mass. (Amherst) (2) Univ. Nebraska *Worcester State College

— Education vs. occupation

In Table 6.8 we look at the relationship between what the members of this group chose to study in their further formal education, and their occupations. As before, the significance of the results is limited by the overall youthfulness of the group. We did not include in the Table the four people who were either primarily students or who had not pursued any further formal education in a serious manner. The Table is arranged by ascending order of age of the remaining seventeen people.

Table 6.8 shows a close linkage between the fields of study that were chosen and the work engaged in at present, with only a very few exceptions. These people clearly knew why they were going to school.

Table 6.8

Relationship of Formal Education to Occupation

Age	*Type of School*	*Degrees*	*Area of Study Concentration*	*Most Recent Occupation*
21	community college		exercise physiology	health club sales and trainer
22	college	BA	political science	owner, games store
22	college, art school		dance	dancer, jazz dance student
23	college		journalism	English teacher in Europe
23	college		pastry arts	waitperson, baker
23	college	BA	fashion design, merchandising	dressmaker
24	college, art school	AA	computer science, business	public relations, office manager
24	college	BS	nursing, abnormal psychology	senior behavior specialist & department manager, rehab facility
26	college		computer science	asst. dir. administrative computing in a college
27	college		computer science	owner of a crafts cafe, technical photographer
29	college		business	screen printing company manager, musician
29	college, trade school	AA	culinary arts	homemade ice cream producer, wholesaler, vendor
33	college, art school	BA	art history	artist, technical illustrator including computer graphics

Age	*Type of School*	*Degrees*	*Area of Study Concentration*	*Most Recent Occupation*
33	college	BA	sociology	R&D contract administrator
35	college		music	musician, software documentation for advanced music programs
35	college		history	supermarket department manager
35	community college		forestry, land surveying	land surveyor

—— Personal comments on education

Some of the remarks made by the interviewees concerning the nature of their post Sudbury Valley educational experiences were interesting. One, for instance, "resented being treated like a kid in college: I am responsible and they shouldn't treat me that way." A second expressed it differently: "I found myself much more motivated than most in college, and much more focussed." Another complained: "I thought I was going to learn all these new things in college, but I found that anything I wanted to learn I could learn on my own, so it was a waste of money."

One person who had taken no formal classes at SVS at all admitted that when he got into college, "I was worried about my academic background, so I worked incredibly hard to get A's." Someone else who also didn't "do classes" at Sudbury Valley said, "Preparing better academically at SVS would have made it easier in the outside world, but it was my decision and I don't regret it because I have been able to do everything I need for my life."

Most members of this group who continued formal studies used their post SVS schools in a very focussed manner to further their interests:

> *I spent my entire second year of college in the library, because I loved to study from books. I study all the time on my own. SVS gave me the self-reliance to educate myself. I didn't get a degree in college because I studied what I wanted*

to know and did well and didn't study anything I wasn't interested in.

I got what I wanted out of my later schooling and stopped as soon as I didn't.

I had an advantage in college academics because every course I took pertained to what I wanted to do.

A number of people in this group expressed their intention to pursue more formal schooling. Three of the seven who had already achieved degrees were planning to continue in graduate school; five others are planning to complete the requirements for degrees; three more have plans for continuing formal education without necessarily receiving certification of any kind. Thus, a total of eleven people (52%) plan to continue their formal education in some manner.

Travel

This group, like that of Chapter 4, also displays a distinct interest in travel. Table 6.9 lists some of the places they have visited. It is organized by age, leaves out four who either have not traveled or about whom we have no information on travel, and is based on incomplete information on the rest. Nevertheless, it makes a pretty impressive set of explorations.

Table 6.9

Travel Experiences

Age	*Places Visited*
21	Quebec, Pacific Northwest, New England, Mexico, cross country USA
22	USSR, England, Israel
22	extensively in Western Europe, Texas, New England
23	throughout continental US, Hawaii, Canada and extensively in Western Europe
23	Pacific Northwest, Mexico, Nevada, Hawaii, cross country USA
23	Florida, Bahamas, Hawaii

Age	*Places Visited*
24	England, Ireland, Western Europe
24	Western Europe, Tortola
26	cross country, Florida, Western Europe
27	Caribbean, Switzerland, Germany, Portugal
27	Mexico, California, Florida, Aruba
29	Indiana, Kentucky, Tennessee
33	hiking, biking and climbing throughout USA
33	hiking, biking and climbing throughout USA
35	skiing and backpacking throughout USA
35	California, Mexico, Western Europe
35	extensively across continental US

Personal Perspectives

Members of this group volunteered many casual comments on their SVS experience. One remarked that "SVS helped to educate me socially; to relate to more people." This was echoed by another person who said, "The most important things in my life are my friends from SVS. I am always with them." Another added: "I relate well to people of all ages due to SVS." The theme of happiness was present in many people's remarks: "I am happy, very independent, and enjoying my life very much." "I enjoy what I am doing, especially outdoors. I am very happy with my life." "I work for the fun of it." One of the oldest members of the group, thirty-five and living in New England, was exuberant: "I love sailing and skippering boats in races year round; also bike racing year round. Life is pretty good and getting better all the time."

A few people commented on specific advantages that their experience at SVS gave them: One person remarked, "Being a Sudbury Valley graduate meant there was no adjustment necessary to freedom and independence, either in college or in 'real life.'" Another said, "At SVS I learned to be ambitious and self-motivated, especially from working on the Dance Corporation." "SVS prepared me for independence, problem-solving, and budgeting time for myself." And, "SVS gave me the ability to accept responsibility without problem."

And again, "I consider myself fortunate because SVS gave me the freedom to not have to rebel against structure and society, so that I could concentrate on what I really wanted to do."

Not all of the comments were positive. One person "found SVS too idealistic and sheltering, because outside, people can hurt you" — an interesting comment in its own right on the atmosphere of the school. Another wondered whether the school might "entail too much moral commitment, and put an unfair burden on students and staff" — an equally revealing impression.

People referred explicitly to how much the school meant to them. One of the youngest, twenty-two years old and freshly graduated from college, said, "Sudbury Valley remains very important in my life and I am still involved with it." A thirty-five year old echoed the sentiment: "Sudbury Valley helped me enormously, and now, fifteen years later, I still feel it was important."

Once again, perhaps the most eloquent comment was the simplest: "I'm a better person because of the school."

7

Reflections of Long Term Students

This chapter is devoted to comments made in the course of interviews for the school's oral history project, which was described in Chapter 5. The segments chosen reflect on the lives of the students after leaving Sudbury Valley, and on what they think they have taken with them from their educational experiences at Sudbury Valley, which spanned at least five years. Of the twenty-one people discussed in Chapter 6, six had oral history interviews, and we have included some comments from each interview. Even though the students come across as six unique individuals, there are common threads to be picked up from one interview to the next.

Here are some comments made by a young man of twenty-six who is now a sociology student and the assistant director of administrative computing at a college. At the time of this interview, he was twenty-two years old.

After leaving SVS, I worked for a year and a half, programming a computer for my dad. I had read a book about programming, and I took an adult evening course while I was at Sudbury Valley, when I was about fourteen. I wanted to learn badly. I was intrigued. Then, after I worked for my dad, I decided to go to school.

So I applied to the college I selected. The interview got me in. It was a neat place up to the last semester I was there. Looking back the only thing

I can really say about it is I must have fallen into a kind of depression because I was sleeping a lot. I lacked motivation; I still took an off-campus course in computers and got an "A" in it but that course was really my major focus, and I kind of lost steam. I did pretty well in my other courses, but I thought, "I can't be here unless I'm willing to make a full commitment and do it right." And the money — it was okay to pay it if I were there taking full advantage, but I wasn't and it was too expensive to sit there and not take full advantage. So I left.

I started working at the job I'm at now. I'm a programmer/analyst acting as assistant manager. The business that I'm working for now used to be a lot smaller then than it is now. Now it's a publicly held company with 300 employees. When I was at school, this guy learned of the programming that I was doing for my father and he was interested. So when I got out of school I wrote him a letter and said, "I'm not in school." I got a call from the VP who said, "Come down and we'll interview you." The interview went terribly, but I was hired.

I was in a unique position; my boss didn't know what the heck I was doing. They just sort of stuck me there because I was the Management Information Systems guy, internal computing in the manufacturing environment. All the rest of the internal computing guys were over in the administrative building so I was the only one. One of my colleagues in the other building helped me out quite a bit and I'd always be calling him up as the guru. He would answer a lot of my questions, and I slowly put a couple of systems together and started to get software running on them as best I could. There were certain obstacles I had to surmount but I could see the benefit in what I was doing for the company. I could see that I was really helping out: that it was kind of a mess and I was straightening it out.

I like a small business with varied duties. I do things such as pulling boards out of computers and changing them, to writing programs and personnel reports. If I need technical information that can be looked up in a book, I find the right resource; or I find the right person and pick their brain.

I think of going back to school. It's always in my mind either on the back burner or on the front burner. Right now it's in the middle. I want to learn more about different areas of what I'm doing now, formally — and get a degree.

The next person was twenty four years old when the interview took place. He is presently the owner of a crafts cafe and a technical photographer.

When I graduated, I wasn't really sure what I wanted to do, but I had a job lined up to work full time, so I figured I could see if I want to work right away. I had taken some college courses at night just to find out what college courses were, and to learn things which, at that time, weren't readily accessible — material on the parts of computer science I was interested in. Everything was high level stuff, for people who had been in computers from the ground floor, and had been working with them for years. Those courses also gave me my first exposure ever to big computers, and to networks. Just to be able to use something so big, so much bigger than just sitting down at a little Apple and typing away. This thing was huge, it filled rooms.

So I worked at my job, fixing computers, for a while longer and then I just more or less got bored. My friend John, who had been a customer at the store and bought endless amounts of stuff, and I'd helped him out a lot, said, "Do you want to come work for me? I'm doing data processing, mailing lists, data bases for different people I've contracted myself out to." We did data processing for retail stores, and started doing magazines and stuff. That was a lot of fun. He had all the computers and we worked right out of his house. I did programming and some entering and stuff. It got to the point where we had tried using so many different things and finally found what worked, that he said "Hey, why don't we try to sell stuff?" So we started selling stuff out of the house. Programs, computers, whole systems, all set and ready to go. Turnkey systems. It's like, "Look, we put this together, and it all works. We're using it right now." I stayed with him for about a year and a half before I went to college.

My interview and letters from people at school were more or less what got me in. I also had sent a resume with work experience with my application. I got an appointment for an interview with someone. I had all the letters sent to him. When I got there, he said, "Well, you've got really impressive records but you don't have any grades. However, after reading everything about the school, I understand." He was really sympathetic. The year that I started was the first year that this school had a college of computer science. This was their guinea pig year. So out of about 5,000 applicants, I was one of the 200 they picked. He more or less said, "Well, look, you haven't had any high school math, you haven't had any high school physics. We'll let you in if you take some kind of introductory course over the summer. Then I don't see any problem if you do well in it. Basically, what it comes down to is, do you think you can do the work?" And I just said, "Yeah, I think I can do the work."

I think it was probably also self-confidence. I wasn't over-confident like "Yeah, this is a breeze, this is a joke." I wasn't like that, but more like, "Yes, if that's what it takes to get through and get by, yes, I can do it."

I learned how to write at Sudbury Valley, and then freshman year in college, I had to take writing. I had to write a research paper. I said to myself, "I know how to do that. No problem." I had prepared myself.

I definitely hadn't prepared myself enough for the math that they bombarded me with the first year, but I struggled through. It was another case of, well, here's the material, yes, I can learn this if I have to. I'm kind of glad that I didn't torture myself when I was younger. College math courses are not for regular people. Because I wasn't forced to learn stupid things like reading, writing and 'rithmetic, I had more of a well rounded, social view — all those things that you're supposed to learn about in college, the reason you go to college, to get rounded, I had done. I learned about art, about literature, and the sciences when I was younger. I wanted to learn them because I wasn't spending all my time doing stupid things. Sudbury Valley was a good school and it was an enjoyable place to grow up because you grew up academically and socially and physically all at the same time. It didn't come in stages. I realize more and more each year what I got from the school.

I still have a lot of things up in the air. I may go to New York. If I go to New York, then I'll go to art school. My girlfriend is into fashion design, and that is something that's always interested me. I've always doodled with that on my own if I have enough time and space to work at it. It's one of those things where I either don't do it at all or I do it and it obsesses me. That's all I do. What you learn in art school, I think, is not something you can put into words. Someone can show you how to do things. But how to mold ideas, the things dealing with the mind, isn't something that you can put down on paper and have always work. Two plus two equals four, you can't change at all, while what is art is really open-ended.

Meanwhile I am going to finish college, no matter what. [He didn't, but is now successfully employed with an innovative business — eds.] It's a lot of money, and everybody keeps telling me — and I finally have come to agree with it — that once you have that stupid little piece of paper, you're worth more and you have more opportunities, but whether it is worth all that hassle, I don't know. Except for my free electives. I've taken all English electives and had a great time: writing, reading, analysis. I've more or less hated everything else. I really haven't gotten excited about the computer stuff that much. I'm learning stuff but the problem is, you get out in the real world and you realize that what they're telling you isn't always what's really happening. You're in class and they say, "Look, this is what's new." And you go out to the job, it's like, "No, we don't do things that way. It doesn't work like that." I definitely learned a lot more on the job. And there are so many prerequisites, all those math courses, and those stupid physics courses. I'm sorry, I just don't need those. I just hate almost everything that they tell me I have to take. Some of the math courses are interesting, the high level ones, like courses in probability and things like that. But calculus: no, I'm never going to use this ever, ever, ever. Everything, basically, I could have learned on my own. The diploma is the only reason that I keep going to college. That and my parents would probably never talk to me again.

Here are the reflections of a thirty-six year old owner of a machine shop and saw mill.

Working in plasticene at Sudbury Valley was a fascination of creating. You were creating things that you couldn't have in real life yourself, maybe, but you could still make them, and by making them, you could have them. I think it was probably one of the most intense things I'd ever done. Villages would evolve. Sometimes you'd be building a gold mining community. Sometimes it would be a bunch of towns with hotels and saloons. Then you'd have battles and wars. You'd be building tanks and airplanes, just one thing after another. But it always involved a lot of buildings, a lot of vehicles, a lot of people and you'd make all the stuff. Then you would enact various scenes with them.

Well, I think about it every now and then, and I'm doing exactly the same things now. Except I'm doing them now in real life. I'm building a factory and making machines and talking to people all day long. Same exact thing. And very intensely. We talk about how to build the things, how to talk to the customers on the phone, all that sort of stuff. Day in and day out, the same exact thing I was doing in plasticene.

I am still interested in drawing. I draw mostly mechanical drawings now. All the time. That drawing board goes with me on airplanes. It goes with me to the store at lunch. I draw as a way of putting my ideas on paper. I used to draw landscapes and things like that, but now I draw designs. I'm always drawing. The clipboard is never gone, it's always being used.

I also write a lot of directions, and a lot of reports on things I've done. In order for me to get my company to work by itself, I've got to be able to put what I know down on paper for people to read, so they can have my knowledge without me being there.

Another thing Sudbury Valley taught me is to enjoy what I do to spend my time. I've never worked at a job that I didn't like doing. Everything is just as much fun as it used to be. I don't do anything that's not fun. There's no point to that. There are times when I wish I could be doing something else. Maybe the snow is falling, but I can't leave the factory. I have to ski, but I can't ski, because there's work to be done in this case. There are problems like that.

What motivates me to do the work is not money. It's the interest in doing what I'm doing, the realization that there's probably not too many other ways to build what I am building, and learn what I'm learning, other than by doing what I'm doing now. So, I keep on doing it. There's always some goal beyond that you're working towards. At one time, many years ago, I could picture that I really wanted a machine shop. I wanted a machine shop with all the usual machine shop tools. I wanted it well set up, and if I had that I'd be all happy and that's all I ever wanted. About two years ago I was walking down the stairs from the office and looked around at all the stuff and realized that I had obtained the goal I had set for myself quite a few years ago. I had gone by it and I didn't even realize it. Because now, there was something else I was looking towards . . . there's always something else. One of my major goals, is to get the business to run itself. That's a real challenge. So that I can leave and it'll still run.

It is wonderful to me. When I was a little kid and I was fixing a tricycle and it had a broken axle, I wouldn't have known how to run a welder even if I had a welder. Now, not only do I know how to do all that stuff, but it would almost be a job that I could do while I was talking to somebody else on the phone. Because I've done that sort of stuff so often and I have all those tools. I'm thinking now of building machines that I could never even dream that I'd be building, and building quite effortlessly. So you're always working on that one machine that you haven't yet done. I want to build a submarine. That's one of the things.

When I used to drive trucks, at the beginning, it was because I wanted to have a truck. So when I first saw my truck, I bought it. Well, now I had a truck. I thought, this is going to be glorious. And I started fixing it and playing with it and getting it running better and better. I started driving it. I needed a trailer, so I bought a trailer for the truck. Now I was driving that around. I got my first load, and I signed all my trip lease papers and someone was showing me how to fill out a log book, and I headed down the road to New York City and I found another load going back to Albany, and then I did this over and over again. I learned more about trip leasing and more about truck repair and more about how to make money, and about insurance and so forth. After quite a while, all of a sudden I knew this inside out. I didn't have to think. After a little while it was no longer quite that exciting. I could have taken longer trips and maybe got a fancier truck, but now I was married and my wife didn't like the idea that I was gone, so I had that pressure, and I just said, "Well, I've gone as far as I can with this at this time."

When I first moved up to Maine, I still had my truck. I also worked for a guy fixing woods harvesting equipment. After a while that became old and was a one way street. I found somebody else who wanted to start a machine shop and went into partnership with him. I just put a lot of time into collecting these tools and learning how to do it, because I wasn't a machinist. I didn't know anything about it other than it was a fascinating subject. I've been in that building that we built, for about fifteen years now. It's been growing. And the more people you have working, the faster it grows. All highly skilled people. We do everything. We design and build custom machinery for people, but the major business is making hardwood flooring. We make custom moldings and log cabin logs. A woodworker nowadays is not somebody who has a fascination with wood. It's somebody who has a fascination with machines and this particular machine just happens to be doing something to a piece of wood. The way to keep it interesting is you have to keep on changing your process and making it better, or doing different things.

I played a lot with farming, but I learned that when I fix something for somebody, I immediately got paid, got a thank you, and the thing was working and I had some money. You don't get that with a farm. Everything that you do now, you only get your gratification six months in the future. And for me, everything I ever did with a farm was a loss anyway! But, I like the fact that I know how to farm. I have a farm, more or less, so if I ever needed to, I could grow my own stuff. I have a lot of food in my place. I like the self-sufficiency that gives me. But even if the economy collapsed I think I'd be more likely to spend my time in the machine shop, fixing other farmers' equipment. I'm probably more self-sufficient now than I ever could have thought I would be. I make everything I need on the farm because my living (my machine shop) is right there. It's only a slightly different manner and, by having a machine shop, I can now make anything I want from farm machinery to woodworking equipment. I build my own furniture. My house doesn't have a lot of the things that people consider a necessity. It does not have indoor plumbing, for one thing. I have an outhouse and I am working on a regular septic system, but I like going out because the outside is something I spend much of my life in and going outside is just a part of living. Particularly in Maine in the winter. I face the fact that when I get up, I'm going to be outside a lot and I dress accordingly and it doesn't affect me.

I'm interested in education now, partially because my education was so different. And I get into conversations quite often with people about education and then I'll somehow end up giving them one of the books about Sudbury Valley. I see a lot of kids in my neighborhood that are being totally raised by television and by what other people think they should be doing.

It's causing people a lot of problems because many people that are my age are living life according to the planned American way. They think, if I do this and this and this, I'm going to have happiness and security. And they're doing all these things and their bills aren't getting paid and they don't have happiness. And they don't have security, because their bills aren't getting paid. They don't know what's going on. They look at me and they say, "You're crazy. You must be really suffering. You don't even have a flush toilet." And I say, "Well, I'm not worried about my bills not getting paid. I've got more money than I want to have."

If at the time I was building my house, a flush toilet had been a necessity, I would have had to get a lot of bank money together in order to do it. I couldn't have built my house where I did because it would have cost too much money to get the electric line in. Probably I could have put in a chemical toilet. And now it would be no big deal. I could just do it like that. But at one time, it would have meant me not putting my time into buying, say, a milling machine. I would have still been working for a guy fixing skidders for $4 an hour. And so to have that flush toilet, I would have been working for $4 an hour; probably I couldn't even have gotten a bank loan to get a house. I would have had to rent. So I would have had my flush toilet and central heat, but every bit of my money would have been going into that. What I did instead is take all this money and buy milling machines, and a workshop and all of a sudden, these things now are making me money. Other people have been dumping all the money into their flush toilet, but I've been dumping mine into something else. Now I can have any number of flush toilets. The problem is many of the other people never really learned what they want, because from the very beginning, they're doing what they think they want. They already knew one step before what they were going to be doing next.

I didn't go to college because I didn't know what I wanted to do in college. My parents had the money set aside. I could have gone to any college. I just didn't know what I would have wanted to learn. Anytime I wanted to learn something, I could picture what I wanted to learn. Like when I wanted to learn refrigeration. I could see these guys working on refrigerators. I knew they were getting a lot of money. It looked like they were having a lot of fun. So I wanted to learn how to do refrigeration. I had a goal. I didn't quit my job and go to refrigeration school. I bought a book. And when I didn't have the book, I asked the refrigeration guys what they were doing. Most guys, if you ask them, they want to tell you. And the more I could learn, the more questions I could ask that made sense, the more interested they would be in telling me. Pretty soon I was doing it. I learned it in a matter of months. Then I got better and better as I did more and more and went into more complicated problems. Whenever I wanted to learn something, I always found I could learn it real quick, so why go to college?

Did the school make me the way I am now? It's something I have wondered often. I don't know if it did. But I wouldn't be surprised if it did.

It certainly helped. And it kept me from wasting my time doing silly things of protest. However, all the time that you are in SVS you worry that this is a school that you're not learning anything and you're going to be a failure and nobody's teaching you how to make money when you get out of school. What are you going to do? And so, there was always that worry. I don't remember ever really doing anything about it, but after a certain time it became obvious — just like, once you had that car and tractor built, you were done with it — that after a certain amount of time the school was something I had to be done wih. I had to graduate. I had to go on and do something else. And that evolved slowly and at the right time, I think. I felt like it was time to graduate. It wasn't like I felt pressed. It came from inside and I was ready. I wasn't sure what I was going to do, but I was prepared to go out and do whatever it was. I don't think I had the confidence to go out until I was really ready. Suddenly, whether I knew what I was doing or not, I knew I had the confidence to go out and try and that I would do the best I could and let things happen the way they were going to happen. I don't "fail" by actually failing, like a guy testing a parachute might fail if he jumped off a big cliff. I would fail by throwing a brick tied to a parachute. If that brick hit the ground and broke, that was my failure. I would test the waters before I jumped, always. And so my failures were never catastrophic, they were just, "Well that parachute didn't work. I'm going to have to build another one." I am very cautious when I do things. I didn't jump out into the real world and do something that would cause me to have a catastrophic failure that would crush me to the point where I would say, "Oh, I'm not going to do that again and I'm just going to pump gas." I always try a little of this, a little of that and so I wouldn't really fail. I still live my life that way. I don't throw all my eggs in one basket.

The paragraphs below were from the interview of a young woman who is now a self-employed artist, as well as a technical illustrator, including computer graphics. She was twenty-nine years old at the time of the interview.

I was very worried about my abilities in school after Sudbury Valley, but I think perhaps that gave me the extra incentive a lot of the other students lacked to prove to myself that I could do it; and I excelled. So really I didn't have anything to worry about. I remember it being a challenge, but one that I was willing to undertake and it was very satisfying to be able to do so well, because I really hadn't come from a structured background. At that point, I realized how different the education was that I had received at Sudbury Valley. I also realized what these other students had missed out on; what I'd had that they hadn't.

There are a lot of things about Sudbury Valley that I think are on a more personal level, as far as building your character, things that perhaps enable you to learn better, that public school students never have a chance to achieve. They don't have to challenge themselves to go out and learn what they want to learn. When you're responsible for your own time, and spend it the way that you want to, you tend to put a lot more enthusiasm into what you do, instead of being a lethargic lump that's molded and prodded into a certain direction. And when you end up the way you want to end up, you know you've been responsible for it. It's a lot more rewarding, I think, than when you end up the way somebody else wants you to end up.

A lot of things that came from the way I learned at Sudbury Valley enabled me to learn in another structure; for example, just being attentive, being able to listen to what somebody says. I think a lot of people can't do that. And being able to really put a lot more into what it is you're trying to do, that extra effort. At SVS almost everybody really tried a lot harder at whatever it was they were doing because it was something they wanted to do. So they really went all out.

When I was in college and a little bit frustrated by some of what I felt were my deficiencies, I may have wondered what would have happened if I stayed in public school where I had been a very good student — if I really would have become some kind of model student with all kinds of scholarships and things like that. But I still did remarkably well. In my entire life as a matter of fact, as far as grades go, I've only had one mark below a B and that was for one paper. All of my courses have always been A's or high B's, so I think that shows that whatever I embarked on I was successful at. But I was very insecure my first semester in college.

My education in the art field was received at a museum school, which was probably the best art education I could have had anywhere. Then when I wanted a degree, I went to a college to get the general education requirements. Most kids who go to college go because of the social life and I was just the opposite. I went because I wanted to learn and I was very sure of that. I loved every minute of all of my education.

After I graduated from college, my husband and I moved to California where I worked as a house cleaner for a year and a half and then I started working for a big company in the art department. At first, though, I couldn't find work in an art related field. It was a big disappointment. In fact I didn't fill out my alumni questionnaire from college because I didn't want them to know that I hadn't gotten a job in the art field yet. For one thing, I was in a new area and I really didn't have any contacts. Maybe if I had stayed around Massachusetts, it would have helped. Plus, unemployment was at 13% that year. And also, in the area I was in, which is an arty area, there are very few openings ever, not just that year, but ever, because people like to retire to that area. If they have an art job, they stay in it until they die. Now I'm a technical illustrator. I'm a supervisor in that same company.

The excerpts below come from the interview of a person who was thirty-one years old at the time of the interview and was then, as he is now, managing a department in a supermarket. However, he is now working in a much larger supermarket.

The one thing I've learned, I don't know if I learned at school. I don't know where I learned it, but I've learned that it doesn't make sense to regret anything. I learned too that it doesn't make sense to be guilty about anything. I wish I had certain innate abilities that other people have, but I don't have them and I think I've made the best of what I have, which is as good as most of the rest of the world. So I don't think I've missed out by not going to any other school or missed out by not going to college. You can't say you missed out. It wasn't right then and I didn't do it then, and I had a choice, too. If you're forced to do something you can kind of regret it. But if you're not forced, you have the choice, so you can't regret it because you still have the opportunity to change it, now.

After I left school, a few of us from school started a natural foods supermarket chain. That took eight years. It was sort of a mixed bag. In some ways it was great experience and I really liked it. I worked hard and maybe half the time was really good and half the time was really awful — I mean, really awful. I probably came the closest to having regrets at that point that I didn't have something else to do. That wasn't anybody else's fault, but it was a feeling I had. That was a scary feeling. I knew there was nothing I could have done earlier to prepare myself for that, but it was an awful position, to feel that you're doing something you don't want to do and you don't know what else to do.

I've learned not to worry about it as much so I'm not so concerned about what I do. I envision some day coming across something that I like doing which will turn into a job. I happen to like sailing. Probably that will never turn into a job, but I imagine something like that will come along some day that turns into a job. (I can always make money.) That's what I'm waiting for. I've found that you can't force it. I've been spending a lot of years just trying to have a reasonable day every day and do things that are fun and a good time and interesting and learn things.

This young man, who speaks so eloquently of his theories of learning, is currently a musician, a jazz pianist, who also documents software for advanced music programs. He was thirty-five years old when the interview was done.

Learning and playing. I'm sure many other people have thought about the process of a kid's adaptation to his environment. I think it's important to have fun when you're a kid in whatever you do. I think it's part of the growing process. This is all just sort of philosophical conjecture and it's not really my field, but I suspect that kids when they play are trying out constructs, mental constructs, that they see other people using. They're not really in a position in the real world to use those constructs, so they play and imitate them and figure them out. If it wasn't fun, they probably wouldn't do it. The motivation for figuring out all this stuff around you is that it feels good to do it. It's kind of like if there were no orgasms, the race would die out very quickly. There would be no sex and therefore no procreation.

We have to understand the world around us because certain information that we need to survive cannot be passed down through DNA and genes. So we have a body of knowledge which we gain after we're born, which is really a cultural knowledge. You learn it as an individual, but it's passed on. That's really what we need to survive, and if it wasn't fun to learn that, we wouldn't learn it. So, for some reason, it's ingrained in us that play is fun, and play is modelling what we see around us. In school I did playful learning. I think it's natural.

When I graduated, I had to present an oral thesis and I had to appear to, or, in truth, to come up with a decision about my life, and so I decided that I was going to be a musician. I've come up with other curiosities since them and followed them and that's been rewarding too, but I'm still a musician. It's hard to make a living as a musician. It's insecure. I'm not buying a house. I have no health insurance. And I have no credit. Nobody will give me any credit cards, because I'm not working for a company.

But anyway, basically, I think it was a little bit of a bottleneck there, forcing me to make a decision and tell people what I planned to do and then prove that I could do it before they let me go. Now I play in clubs in Los Angeles, Latin music, and I have been in a band for a few years in a row at the same club and I can leave my stuff there. If I freelance, I can work just as much, but I have to carry the equipment every night. The plus is that I get to play with a lot of different musicians and read different charts. It's fresher, more variety. You're never quite as musically satisfied as you are with a steady band. After playing the same tunes for a year and putting on little additions, and everybody knowing what everybody else is going to play and how fast we're going to play it and everything, the music starts to sound pretty good and feel good and it's really what they call "tight." You don't get that as a freelancer, but that's more of a personal challenge. I play three nights a week, four nights a week. It gives me enough money to have free time for the other nights, and it gives me the days. I really prize my time almost above everything else.

When I left Sudbury Valley and entered music school I was weak in mathematics, which I later became interested in and studied somewhat. I was able to relate it to music and that's why I was so good at it, because when they were talking about the different parts of a triangle, those were like the different notes that are in a chord, chord members. And there was a relationship between them and vibration numbers. So it was very easy: I had another model to map that over so it made perfect sense to me.

The reason that college was easy was that I already knew all this and all they did was give me the names for it. I knew it because I had the time to play around, I suppose. I mean, there have been true prodigies who come up with this stuff when they're five; to know it when you're sixteen is not really that much of an accomplishment. But I felt like it was good to be able to have come up with it, to have the free time. Looking back, I think that's really good, to sit around and play all day.

At Sudbury Valley I really got a sense of my own investigative powers and I still use them. I can learn just by reading books, by reading a glossary. All I need to do on many subjects is read the glossary and I understand a lot right off. I often don't really even need to read the book. It's the terms. A good definition of a term in a glossary written by somebody who's articulate is a whole lesson in a single paragraph. It's as if somebody defines polarization in the back of a camera manual, and they do it well, and that teaches you about light and about the camera and about a lot of stuff in the paragraph. So that's what I like to read. It's really encapsulated.

Most of my musician friends have a smaller range of music that they're interested in than me. I have a lot of different friends, so that I can keep interested in lots of kinds of music. I don't know if that's child-like or not, but I'm more of a "know a little bit about a lot of things" rather than a "know a lot about one thing." Most of the really good musical masters, on a particular instrument or whatever, have just studied that instrument in one idiom all their life and I'm more the kind of person who likes to spread out and unify things, find the similarities in everything and learn new things. It seems like the more I know, the quicker I can learn other things because so much of knowledge is organized in the same way.

All subjects are basically organized in a nested structure where you have — well, let's see, what's a good example? Geography. You have the country and you divide it into states which are divided into counties, which are divided into towns. That's a hierarchical nested structure. And that structure is used in many bodies of knowledge and often when it's taught, it's taught that way. Once you know that, it's very easy to map a new subject onto that and see what's going on. I find similarities in things. One of my idols is Buckminster Fuller who is a generalist. He called himself a generalist rather than a specialist. I like that. My models are becoming more general now. I'm able to apply them to bigger things, larger groups of various things. I enjoy evolving my mindset to make sense out of more and more things.

It's hard to compare yourself to what you might have been had you grown up differently, or even to other people you know, because it's hard to tell what part of you is your personality which would be the same no matter what happened to you.

I wrote a manual for a music computer a couple of years ago. What taught me to write and really helped me articulate my thoughts was computer bulletin boards. You have these dialogues with people that are halfway between a conversation with somebody face to face — which is reasonably quick and a lot of exchange and you make mistakes in your grammar — and writing letters to somebody which takes maybe a week to get a response. This is like a conversation in that you get your answer in a day, but it's nice because nobody interrupts you while you're typing. Some deep discussions go on, in text. I really enjoyed it, being able to straighten out my thoughts and put them down where somebody else could read them quickly and respond. It's fun. It's enjoyable being articulate and having someone discuss something with you, even if it's an argument. I would say it definitely improved my writing. I was ready to write after doing that for a couple of years and it just so happened that the manual came up about then.

I am very interested in photography. It's different than music because you're taking pictures of things that exist in a way that, hopefully, will portray some kind of mood or view. When you make music, you're actually creating the subject, unlike photography, and there's a mood that goes along with it too, you know. You create subjects, probably to inspire a mood in somebody, whereas in photography it's like trying to get other people to see things the way you see them. You take a picture of something that you like and show it to somebody and if they get a similar reaction to it, then I guess it's successful photography. I like it because it's visual, and I also like to do computer graphics.

The expansion of your awareness of things around you I think of as relating to a bubble. Everything within the bubble I know and understand and it's part of my world. Outside, I haven't learned yet, but I may be aware of it. That bubble expands as you grow. One year when I was about thirteen or fourteen, I became really aware of that growth. Before that you're not even aware of your own growth. You're just learning, and the things you know are all you know. But eventually you become aware of your own process of learning which is kind of interesting. It's sort of a meta-awareness or something. And I guess as you get older, you can abstract to any level. Any thought that you have, you should be able to step back from and be aware of and that's when you know you're conscious and aware and intelligent. That was kind of fun. It was interesting to me, to become aware of myself and even now I still feel like there are things that I'm aware of which are still not inside my bubble, and I'm still growing. I follow my curiosity and then bring it into the bubble. I don't purposely try to study things that I'm not interested in.

Part IV

Short Term Students

8

Students Who Were Enrolled in Sudbury Valley For Their High School Age Years

This chapter and the next are about those people who came to Sudbury Valley for what is generally considered to be their high school years. All of these former students spent either three or four years at SVS, and they considered their stay the equivalent of having gone to high school. Whether or not they completed the requirements for graduation, they left feeling that their basic schooling was completed. This group differs from the group discussed in Chapter 6 in the number of years spent at Sudbury Valley, which is reflected both in a higher entry age and a greater exposure to more traditional schooling before they enrolled. Because of these factors, the adjustment to Sudbury Valley must have been much more difficult for these individuals than for those in the preceding groups. They were undoubtedly not accustomed to the level of control over their own activities that they encountered at Sudbury Valley.

There were fifty-three people in this group, of whom fifty were respondents in the study, for a response rate of 94%. All of the data presented in this chapter will refer to the fifty respondents only, of whom thirty (60%) were male, and twenty female.

Thirty-seven (74%) of the fifty received diplomas before leaving. The fates of the thirteen who did not receive diplomas did not seem to be adversely affected by the absence of this particular certification. Four of the thirteen got university degrees, of whom one became a university professor, one became a physician, one received a masters' degree in theology, and one received a bachelor's degree in nursing. Three went on to manage or own businesses. One became a carpenter and fireman, one a computer programming specialist, one a musician, one an artist, one a parent and a student of photography. The only one of the thirteen who remained in an unskilled job was the only member of the group — and one of the few in the history of the school — who because of his conduct was not allowed to continue as a student.

Basic Demographics

—— How old are they now?

Figure 8.1 shows the distribution of this group by age on January 1, 1991. As might be expected, with this group we are beginning to get a slightly older set of people, ranging in age from twenty to thirty-nine. The average age of the group is thirty, and the median age is thirty-two.

Figure 8.1

Distribution by Age, January 1, 1991

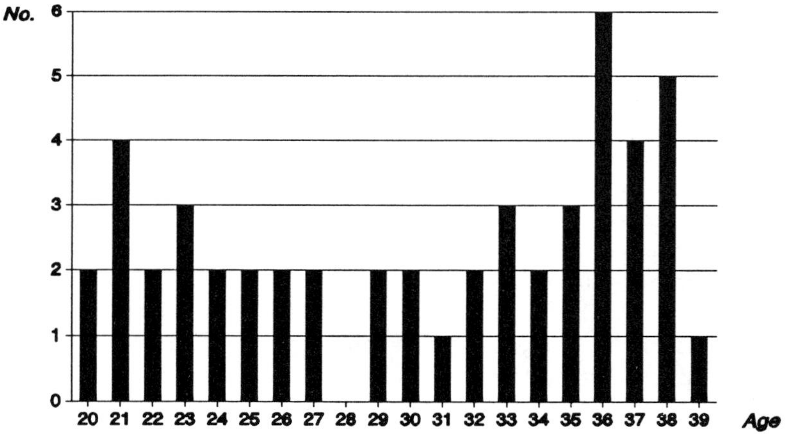

— Their marital status

Of the fifty people in this group, twenty-one were single (42%); twenty-three were or had been married (46%) — eight were divorced, one of whom was remarried, one living with a significant other, two engaged to be married again; and six were living with significant others (12%). Five people were married ten years or longer, one for seventeen years. This group of fifty had a total of twenty-four children, ages one to fourteen; whereas the first two groups together, consisting of forty-eight people, had a total of five children. In this group, fourteen people (28%) were parents; two had three children each, six had two each, and the balance had one. Thus, in general, this group tends to be somewhat older and more settled than the other groups.

— Where do they live?

Table 8.1 shows where these people live. Twenty-eight of them (56%) live in Massachusetts, all but three of them in towns that are considered to be in the school's catchment area.

Table 8.1

Current Geographical Distribution of the Group

No.	*Town*	*State*
1	Agoura Hills	California
1	Daly City	California
2	Los Angeles	California
2	Oakland	California
1	San Diego	California
1	Boulder	Colorado
1	Washington	District of Columbia
1	Largo	Florida
1	Lawrenceville	Georgia
1	Hayden Lake	Idaho
2	Ashland	Massachusetts
2	Framingham	Massachusetts
1	Harvard	Massachusetts

No.	*Town*	*State*
1	Holliston	Massachusetts
1	Marblehead	Massachusetts
4	Marlboro	Massachusetts
1	Milford	Massachusetts
2	Nantucket	Massachusetts
1	Salem	Massachusetts
1	Shrewsbury	Massachusetts
1	Somerville	Massachusetts
2	Southboro	Massachusetts
1	Sudbury	Massachusetts
2	Walpole	Massachusetts
1	Woodville	Massachusetts
5	Worcester	Massachusetts
1	St. Paul	Minnesota
1	Lavina	Montana
1	Hudson	New Hampshire
2	New York	New York
1	Providence	Rhode Island
1	Seattle	Washington
1	Toronto	Ontario, Canada
1	Vancouver	British Columbia, Canada
1	Hong Kong	Hong Kong

— How old were they when they enrolled?

Figure 8.2 shows the ages at which this group entered the school. The ages range from thirteen to eighteen, with both the average and median age of entry being fifteen.

Figure 8.2

Distribution by Age of Entry

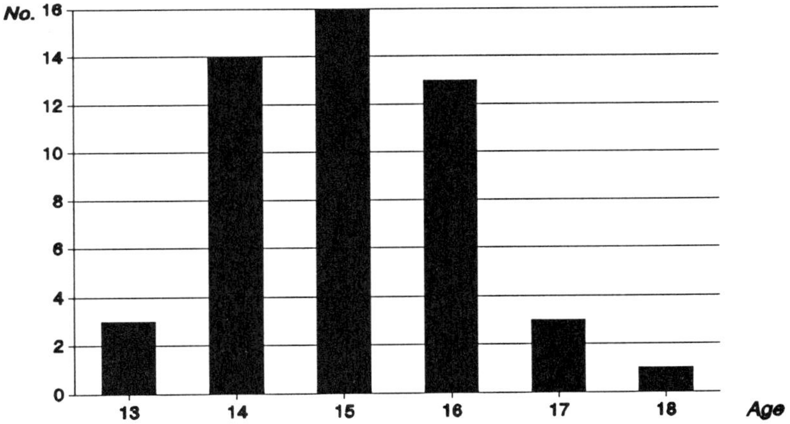

— What was their prior schooling?

Every member of this group had extensive exposure to more traditional schooling before entering Sudbury Valley. Figure 8.3 details the number who went to various categories of schools prior to SVS. We distinguish between private and public schools. Since a person may have gone to both private and public schools at any level, the total number at each level is higher than the actual number of individuals who went to school at each level.

Figure 8.3

Schooling Prior to Sudbury Valley

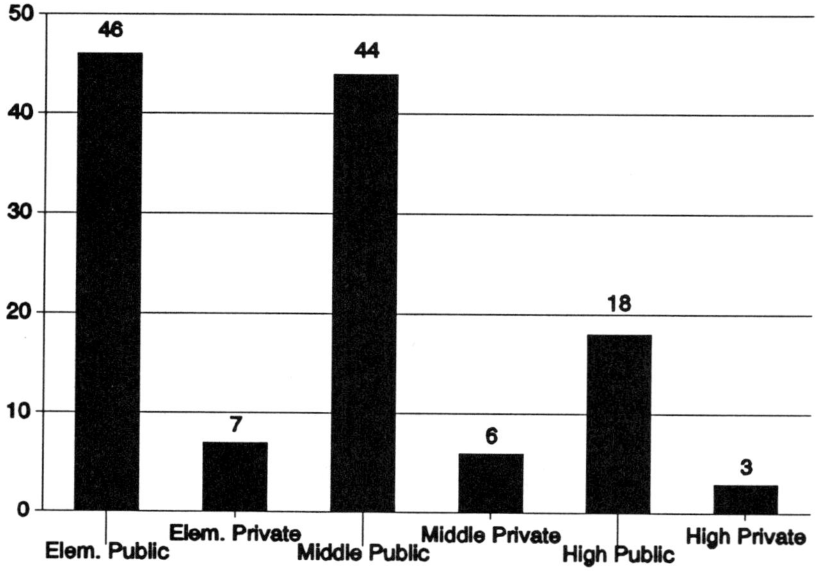

Of the fifty, all attended elementary school. Forty-seven (94%) attended middle school. Twenty (40%) attended high school. Of the six students who went to a private middle school, four had also attended a private elementary school, and one went on to attend a private high school. (That one student also tried public elementary, middle and high schools.) Out of the entire group of fifty, eleven different people (22%) attended a private school at some time before entering Sudbury Valley; only two of these eleven attended private schools exclusively. Thus, thirty nine people (78%) had attended only public schools, and forty-seven people (94%) had attended public schools at some time. These figures show conclusively that this particular population was not drawn from among families who traditionally send their children to private schools; in fact, such families were very much the exception.

—— How old were they when they left the school?

This group includes only people who stayed at the school for three or four years.[1] Out of the fifty, thirty one (62%) stayed three years. Figure 8.4 shows the ages at which members of this group left the school. Both the average age of leaving and the median age of leaving is 18.5, slightly higher than for the first two groups, where the averages and medians were both 18. The person who left school at twenty-six had been enrolled for three years, left school to pursue an entrepreneurial career for several years, and then returned to school in order to continue his education and then to defend his thesis and receive a diploma.

Figure 8.4

Distribution by Age at Leaving

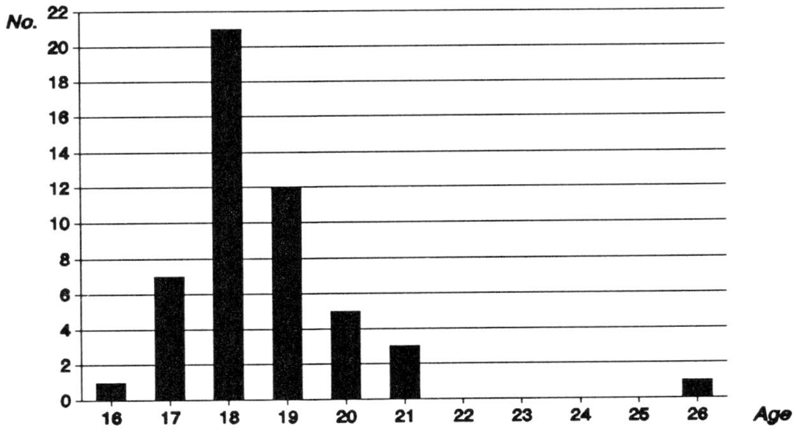

[1] We count only years actually enrolled in the school. For students who left Sudbury Valley for a time and subsequently returned, the time spent away from Sudbury Valley is not included in the calculation of the length of stay at school.

— Where did they live?

Table 8.2 shows the geographical distribution of this population at the time that they were students here. This group was drawn from a much larger number of towns and a generally wider radius of commute than the other groups. There may be some connection between the length of time these families expected to spend as members of the school community and their willingness to take on a very difficult commute; the fact that most of the students reached driving age during their stay at school may also be a factor.

Table 8.2

Geographical Distribution While in School

No.	*Town*
2	Acton
1	Ashland
1	Boston
1	Concord
9	Framingham
1	Franklin
1	Harvard
2	Hingham
5	Holliston
1	Hopkinton
1	Hudson
3	Marlboro
1	Medway
2	Needham
3	Newton
1	Northboro
1	Roslindale
2	Southboro
1	Stow
1	Sudbury
1	Walpole
1	Wayland
1	Wellesley
2	Westborough
1	Woodville
4	Worcester

Occupations

— What are they doing now?

Table 8.3 summarizes by category the variety of occupations presently engaged in by members of this group. Occupations marked with an asterisk denote entrepreneurial or self-employed situations. Any individual can appear in more than one category of occupation. The category "Parent" appears here for the first time because this is the first group in which members were full-time parents.

Table 8.3

Present Occupations (Arranged by Categories of Occupation)

Category	*Number in Category*	*Specific Occupations*
Business Management	12	consultant in international strategic management
		shoe store assistant manager
		clothing store manager
		gas station assistant manager
		health club supervisor
		bar manager
		funeral home manager
		*animal husbandry
		*owner, manager of computer store
		*owner, crafts business
		*owner, construction business
		*owner, bio-electric shield company
Office Manager/ Executive Assistant	4	office manager
		secretary
		medical transcriber
		counselor, planned parenthood
High Tech	3	computer software technician
		*computer accounting systems consultant
		design engineering assistant

Category	*Number in Category*	*Specific Occupations*
Professional	10	physician •chiropractor nurse (4) clinical psychologist medical insurance claims adjuster epidemiological research project manager journalist US Air Force reserve officer
Parent	2	parent (2)
Education	4	professor of mathematics aerobics instructor museum guide college physics teaching assistant college English teaching assistant
Marketing	2	network marketing (2)
Trades	7	hotel chef cook, butcher, bartender hairdresser fireman auto mechanic carpenter (2)
Design	1	fashion design
Creative Arts	6	•Native American crafts reproduction •freelance author (2) song writer (2) composer
Performing Arts	5	•musician in group (4) musician in symphony orchestra
Unskilled Labor	7	waitperson (3) commercial office building cleaner (2) retail clerk (2)

Category	*Number in Category*	*Specific Occupations*
Student	9	physics (PhD program) pastry arts liberal arts psychology history theology (graduate program) photography music film-making

Table 8.4 lists the occupations in which each of the people in this sample are currently engaged. The list is in ascending order of age. There is no predominance of any category of work in either the younger or the older part of the group.

Only one person is an unskilled laborer and not at the same time a student; he is the person referred to above who left school because he was asked not to return.

Table 8.4

Present Occupations (Arranged in Order of Age)

Age	*Present Occupation*
20	pastry arts student
20	music student
21	liberal arts student, carpenter
21	psychology student
21	shoe store assistant manager
21	hairdresser
22	planned parenthood counselor, waitperson
22	film-making student
23	nurse
23	nurse
23	clothing store manager, waitperson
24	carpenter
24	computer software technician

Age	*Present Occupation*
25	gas station assistant manager
25	history student
26	Native American crafts reproduction, commercial office building cleaner
26	aerobics instructor, health club supervisor, secretary
27	musician, commercial office building cleaner
27	owner of crafts business, office manager
29	musician, song writer
29	bar manager, cook, butcher, bartender, waitperson
30	physician
30	owner of construction business
31	network marketing
32	retail clerk
32	professor of mathematics
33	clinical psychologist, freelance author
33	photography student, retail clerk
33	network marketing
34	physics student (PhD program), college physics teaching assistant
34	computer accounting systems consultant
35	nurse
35	fireman
35	nurse
36	journalist, freelance author, college English teaching assistant, museum guide
36	parent
36	carpenter
36	consultant in international strategic management
36	animal husbandry, medical transcriber, US Air Force reserve officer
36	design engineering assistant
37	fashion design
37	auto mechanic, musician, composer
37	musician in symphony orchestra
37	chiropractor, medical insurance claims adjuster, owner of bio-electric shield company
38	funeral home manager
38	parent
38	hotel chef, musician, song writer
38	owner and manager of computer store
38	epidemiological research project manager
39	theology student (graduate program)

— Range of occupations

Table 8.5 presents as complete a list as we have available of all the occupations engaged in by members of this group after they left school (including those in the above Table of present occupations). As in Table 8.3, occupations marked with an asterisk denote either entrepreneurial or self-employed situations. The category of "student," shown in Table 8.3, has been dropped, since a subsequent section will take up in greater detail the education pursued by members of this group.

Table 8.5

Occupations Engaged in Since Leaving Sudbury Valley (Arranged by Categories of Occupation)

Category	*Number in Category*	*Specific Occupations*
Business Management	22	consultant in international strategic management
		shoe store assistant manager
		clothing store manager
		gas station assistant manager
		convenience store assistant manager
		health club supervisor
		bar manager
		restaurant manager
		funeral home manager
		auto rental business manager
		grocery manager (2)
		drive-in supermarket manager
		ice cream business manager (2)
		*animal husbandry
		*owner, manager of computer store
		*owner, crafts business
		*owner, construction business
		*owner, bio-electric shield company
		*real estate management
		president, clothing manufacturing co.
		*music and recording management co. (2)
		*owner, house cleaning business
		*truck rental business

Category	*Number in Category*	*Specific Occupations*
Business Management *(cont'd)*		•partner, natural foods supermarket chain •sewing machine sales & service business •owner, auto repair business
Office Manager/ Executive Assistant	14	office manager (4) secretary (4) medical transcriber medical assistant in doctor's office counselor, planned parenthood childbirth counselor job developer for refugees drug rehab facility supervisor warehouse supervisor bookkeeper employment advisor, personnel agency
High Tech	6	computer software technician •computer accounting systems consultant computer programmer supervisor, computer department of insurance company design engineering assistant •computer consultant (2) electronics technician
Professional	13	physician •chiropractor nurse (5) EMT clinical psychologist manager of mental health facility for adults physical therapist medical insurance claims adjuster epidemiological research project manager journalist US Air Force reserve officer military historian member of a lay Catholic service order
Parent	2	parent (2)

Category	*Number in Category*	*Specific Occupations*
Education	8	professor of mathematics aerobics instructor museum guide college physics teaching assistant college English teaching assistant day care center worker (2) skating teacher Sudbury Valley School staff member
Law Enforcement	2	*detective assistant to head of juvenile services with juvenile court
Marketing	3	network marketing (2) insurance sales
Trades	24	hotel chef cook, butcher, bartender baker candy and ice cream maker head waiter hairdresser fireman letter carrier logger auto mechanic sewing machine maintenance air craft maintenance machinist welder copier technician lab technician (3) USN submarine crewman clothing alteration medical orderly model caretaker of an estate carpenter (11) *carpenter (self-employed) painter

Category	*Number in Category*	*Specific Occupations*
Design	1	fashion design pattern maker
Media	4	assistant producer, cable TV assistant producer, radio radio announcer researcher for radio station disc jockey
Creative Arts	7	*Native American crafts reproduction *freelance author (2) song writer (2) composer craftsperson
Performing Arts	10	*musician in group (4) musician in symphony orchestra dancer singer actor technical director of a repertory theater live sound engineer
Unskilled Labor	26	waitperson (12) commercial office building cleaner (2) bank clerk retail clerk (11) office clerk (2) data processor hotel clerk delivery person (2) warehouseman (4) truck driver (2) cab driver bus driver limousine driver mate on a ship gas station attendant (2) farm hand

Category	*Number in Category*	*Specific Occupations*
Unskilled Labor *(cont'd)*		kitchen help (2) camp counselor veterinary assistant stable hand factory worker security guard carnival worker (2) ice cream vendor

While they were attending school at Sudbury Valley, thirty-eight of the fifty (76%) held jobs. Some of the jobs were relatively advanced, such as music store assistant manager, carpenter, model, hospital ward secretary, cook, and custom embroiderer. Six had apprenticeships: one as a pattern maker (the same person who was a custom embroiderer), one as a pathology lab technician, one as a biochemistry lab technician, one as a radio technician, one as a leather worker, and one at the Loeb Drama Center. The other jobs were more routine, typical of those held by high school students: waitperson, grocery clerk, retail clerk, camp counselor, potter's helper, nurse's aide, kitchen help, warehouseman, house cleaner, paper deliverer, gas station attendant, stable hand, and photography assistant.

— Where have they worked?

Table 8.6 lists some of the places where members of this group have worked or currently work. The table is arranged by job category and contains only a sampling; we have included it to give an idea of the kind of work environments this group has chosen.

Table 8.6

Places of Work (Arranged by Categories of Occupation)

Category	*Company or Institution*
Business Management	McKinsey & Co.
	Gemini Corporation
	Herrold's Ice Cream
	Fayva Shoes
	Shirt Tales
	Lincoln Sewing Center
	Sunoco
	Park West Hotel
	Market Express
	Truckaway
	New City Builders
	Store 24
	Reynolds Management & Entertainment
	Natural Grocer
	Nature Food Centre
	Auto Repair of Boston
	Micro Muse
	Bio-Electric Shield Co.
Office Manager/ Executive Assistant	Planned Parenthood
	Stanley Steamer
High Tech	Stratus Computers
	Consumer Value Stores
	Reynolds & Associates
	First Micro Group
	Analog Devices
	DBX Company
Professional	Newton Wellesley Hospital
	TLC Nursing Agency
	Kaiser-Oakland Hospital
	Cambridge Hospital
	Kew Beach Chiropractic
	Spaulding Rehabilitation Center
	University of Massachusetts Medical Center

Category	*Company or Institution*
Professional	US Air Force Kaiser Permanente Boston Phoenix Boston Globe
Education	Sudbury Valley School Cornell University Georgia Institute of Technology University of California, Berkeley University of California, San Diego Tufts University Society for the Preservation of New England Antiquities
Law Enforcement	Worcester Juvenile Court
Trades	Maxim's in Waban Alcoba Pandolfino's Bert Development Corey's Beacon's A-Copy Professional Copy Systems Hill Construction Co. Nantucket Fire Department Clair Motors Beverly Hills Hotel Boston Harbor Hotel
Design	Perry Ellis Calvin Klein
Media	WICN WMJX
Performing Arts	Chevy's Fraser Young Production Pioneer Village Thundertrain The Sound Company Hong Kong Philharmonic Orchestra

— Personal comments on employment

The casual comments these people made about their work stressed similar themes to those we have already encountered. Many talked about the pleasure their work gives them and the rewarding challenges they meet.

Carpentry work gives me satisfaction and suits my abilities.

I enjoy the challenge of writing well, and seeing my words in print.

Allied health work gives great satisfaction — saving lives, meeting a whole spectrum of humanity, getting acquainted with a lot of areas of knowledge.

Working as a doctor is satisfying because I can make a difference socially, plus work with my hands. I also enjoy writing stories, poetry, and painting on silk.

Work in the fitness field gives me much satisfaction, helping others achieve their goals.

Undertaking is draining but very rewarding emotionally. It is the hardest time of life for people. You help them out, advise them, counsel them, and they come back over and over again to talk.

Work as a musician, photographer and chef, has given me the opportunity to flex my artistic muscles.

I get satisfaction as a consultant from teaching and developing people, problem solving.

I like private duty nursing because I give one-on-one care.

Fire fighting is very satisfying because it impacts people's lives. It is rewarding to help people and save lives.

All work gives you satisfaction when you are doing the best your can. I don't like a job which I don't have a say in. I like to be able to go to higher ups to share ideas.

I love handiwork, especially fixing cars.

I find music the most satisfying activity, especially when playing with friends for applause, not money. Construction is also enjoyable work because it gives tangible results.

I like my current work in the electronics field. I always knew I would do this, even in my SVS thesis in 1972.

One after another these people seem to be working in fields that really interest them. As one person said, "I always changed jobs to something I wanted as soon as I wanted to."

Further Formal Education

— Where did they continue their schooling?

Out of the fifty members of this group, forty-five (90%) have at some time or another attended formal classes in order to further their education. Twenty (40%) completed the requirements for one or more degrees. Table 8.7 lists the schools attended after Sudbury Valley; however, our list of these institutions is incomplete. Schools marked with an asterisk are those from which degrees have been received. In several categories there are more school names than the number attending. This is because several students attended more than one school.

Table 8.7

Schools Attended After S.V.S.

Type of School	*Number Attending*	*Number Completing Degrees*	*Names of Schools*
art schools	5	n/a	Worcester Art Museum Boston Museum of Fine Arts School Boston Film-Video Foundation Musician's Institute School of Contemporary Music

Type of School	*Number Attending*	*Number Completing Degrees*	*Names of Schools*
trade schools	9	n/a	Connecticut School of Broadcasting Keefe Tech (2) Massachusetts Fire Fighting Academy Blaine Hairdressing School Peabody School of Fashion Design Fashion Institute of Technology USAF School of Health Care Sciences Mercedes-Benz of North America; Porsche Cars
miscellaneous	5	n/a	The Tracker School Dynamy Outward Bound Brookline Adult Education Center Cambridge Center for Adult Education
community college	6	AA (2)	Mass Bay Community Coll. (5) Quinsigamond Community College (2) Middlesex Community College *Berkshire Community Coll. *Greenfield Community Coll.
junior college	7	AA (3)	*LaSalle Junior College Pine Manor Junior College Dean Junior College (2) *Catherine Laboure College *Newbury Junior College (2) Holliston Junior College North Idaho Junior College

Type of School	*Number Attending*	*Number Completing Degrees*	*Names of Schools*
college	31	BS (5)	Assumption College
		BA (7)	Bennington College
			Boston Conservatory
			*Boston University (4)
			*Brandeis University
			Catholic University
			Clark University
			Framingham State College (5)
			*Framingham Union Hospital
			Friends World College
			Johns Hopkins University
			Johnson & Wales University
			Keene State College
			Mass. College of Art
			Merrimack College
			Mt. Ida College
			Nichols College
			*Northeastern University (3)
			*Park College
			Parsons School of Design
			Salem State College
			San Francisco State College
			Santa Barbara City College
			Santa Monica College
			Simon Frasier University
			Sonoma State University
			Swinburne College
			*University of California, Berkeley (2)
			*University of California, Los Angeles
			University of California, Santa Barbara
			*University of Denver
			University of Grenoble
			University of Lowell (2)
			*UMass Amherst (4)
			*UMass Boston
			Worcester State College

Type of School	*Number Attending*	*Number Completing Degrees*	*Names of Schools*
graduate school	8	MBA (1) MD (1) MDiv (1) MS (3) PhD (1) DC (1)	*University of Southern Cal. School of Medicine *Harvard University School of Business *Catholic University *Johns Hopkins University *Palmer College St. Mary's College *University of California, San Diego *University of Wisconsin University of Minnesota

— Education vs. occupation

In Table 8.8 we look at the relationship between what the members of this group chose to study in their further formal education, and the occupations they are currently engaged in. We did not include in the Table the twenty people who were either primarily students or who had not pursued any further formal education in a serious manner. The table is arranged by ascending order of age of the remaining thirty people.

Table 8.8 shows a remarkably strong correlation between subjects studied in formal schooling and current occupations. Members of this group obviously, for the most part, used formal schooling as a tool of vocational education and to fulfill certification requirements.

Table 8.8

Relationship of Formal Education to Occupation

Age	*Type of School*	*Degrees*	*Area of Study Concentration*	*Most Recent Occupation*
21	junior college		media	assistant manager, shoe store
21	trade school	cert.	hairdressing	hairdresser
22	art school		art	planned parenthood counselor, waitperson
23	junior college	AA	nursing	nurse
23	college	BS	nursing	nurse
23	college		social rehab	clothing store manager, waitperson
24	junior college art school		computer science	computer software technician
26	misc.		outdoor survival	Native American crafts reproduction, office cleaner
26	junior college	cert.	human movement, psychology	aerobics instructor, health club supervisor, secretary
29	art school		music	musician, song writer
29	junior college		business	bar manager, cook, butcher, bartender, waitperson
30	college, medical schl	BA, MD	anthropology, medicine	physician
30	college		drama	owner of construction business
31	college	BA	sociology	network marketing
32	college, graduate school	MS, PhD	chemistry, mathematical mechanics	professor of mathematics

Age	*Type of School*	*Degrees*	*Area of Study Concentration*	*Most Recent Occupation*
33	college, graduate school	BS, MS	psychology, writing	clinical psychologist, freelance author
35	college	AA	nursing	nurse
35	trade school	cert.	firefighting, EMT	fireman
35	college	BS	nursing	nurse
36	college, misc.	BA	theater, film, visual arts	journalist, freelance author, college English teacher, museum guide
36	junior college, trade school	AS	physical therapy, dressmaking	parent (former physical therapist)
36	community college	AA	geology	carpenter
36	college, graduate school	BA, MBA	economics, business	consultant in international strategic management
36	college, trade school	BA	health sciences, management	animal husbandry, medical transcriber, USAF reserve officer
36	college		electrical engineering	design engineering assistant
37	trade school		auto mechanics	auto mechanic, musician, composer
37	college		music	musician in symphony orchestra
37	college, graduate school	DC	Chiropractic	chiropractor, medical insurance claims adjustor, owner of bio-electric shield co.
38	college	BS	nursing	parent (former nurse)
38	college	BA	sociology and law, french	owner and manager of computer store
38	college, graduate school	BA	health arts, health administration	epidemiological research project monitor

— Personal comments on education

This group too offered spontaneous observations on their educational experience. For some, their college experience was a kind of culture shock:

> *I found college very frustrating: they would say "read these books." I'd come to the tutorial and I had read, but no one else would have read them, so they'd talk about something else.*
>
> *I hated college. It was like public high school. But I proved to myself that I could do the academic work.*

For others, their continued schooling posed no special problems: "I had no trouble getting into college with essays and life experience," said one. Another noted that "I had an easier time with university work than others around me, as I was not concerned with my grades." One person commented, "Sudbury Valley School prepared me for college, because I knew I was responsible for making it or not making it." Another was in no rush. He said: "I'm taking college one course at a time until my children grow up. I'm going to school for refinement and depth of knowledge, because I want to understand technical things better."

Several people in this group expressed the intention of pursuing more formal schooling. Six of the twenty people who have already achieved degrees were planning to continue in graduate school. Eight others are planning to complete the requirements for degrees. Seven more have plans for continuing formal education without necessarily receiving certification of any kind. Thus a total of twenty-one people (42%) have plans to continue their formal education in some manner.

Travel

Like the earlier group, this group also appears to display a distinct interest in travel. Table 8.9 lists some of the places they have visited. It is organized by age and is based on incomplete information. Twenty one of the fifty members of the group are not included, either because we lack information or because they actually have not travelled extensively. Due to our uncertainty about the information, it is impossible to draw conclusions about whether the percentage of people in this group who are drawn to travel is in fact significantly lower than the percentage for the preceding groups.

Table 8.9

Travel Experiences

Age	*Places Visited*
20	all over the USA as a "Dead-head"
20	cross country USA
21	California, Oregon, Washington, mid-west, Tennessee, New England
22	London, Paris
22	England, France, Switzerland, Mexico, cross country USA
23	Caribbean, France, Spain
23	Ireland, extensively in USA and Europe
24	Europe, USA, Canada, all extensively
25	Israel, Europe
29	throughout Europe and USA
29	Eastern Europe
33	England, Europe, USA
33	California
33	cross country USA
34	Bali, New Zealand, throughout USA
34	extensively in USA
35	Jamaica, Virgin Islands, Bahamas, California
35	England, Ireland, Europe, throughout USA
36	England, throughout Europe, Canada, Western USA
36	extensively in southern USA
36	Far East, Israel, throughout Europe, USA
36	Western Canada, every state except Hawaii
36	continental USA
37	Italy, Austria, Germany, Great Britain, Virgin Islands
37	Western Europe, eastern seaboard to Canada
37	Far East
37	Egypt, India, Sri Lanka, Burma, Thailand, Japan, Costa Rica, Mexico, Canada, and 44 states
38	England, California, New Mexico
38	Australia, Japan, Hong Kong, Philippines, France, Europe

Personal Perspectives

The people in this sample offered many comments on both their SVS experiences and their lives. Some dealt with the theme of happiness:

> *I am very content. Sudbury Valley allowed me to bond with people and to learn to trust people. No one shot down anyone's dreams at Sudbury Valley. I am capable of dealing with defeat and I have no fear because of Sudbury Valley.*
>
> *I enjoy teaching and like research in mathematics. I enjoy the outdoors — hiking, canoeing, gardening. I love music. I love to spend time with my family.*

Several stressed the values in their lives:

> *Liberation work is very important to me, including women, young people, reproductive rights, people of color, and ending oppression in the world.*
>
> *The main lesson Sudbury Valley taught me is that everyone is an individual and has a right to be an individual.*
>
> *Much is important in my life, but money is not. I feel society's laws give a base to life and allow safety with movement. I am very interested in spirituality.*
>
> *Sudbury Valley gave me the apparatus to move on into the world. The school taught me essential lessons about life, and the value and equality of persons, that still guide me in my work today.*
>
> *My wife and I are a team. Every marriage should be that way. Family is what is important right now. I am a good father and really enjoy it.*
>
> *I do community work with people with AIDS.*
>
> *I, with my wife, share a strong commitment to spiritual development.*

Some reflected in general terms about what the school did for them:

School prepared me well and gave me a lot of confidence.

Sudbury Valley let me be who I am. It didn't try to mold me. I could be an individual and be happy about it.

At Sudbury Valley I learned it is okay to do what interests me. I always could move on to something else.

Sudbury Valley gave me the freedom to figure things out for myself, and to figure out my life. I do it now and will do it for the rest of my life — I am always figuring things out.

Sudbury Valley gave me time to figure things out.

Sudbury Valley, without question, was the best experience I have ever had.

Others were a little more specific about the effect of the school on their lives:

Learning primitive living skills is very important to me. I got a general feel for roaming the woods while at Sudbury Valley. I had time to get acquainted with the woods.

I got into music at Sudbury Valley. I learned to play guitar by just playing. I had the time to do what I really loved. Now I am one of a group of thirty musicians who form different bands playing all kinds of music at all sorts of occasions. I love my work.

Sudbury Valley provided the environment in which there was time and freedom to learn to play the guitar. I learned to play from other students at school. [He is now a musician.]

Sudbury Valley gave me a chance to develop what I really wanted to do, to be a musician, to do what I felt passionate about. I have continued the development of my music career in "melodic rock." Sudbury Valley was like a family for me.

A new theme appears with this group, not unexpectedly. Quite a few people referred to their other school experiences and talked about how being able to become a student at Sudbury Valley made a crucial difference in their lives.

I am happy with my life. Sudbury Valley definitely prepared me to do things that I couldn't have done had I stayed in public school.

Sudbury Valley built my self-confidence. I learned to be more independent and open-minded. It made me blossom.

Sudbury Valley got me to do things instead of letting people do them for me.

Sudbury Valley changed my life by forcing me to realize what was going on with myself. I had the opportunity to think out my problems without pressure and learn to cope with them.

I am very happy I went to Sudbury Valley, and feel that if I hadn't, I never would have finished high school or gone to college.

At Sudbury Valley I went from very shy to grown up by learning how to interact with people.

The most important thing about Sudbury Valley was that I could graduate before I turned sixteen. It allowed me to get a leg up on taking charge of my own life. Being able to pursue my own interests in an unstructured environment changed my life significantly.

Sudbury Valley was what I needed at the time. I was going insane in high school.

I feel I owe Sudbury Valley a lot. I was rotten to the core when I first came to SVS, and it turned me into a normal person. I learned a lot from other kids at the school.

One person added a sweet nostalgic note: "Sudbury Valley helped me get things together, realize that I had to do for myself and be responsible. It was the best thing that ever happened to me. I wish I was still there."

9

Reflections of Short Term Students

Some of the people who were interviewed for the oral history project were part of the group of former students who spent three or four years at Sudbury Valley School and then went on to adult pursuits. We have included excerpts from several of their interviews in order to allow further glimpses into the development of their lives and characters.

The following comments are from a young man who was twenty-one at the time of the interview below, and has since developed his interest in Native American ways, described below, into his lifestyle and career:

Last summer everything started snowballing, and now it just moves faster and faster. I finally got time to build a tipi and all kinds of other little projects. I just kept plugging at it. I had wanted to buy one, or get a sewing machine and make one, for so long. Then I went out and got the damn canvas when I had the money, threw it down and took a needle and thread and started working and just kept going.

At the school people can't really hide under superficial things, so you really get to know somebody a lot more deeply. You can't hide who you are from people. I learned that I don't have too many deep, dark secrets because I'm just used to who I am. It's good because you learn to deal with things being out there, you learn to grow and know that who you are is who you are, and you can't be ashamed or try to hide who you are. Some of the other lessons I learned there, I'm just starting to realize. One was not to categorize people by age, and with those categories gone, you have a lot more freedom just to meet people and get to know them. The freedom to make decisions, democratic decisions, has become more valuable. Sometimes it doesn't work out that well in society because I'm used to these rights in America and then going to Sudbury Valley on top of being in America, you get really used to having your rights!

It's funny that the more simply you live the less you have to just rough up things. You have to take less from nature as you learn more, even though I still disrupt the land quite a bit. I have learned a lot on my own since I left school, but it's a lot slower. It's a lot more work, it's more money for books because sometimes you have to buy a book just to get one chapter's worth of information. Other books, of course, just fill me to the brim.

I am really looking for a teacher now. I hope to find somebody to apprentice to, or at least somebody to learn with and eventually some kind of small group of people to share with, one way or the other. I'd like to have somebody walk beside me before I start teaching some younger kid. But before I go to too many people, I want to see my own feet where I want them so I have something to offer them.

If we have time, if the earth survives long enough, I should survive too.

The young woman from whose interview the following comments were taken was twenty-six at the time. She is now thirty and has completed her medical training.

I think there's part of me that is just a problem-solver and has always looked at people and tried to figure out, first, how to help myself, but then how to extend that to other people and do something that I felt was worthwhile. Sudbury Valley is just part of that in the sense that there, something was being done right, and I wanted to be part of it. It was a way of fixing one thing that was wrong: I didn't like the way school and education were, and here it was being done right.

People have said to me they felt like they might have gone to college sooner or they might have had an easier time in college if they had gone to a regular high school. I don't feel like that. I mean, I feel I could have used the school more to my advantage as far as learning the things that would get me through college, but the school was the perfect place for me in the sense that I really knew exactly what I wanted, and at that time I didn't want to go to college. It was not in the plan, at least not in the sense of finishing high school and then going to college. It was only in line with very specific goals that I ever thought about going to college. For me, Sudbury Valley was a very clear goal, and when I found out about my next interest, that was a very clear goal for me. I was a very "one-step-at-a-time" person. I had to do things one by one.

My last year at Sudbury Valley I got involved with a natural foods store and I spent a lot of time with the store. At that point in my life I wanted to make money and I wanted to leave home. The only way I could continue to go to the school would be to live at home and I just didn't want to. So I left school, and I worked at the store I think for about six months and then I quit that and went to work with a friend. We started an apartment cleaning business. It was hard, but it worked out pretty well. I made a lot more money than I made at the store.

I did finally go to college. I started going to a community college and I took whatever I wanted. They had classes there for people who didn't take them in high school, but I never took any of those classes. I just went straight into the college courses.

The first thing I took was a Spanish class because I was living in Southern California and I wanted to learn how to speak Spanish. When I started going to school it was for reasons like that. I just wanted to have fun. I took drawing and painting classes and I took acting classes. That's how I started. Then more time went by and I felt that I've done waitressing and cleaning apartments, now what? I had a very good friend at school whose mother was a midwife and I started thinking more and more about that. About six months after I met her, I started school doing the full nursing curriculum. I was going to get my RN first and then I was planning to go to midwifery school. At some point when I was in the nursing curriculum I decided I was going to go all the way and become a physician and not have all the problems and things that midwives have, as far as being accepted.

Sometimes I think that if I had become a midwife I could do all the things I wanted to do and I wouldn't have had to spend so much time going to school and studying and learning a lot of extra things which I'm not really that interested in. I could have done what I wanted a lot more directly. But I like the idea of being a physician and having the flexibility to work in an academic setting. I can teach other doctors, I can do so many things as a physician. It's very, very open ended. And there's a lot of people who need help who aren't going to go to a midwife for it. They can still use the kind of skills that I'll have, even if they aren't going to say, "I want a home birth and I want everything all natural." They don't have to think exactly like I think to be able to take advantage of some of the things that I'll know.

Once I decided I was going to medical school, I transferred to a four-year college and I took everything I had to take to go to medical school. There were certain things that were hard for me. I didn't know how to take notes. The first chemistry course I took, I would go to class and listen, but I was not an auditory learner. I usually have to learn by reading. Other people would take their notes and read them later, but I'd come out of there with no notes. I had a friend who took very good notes and I studied together with her and I think that's the only thing that got me through that class. As a matter of fact I ended up getting a better grade in the class than she did which really got her mad but, since I didn't take notes, I did all the problems. I always liked math because I liked doing problems and chemistry was the same thing. Taking notes was just a skill to learn and I learned it. Maybe I would have learned it in high school and maybe not.

I think one thing I got from Sudbury Valley was more of an acceptance of not having to do certain things and still be ok. I never felt that I had to go to college in order to be thought of as educated, or smart. That's one thing the school gave me; I just figured I was that way anyway, that college had nothing to do with it.

To get into medical school, you have grades, interview, you write an essay and you have recommendations. It was a combination of all of those that got me in. My grades were kind of a mix. My first overall year in college I had a C average and I didn't really care. I was just there for fun. But what was good was that I had an explanation for everything. I could talk to them about it. Once I decided to go to medical school, my grades were pretty much A average, so there was no problem after that. I just explained that I've always been very self-directed and motivated, and when I decided to do it, that's when my grades got better. They were happy with that answer.

When I first decided to go to medical school I was very confident. A couple of years of hanging around with pre-med students started to really erode my confidence because everybody was so uncertain and so unsure. When you're always around people who are very worried and very unhappy and very afraid that they're not going to make it, it does start to have an effect on you. At least it did on me. I had friends who had much better grades than me and they didn't even apply to good schools. They applied to the bottom of the barrel because they didn't think they'd get in.

I do less of the things I don't like than most people do, and I find I try to do more of the things that I like. That's one thing maybe going to Sudbury Valley taught. I have very little patience for doing things that I don't like and so I find I try to maximize the things that I do like doing and I learn those things and I kind of just get by with everything else.

I think for me it's very important to know that what I'm doing actually works. I know that I can help people have a nice birth, and I know that I can learn how to be a good surgeon and I know that I can have the skills to talk to people about their problems and about their sexuality and things like that. I know I can do all those things and I think I can be good at them.

At thirty, when his oral interview took place, the person whose comments follow had not yet begun the career he had established at the time of our survey, that of consultant to non-profit companies setting up computerized accounting systems.

I graduated before I turned sixteen. I considered myself a very smart person, which may sound self-centered and it's not meant to sound that way, but I considered myself a very able-bodied person physically, emotionally, and psychologically; and also in my ability to learn something very quickly. So I had no fears about anything. I never had any fear of making my way in this world. I was proved to be correct in those feelings because I was out working full time at the age of sixteen.

To a certain extent I also had the advantage of having a natural ability to manage, and to control situations. For instance, in jobs I've had, I don't need to spell and I don't need punctuation because I dictate things to secretaries. I'd never be in a position where I needed it, for the same reason that I don't know how to fix cars, because the minute you know how to do something, you end up doing it. Not all the time necessarily, but if you learn how to fix vehicles, you end up being your own mechanic. I have no desire to be a mechanic. I have no desire to tear engines apart or to fix things when they go wrong. I have no desire to have to write and type my own letters so I've always just placed myself in positions where other people have to do that for me. When I was in corporate America, I had secretaries. At one point I had a secretary and a staff of twenty people. I figured that out when I was very young.

For me, SVS was a very positive time. The school gave me the freedom to interact with people. Also because of the wide diversity of age groups and, with myself about in the middle of that, it gave me the ability to grow up faster, by having access to interaction with people who were three, four years older than me, but it still also allowed me to interact with younger people who were four, five, six years younger than me, so that I never lost the sense that there should be a child in all of us. No one should grow up completely. But in a general sense, it gives everyone that goes there the opportunity to shape their own lives as opposed to having their lives shaped by what the "majority norm" is, which is what public school systems do.

The way I used the school was as a place to interact with people. I didn't need staff, except as individual human beings to interact with. They were ten more people at the school to interact with and learn something from. But had those ten people all been under twenty, that still would have been ten more. Obviously, they would have had less life experiences and less learned knowledge than the staff, all of whom had obviously experienced a lot more of life by virtue of their age, but they weren't really a governing body. I just looked upon everyone on the staff as part of the mainstream population at the school. The pivotal, important point about the school is that it allowed me all the freedom I needed to pursue anything I wanted to pursue. People learn as much as they want to learn.

I didn't look upon going to Sudbury Valley as a radical thing. I looked upon it as what the norm should be and that the rest of the school systems were radical because they were radical departures from almost any other situation that any human being goes through in the United States in their lives. Once we reach eighteen, we're all in control of ourselves within the structure of the law in the U.S. We are not placed in the position where legally we have to be in a building "x" number of hours a day and we have to listen to someone. Schools are basically set up as dictatorships, which is why as children develop in public school systems, they end up developing in the same way that prisoners in prisons develop: they tend to become mentally sluggish and submissive.

I graduated and took that summer off, just hung out, went to the beach. I was interested in possibly pursuing a veterinary career, so I got a job at an animal clinic. After that, I decied I wasn't really interested in being a veterinarian so there was really no reason for me to stay there. I had been working there making less money than I felt I should be, simply because I wanted the hands-on experience. I used to hold animals and help doctors, even during surgery. I got as close a look as one could, without actually being a veterinarian, of what it would be like to do that as a profession and I decided I was not going to go through eight years of college, which is approximately what it would be, to become a veterinarian and do that for the rest of my life. I thought it would be interesting to be a veterinarian for a couple of years, but I wasn't going to spend eight years learning how, just to do it for two. It's a waste of time. So then the whole thrust of what I was doing turned to making more money.

I worked at my next job for about nine months. I was making very good money. I was still living at home. I was seventeen, but just before I turned eighteen, I decided I wanted to be out on my own. I now had enough money. I had a car, which I had bought myself, and quite a bit of money in the bank. Partly because of doing night work, I didn't have time to spend any money. So I quit that job. I was going to take some time off, but what I ended up doing was selling my car and all my personal belongings and moving out to L.A. I got tired of Boston, I got tired of Massachusetts, and I wanted a whole new change of scene.

It took a while to get to L.A. I stopped in a lot of states in between. Finally I ended up in Los Angeles, got a job the next day driving brand new rental cars. Fun job, pay was OK for my needs. Got to know a lot of the Mexicans out there. That was very interesting. Just talking about what life is like in Mexico. Finding out about their life experiences and sharing my life experiences. I did that for a while, got tired of that, decided I didn't like Los Angeles, went back to Massachusetts, got a cab license, drove a cab in downtown Boston. Made money hand over fist doing that. Most big companies, like law firms, use cabs as messengers to transport documents from one place to another. Often extreme distances. All of them have charge accounts. Most of them are billing their clients. When it finally got down to it I was only dealing with three companies. I almost never drove people. That's nuts when you're a cab driver! If I had three people in my cab all day long, it was a big day for having people in the cab. I was doing packages. I made my own hours. I went to work around 7:00, I knocked off at 3:00 in the afternoon. I only worked four days a week, Monday through Thursday.

Next, I went to work as a house detective, licensed by the Boston Police Department at a large Boston hotel, 1200 rooms. I had some amazing experiences there! Once, I came upon somebody in the hallway that I thought was having trouble getting into their room. It wasn't their room and I had a 38 pointed an inch from my head with a nut who was obviously on drugs telling me he was going to blow my head off. I stared the guy down. I tried to look as mean as I possibly could. I tried to look as though, even if he pulled the trigger, even though he might kill me ultimately, I'd kill him before I died. And he backed off and ran away. Later, after driving a cab for a while again, I moved inside and started working as a clerk in the accounting department of the cab company. I started as a little clerk there. In nine months they made me the head of the accounting department. I didn't like the actual work when I was a clerk, but when I became the manager of the accounting department very little of it really had to do with figures. It had to do with organizing other clerks and bookkeepers. Then, on top of that, I took on the job as administrator of the pension fund. I did that for five or six years, running an office with a staff of twenty that also interfaced with two other corporations owned by the same man.

When I became manager, I said, "Dress code change!" I wore sneakers, jeans and a shirt, open. They came to me and said, "You're a manager now, you can't dress this way," because none of the other managers did. I said, "It's real simple. You want me to wear a suit and a tie? You pay for the dry cleaning." And I had my suits dry cleaned every day. Then they said, "Well, wait a minute, wait a minute." I said, "That's it, that's the deal." And they backed off. I learned a lot in that job about getting things done expediently in the corporate structure. It was a great education. I had everything I wanted because all I did was do it. I didn't go through committees, I didn't go through anything. I just instituted the policy and I had a big enough staff that once the policy was instituted, my staff was loyal to me. I am currently managing and marketing and promoting new music, primarily rock and roll. Bookings are no problem. I book bands, I can get them playing out. But they don't make money. Nobody's making a living. All of them have regular day jobs. There's not a lot of money in this. You make it when you get a label and you're getting a salary and you've got a commitment for four or five more albums. That's when you make it big and even some of those people go right down the tubes. So its a very tough business. I charge a fee for booking, regardless of whether there's money involved in it or not. And when you're dealing with 75 bands, it works out. I'm in a position now where I sit on sets way in advance. I'm a professional business person in the sense that I'm not some guy from a band that says, "We play great music. We really get into our music. We don't know anything else but we play great music." Club owners don't want to hear that. Club owners want to hear that there's somebody that understands that the bottom line in the business is to get people into the club so that they'll buy booze so the club will make money so the owner can own a yacht and a Cadillac and vacation. I'm very well organized. Bands are often very disorganized. I force organization onto the band which in turn usually results in them having a better draw because they're well organized in sending out tickets at the right time, promoting themselves. So that's the promotional marketing aspect of the business. With me the clubs are dealing with someone who is a business person and understands that what they're really interested in is the draw. So it's very easy for the clubs. Whoever is doing the bookings is in charge of entertainment at the club. They give me a bunch of sets. They can just do that in two minutes and say here are all the dates — do what you want with them — I get back to them when it's all booked and send them something tight and that's it. They haven't had to talk to twenty-four different bands and explain the same information over and over again. This is when you load in, this is how long your set is, this is when you start, this is when you stop; I do all that.

A nurse with a lifelong devotion to health care, the man below describes his path into his career. The interview was done when he was thirty-one.

My confidence was shattered from my early educational experience almost from the word "go". Things didn't come as readily to me as other kids, which is ok, but it was coupled with the fact that I had some confused or ignorant early teachers.

By the time I left Sudbury Valley I felt differently about myself, especially if there was any particular avenue that I was interested in. I thought when I first got out that I was interested in going into construction, and I went about doing that by working in a geotechnical engineering firm. I saw what the planning end of construction could be and then I worked as a carpenter's helper with a good friend of mine who had his own construction business. I enjoyed it, but it didn't really seem right to me. I hadn't even been out of school a year yet. That's when I first decided that what I was really interested in doing was going into the Allied Health professions.

So the way that I went about doing that is I cut off most of my hair and got a job at a large teaching hospital. The first job I had was a nuclear medicine orderly. It was great because, since it was a teaching hospital, I got to go through the whole hospital and see all the different areas that were available to get involved in, whether it was occupational therapy, physical therapy, respiratory therapy, nursing, medicine, the whole gamut. From being right in that environment, I knew what you had to start to work on specifically, in terms of preparation for sciences. I remember one thing that was particularly useful to me, a book I got out of the reference section of the local library. It was a health career guidebook that the U.S. government put out and it gave job descriptions, from a candystriper all the way through to neurosurgeon — what you had to do for basic preparation, where the schools were, what the procedure was for applying to the schools and all that. So through time I just put it together and one thing led to another. I went from being a nuclear medicine orderly to being an Emergency Medical Technician. I did that and was still interested in going on. I kept going to school part time and ultimately became a registered nurse.

I had gone to school on a part-time basis at a lot of different levels and places. Everything from courses at the Center for Adult Education to private tutoring (just to bone up on some math that I needed to master chemistry), to Northeastern University, Mount Ida Junior College, Mass Bay Community College — I did all that prior to going to school full time. I took courses specifically to go into nurse's training: chemistry, anatomy and physiology, some humanities, sociology, psychology, some general ed courses, English.

I did pretty well in my courses at first; maybe not as well as I could have because I had to make myself learn how to go about being disciplined in studying and that was a little bit awkward. But, as far as the motivation, that I never lacked, because I was ready and it was something I wanted to *do. It was clear in my mind what I wanted to accomplish and I set out about doing it.*

It was hard for me to get into nursing school only because I applied late. I hadn't taken SAT's, and that worked against me because they wanted that. But the thing that I had to my benefit was the fact that I had worked in an Allied Health setting for a while. I was a nuclear medicine orderly and I was an EMT and I had references written by physicians, nuclear physicists, other technicians, and management in places I worked, which talked about my character and my motivation. I also had taken a good biology course at an adult education center and I did really well in that, and then I took a basic college chemistry course and I got an "A" in that. I was accepted within a couple of weeks.

At that particular time, people wanted to go into nursing a lot more than they appear to want to now. I initially applied to some community college nursing schools which cost almost nil in tuition. But for that reason they were very, very competitive. People who were entering had to have like a straight "A" background from their high school experience, or whatever. So from that point of view, I did have a problem, but that didn't discourage me, because if you can get adequate grades and want to go to any private nursing school, they're going to take you ultimately.

What makes you a good nurse is how current you are in keeping certifications beyond your basic license. You have to achieve in the area that you work in. For example, I'm involved in emergency medical services, and I have to have an ongoing certification in Advanced Cardiac Life Support. That's just an example. In my last position, I was an R.N. for less than two years cumulatively, and I became the full time charge nurse on the evening shift in the emergency room that I worked in. That was a little bit awkward for me although I was very glad to have the opportunity to do it. I had that titled position over some people who had been in nursing for ten to fifteen years, so there was a lot of resentment — if not on the surface sometimes, then subconsciously. It all worked out in the end because I had a really good working relationship with these people and conveyed to them my appreciation of their role in cultivating me as a new nurse (relative to them) in the area that we worked in, even though within the hospital structure I was considered their "charge nurse." That was a pretty awkward thing, but it worked out fine.

The young woman below was thirty-three at the time of the oral history interview excerpted below and still excited about the early experiences she describes:

Once I realized what I would like to do for work, I knew it was something I would be happy to do — I imagined, forever. Fifteen years later I still love to do it. So I think I was right. I developed the idea through working with a designer in Boston with whom I had an apprenticeship. Then I went for an interview at the factory where I was going to work. I think it was in March. I wanted to stop school right then and go to work and my boss said, "No, you're going to finish school and come back in June." I was so scared he would forget about me and I'd call up in June and he'd say "Oh, sorry, I forgot about you and you have no job," and I'd end up waitressing all summer. But he did remember me.

I worked there for three years. It was an old fashioned garment manufacturing company, the real traditional working class craft stuff. I learned from the cutters, I learned from the sewers, I learned from the marker makers, I learned all the basic stuff. I was assistant pattern maker, but you interact with all the different people. When you're pattern maker you're at the highest rung of all the production people, so you work together with all of them.

First of all I worked for $2.00 an hour. I started in June and, if I didn't do really well, at the end of the summer I would be gone. That was the agreement, because my boss couldn't believe that an eighteen year old girl would want to work in a dirty factory with a whole bunch of men as old as her father. It was not so interesting to him, and he couldn't believe that my interest in pattern making wouldn't wane within a few months. He said, "Can you absolutely say to me that you want to do this for the rest of your life?" And I said, "Well, as much as possible." He called my father to make sure it was OK with him if I worked in this factory because he was afraid there would be rough language. It's really funny!

It was a little hard at first. I mostly was a gofer. Pattern makers work from existing patterns from a previous season and they're all stored on racks, and somebody has to go get them. I would do that. I really started out doing errands, and then started tracing and cutting for other people, and eventually doing my own work. Everybody taught me in that whole factory, which was so unbelievable and so wonderful because most of these people were very jealous of their jobs. Somehow I just charmed them — I think mostly because, when you've been doing something your whole life that, in this country, is not terribly respected and a young, obviously more middle-class girl comes in and is so excited because you'll teach her and really pays attention and just loves that you can teach her this, how can you not like it? That wasn't a conscious effort on my part — it was just true. Every minute of it, I loved. My first couple of years working, I would learn so much in a day that I would go home and go to sleep at 8:00 o'clock because I just took in so much and I really, really loved it. I didn't love the dirt, I didn't love *getting yelled at in Italian — there were things that I didn't love, but the first year and a half or so was just so exciting.*

I remember when I went for my interview and my future boss brought me upstairs to the cutting rooms, I looked in and it might as well have been a magical garden. This big, dirty room with tables twenty yards long, sixty inches wide with guys laying up fabric and making markers was just magic to me and it still is. So I worked there for three years and then they transferred everything either to New York or down South where labor was cheaper. Guys who had been working there and whose fathers worked there were getting pink slips on Friday and told not to come back on Monday. The woman whom I had been assisting, who was making a good amount of money, was let go and they expected me to do her job. I said, "Well, you have to double my pay if I'm going to do this." I was checking on the work of people who were making four times as much money as me. So I marched right up to the office and said, "Double it or I'm leaving." And they really tried to keep me, but the head office just wouldn't give them money, so they had to let me go.

That was very depressing. I went on unemployment, which I didn't feel bad about at first, because they laid me off, but there were no other jobs. I looked and I looked and I looked. There were no jobs.

I went to New York. I thought that everybody there must know a lot that I didn't know so the first job that I took was really less than I could do, and eventually I made them raise me a lot in both responsibility and money. They pretty much doubled my salary in the first year. Initially I worked for mostly small companies run by women because I was so young. I was twenty-two when I went to New York. Most pattern-makers even today are Italian men in their fifties and I was a little red-headed girl of twenty-two who looked about eighteen. And nobody would believe that I knew what I was talking about. But the young women who owned their own small companies didn't like having these men come in who thought they knew everything and would tell them what they could and couldn't do, so they really liked having me work for them. Also, I had much more artistic sense than the men who were available and wouldn't take everything that they designed and make it look exactly the same. So I worked or freelanced for several of those. Then I decided I really wanted an established company and I wanted security now that I was old enough and had enough experience.

At the time of the interview, the woman whose musings follow was thirty-four years old and working as a staff member at Sudbury Valley School; now she and her husband own and run a computer hardware and software business.

From all my experiences of talking with staff and spending time thinking, absorbing, I realized that I was a very different kind of person from what I had thought I was and that was really interesting to know. I hadn't understood that I was a really intellectual kind of person. I didn't know that at all. I went from an environment where everything was superficial and weird and hard to understand, to understanding a little about what kind of person I was, a lot more about what kind of a world it really is and sort of being able to analyze how to go about getting the things I wanted out of my life and out of the community, and contribute at the same time.

At the time, I felt I had absorbed what I needed the most, and I was ready to go on. My self-confidence and self-esteem had risen so enormously that I was really excited about getting out into the world and trying out some things. I had theories as to what I would do and how I would go about it all cooked up and I wanted to go out and try out my experiments and see what would happen.

The first year after I graduated was, amazingly, just wonderful. It was just a fantastic year. I had prepared for it and worked it all out during my last year at Sudbury Valley. I went to live in France for a year. I found a room through the University, I found out about classes, I got myself a little motorbike. I had a big group of friends and every day was full of exciting conversations about literature and art and philosophy. I had three goals: to improve my French, to write and to sing. I wanted to have a career as a singer at that time. So I joined a group of folk singers in Grenoble and we sang every week in some cafes around the whole region. I sang both in French and in English. It was wonderful. We sang at a big festival once for about two thousand people. That was pretty heady. It was very scary for me because I was fairly stage shy. So I was really confronting what I needed most. I needed to overcome some of those fears, so I went and challenged all the things that I was really afraid of. It was amazingly good and very successful. But I ran out of money and I hadn't planned for that possibility. I thought, "Oh, I have to go back and make more money and then maybe I can come back here again." So I returned to the U.S. and, for some reason once I got back here my intuition was that I shouldn't go back to France, that I should stay here and work out my life, my real life.

I worked part time for a lawyer. He gave me the most boring job in the whole world, photocopying a million pages and then cutting them up into tiny pieces and remaking a telephone book. I thought I was interested in law and here I was, trying to come to grips with myself, my life. I had been interested in singing and I was dropping it because it wasn't working for me at that time. I didn't know whether I wanted to go to school, and I thought maybe I'd be an entrepreneur. I had a lot of different thoughts. In the end, I opened a juice bar. But, in the meantime, I was just going to have to stay here for a little while and deal with the insecurity which had set in because I hadn't worked out what I was going to do after France. It's one thing to make a certain amount of money and go some place and spend it for a year and really live the way you want to live. But then it runs out and you have to make money to support yourself and try to live that lifestyle at the same time, which is another whole story and I didn't have the energy to do both at once.

So I went into this entrepreneurial thing feeling that maybe I should do what the family has always done — have my own business. I tried that for about a year. I made a living, met a lot of people, had a ball. I worked very hard, but you don't care if you're having a lot of fun. I was writing poetry and I started a writing class. It was a wonderful year once I got back on track.

A year of that and I realized I'd never make any money because I couldn't stand to charge a lot. I wanted to make it fun for people and make it possible to buy natural juices and things, and I had the most wonderful customers. But I didn't want to start figuring out all the angles so I decided I'd go to school because I wanted to make a contribution to the community and the best way was to go to school. I followed my interest which at that time was working with different groups of people in the community, disadvantaged people, different kinds of people. I took courses on public and community service and I got my degree. It really wasn't hard. I was doing the juice bar and going to school.

The classes were pretty dull. It wasn't what I wanted. I wanted to work with people who were really excited about what they were doing and the people there were mildly excited about what they were doing. It was fairly boring and humdrum, but I learned something. Later, after more extended travels, I worked for a couple of years as a job developer with Indo-Chinese refugees. It was absolutely wonderful. I found them work; I talked to employers; I helped them to get acclimated and start working and figure out what to do.

I feel as though the process and the environment which is created at Sudbury Valley is a really valuable one. It's tragic to me that people can come through all their educational years in this culture and not realize that we're practically like gods — we can do so much. People aren't in touch with the fact that they really have so much power and so much ability. What I think is magical about Sudbury Valley and so wonderful is just that so many people who go through there can feel that sense of control over their lives when they leave. No matter what they do afterward, they know that can exist because they experience it there at the school.

At thirty-five, this person was just beginning a new life which includes one of her earlier interests, animal husbandry, as well as her later ones:

Something lasting that I started to learn at Sudbury Valley, and I'm learning more about very slowly, is about people being more alike than they are different, and not to be put off by someone because they seem totally different from you. People are so different, but there's a lot in common and no matter how peculiar or different from you someone is, there's always something to share and people are usually willing to share with you. That's something I explored at the school, pursued. I enjoy a lot of different people in different age groups. I feel like I can adjust, I can go up and talk to a stranger very easily. Sudbury Valley was the beginning, because there's so much mixing and so much recognition of people's value.

Another thing I learned was the importance of just reading the rules and all that real well. For instance, in Officer Training School, we were involved in some sports. I'm a complete klutz at sports. I was a great little soldier, but I was really losing points as an athlete. But once I managed to read the rules and find out that the opposing team had broken some obscure rule and I won the whole game for my squadron.

I was basically happy at Sudbury Valley. There were minor ups and downs, and there were times of self doubt. And there probably are all through life. You know, "What am I doing here?". But you take them in stride and learn to question what you're doing. I made a big career change two years ago. I started asking "What am I doing," questions and finally decided I'm not doing anything I like and it's up to me to change it. You have to let yourself question, ask yourself the big questions. And that's exactly what most of us were doing at school.

I left SVS at the time I did because I knew what I wanted to do next and I was prepared to do it. It was work with horses. I enjoyed the work. I could support myself in a miserly fashion. I had an internship with a stable while I was at school, and they hired me after I left school. I worked there full time for quite some time, grooming horses, doing some exercise riding, just taking care of horses. The work was hard and the pay was terrible. But I really liked it. I learned a lot. I rode quite a bit, but I shovelled a lot of shit. And I really learned how to work hard.

I worked in New Hampshire for a while, then at a show stable in New York for a year, where I worked even harder. I got paid even less, it seemed. And then racetracks, harness horses. It was all really interesting. It got me away from home into a different environment, being an adult, living my own life. I was being self-sufficient.

A friend who had worked in the stables had gone on to a junior college. She was learning paraveterinary work and that appealed to me, but working in the human side of medical science appealed more. So I got into a two year program for medical assistants. I just whizzed through. It was easy for me. I loved it. Some of the classes were tough. Anatomy and physiology was one. But everyone was struggling with that, and with medical terminology. Those were tough courses but I worked hard. After that, I had my little degree as a medical assistant and the next step for most people would be to get a job in a doctor's office and get an apartment. But I really didn't want to do that. I had a friend, a real hippie type friend who had gone in the military and become a Marine and loved it, which was totally bizarre. There's nothing more establishment than the military. But I thought this might be a good idea and started looking into different services and got to know all the recruiters, Army, Navy, Air Force and Marines, because they're all on the same block in downtown Framingham. Basically I hung out and persisted until I got the best offer any of them had for me.

I was twenty-two. I settled on guaranteed training as a lab technician in the Air Force and I had everything in writing. I know it seems really out of character and no one believed it. But actually, it was totally in line with what I wanted to do because for one thing I had a goal. I knew I loved lab work, so I would get to be a lab technician and I had talked to enough people — for instance, before I even got officially recruited, I drove all the way out to Colorado to go to the Air Force Academy, begged my way onto the grounds, and got someone to give me a tour of the hospital at the academy. I went and talked to lab technicians and asked them, "What is it really like?" I wanted to know first-hand. I wasn't going to let the recruiters pull the wool over my eyes. So somehow I got smart enough to figure out what I was getting into before I got committed.

I loved basic training. It was a game and I just did it. I could make those toilets stand at attention for inspection with the mop gang! I had done shitty work before, like in the stables, and I knew that if that's what you need to do, you just do it. Just follow directions. I didn't look at it as a threat to my independence. I just figured that this is basic training. It's a temporary condition. I'll just do it and make it easy on myself and get through it. I kind of had fun with it. I was getting fed and getting sleep at night. It was kind of relaxing, and I wanted someone to tell me what to do for a while. I wanted some kind of financial security and I knew the educational benefits would be good. It turned out to help me a lot. It was sort of a challenge to put myself in a position where people would send me places with a job to do and I would not have to make a decision. I would just do it. Because, you know, when you're a girl growing up in the late '60's, early '70's, in a totally permissive society, it is damn hard to make decisions. I knew that I didn't know what I wanted to do specifically. I had some ideas. But I knew that my career wasn't decided. I hadn't decided if I ever wanted to get married.

A lot of things were totally undecided. I kind of thought about something like Peace Corps, except I wasn't really marketable. I didn't have enough to offer. I didn't have any particular reason to want to go to college and get a Master's in biology or something. I wanted to earn my keep and do something constructive. I had a lot of doubts about the military, but I wanted that guarantee of being in the medical field in the military.

In the Air Force, there are all these competitive things for Airman of the Quarter, Airman of the Year. I started competing in those things and winning them. You'd shine up your shoes, put on your uniform and go into a board and they'd say, "Well, Airman, tell us about yourself." They'd ask you all these questions and it was competition based on how well your supervisor said you did and how good an overall citizen you were. I did a lot of volunteer work in the community, things like that. I had a reputation as a good little person. The board would evaluate you. Questions on military history and customs and courtesies and current events. One question I remember the board asking me was, "Well Airman, what do you think of limited nuclear warfare?" I just looked this Chief Master Sergeant in the eye and said, "Well, sir, I think it's about as viable as limited pregnancy." They all cracked up and I won. I won Airman of the Year and won a great ride in a fighter. An F-111 — 1.7 hours in that thing. I felt like I had been run over. I was beat up. That's hard work.

Each base has a historian who has his or her own office, gathers day-to-day data, everything from logistics to personnel to what's going on in court-martials to how well the jets are flying, or breaking, to how well we can go out and do the mission, where you'd get into all the classified stuff. Eventually I was offered this position. This involved getting a Top Secret clearance, and getting my own office and working on the Commander's staff. With three years in the Air Force, I knew so much about what was going on at that base. And it was fun. I went with the Commander on speaking engagements and really had a ball. I did some writing. I did some actual documenting of history and writing it. There were a lot of trials and tribulations, but I enjoyed it because I could interview anybody on the base and I loved it. I ate it right up. I did that job for three years.

From there I applied for Officer Training School. I wanted to get my commission at that point. And I wanted to fly. My eyes disqualified me from being a pilot. I'm nearsighted. But I could be a navigator. I wanted to be a navigator on a tanker. That'd be a neat mission. So I applied. There were very few slots available cause it was broken down into how many of them would be women. I was probably twenty-six. I was getting right up near the limit. So it was now or never. I went half way through Officer Training School before they started looking at spinal x-rays and decided that I might have spinal arthritis, and took me out of the program, which was devastating because I was at the top of my class. I was leading all the troops around. But after six weeks of that, and thinking I was doing great, they told me I couldn't fly and there was no other slot for me to do anything else. I had to go back to being enlisted. But the whole time I was being really cool. You know, through my tears, "boo, hoo, hoo," I was just saying, "Well, there's a lesson in this and I haven't really had any hard knocks in my life. This is the first one and I'm going to learn to have a little compassion for other people going through this kind of stuff."

By then I was married. I got married just before that. I reapplied as a maintenance officer and did that for a few years. I spent a year in Alaska. I got to fly my airplane up there, from Louisiana. The day I started my flying lessons, I said, "I'm going to learn to fly and I'm going to buy an airplane". And they all said, "Ha, ha, ha". But I did. When I accepted this job in Alaska, I informed the Air Force I would accept it if they would allow me to take my privately owned vehicle. They didn't know the privately owned vehicle was the plane. They wound up paying for me to fly it up there. It was terrific. I took a month's leave and just camped through British Columbia and the Yukon.

In the course of all this stuff, I got my Bachelor's degree in business management. Then I went on to take Master's courses. Unfortunately that was square filling, to meet the requirements for Officer Training School. I didn't learn anything. I just passed courses. So I had some regrets about that. With my leftover GI bill, after I got out of the Air Force two years ago, I took a bunch of classes again. I got out and became a reservist. I drew on my old skill as a lab tech and wound up doing lab work in two different doctor's offices and I love it. That's what I'm doing now. I'm also doing medical transcribing, which I learned to do just using up my GI bill. But the transcribing is something I know I can do in a home office some day. Or maybe start running a little service.

I don't think I've ever been bored in my life. I mean, I'm easily entertained. There's always so much to do.

The older brother of the young woman above has also pursued many careers, all in the arts. He was interviewed for the oral history project at thirty-eight, contemporaneously with the current survey.

I just have so much going on. I always have done so many things I've really wanted to do, and I continue to.

For instance, I worked in a circus. I was in a horse act and I rode unicycle, and I helped put up the tent. That was only for a few months, but

I had to join the circus! Also, I leased an ice cream truck and I had my own ice cream route a few years ago. Greatest job of my life. Fantastic. I loved it because once you get that truck, you load it up not only with the candy and the cookies and the ice cream, but then you fill up your top row with little parachute guys and little bombs, little guns, little cool things. The kids loved me. "Cowboy", they called me. I did that for a whole summer, and made good money. It was a great job. I loved it.

Then I moved to California. That was my first restaurant work. That's when I got into food service. I apprenticed at a Beverly Hills Hotel under a really great French chef there. Totally the "wait and see" Sudbury Valley attitude, getting into that, you know, because I didn't really know what I was doing and most of the guys coming into that business go to culinary school. So I kind of slipped through the back door, did a lot of learning, kept my eyes open.

I had my music career, which is what I'd gone to right after I left Sudbury Valley. Played in bands for the better part of the last twenty years and did some records. That was my living through most of the '70s. It was a starving living. We bought our own twenty foot truck and our own light system, our own sound system. Had three or four guys working for us and we were on the road all the time. We had a following, newsletters and mailing lists and we were putting out records, one every six months or so. Then the band broke up after five years. Financially things were changing. The drinking age was raised from eighteen to twenty-one, which had a big effect on our audience. And the gasoline price doubled, so our truck and everything got really expensive. A lot of things changed. I stepped back and made a film at Sudbury Valley and went and joined the circus and worked a few other jobs and was kind of cleansing rock and roll out of my brain.

Then my friend J.P. called, and I joined forces with him. I was co-writer on all the material. I'd write the words and the musical line that the words would follow, and he would write the guitar part and the musical line the guitar would follow, and we would meet so that my singing would meet his guitar. We had a drummer and a bass guitar and that's the essence of a four piece rock band.

We were starting to get successful. It had taken us a while to get a new record deal, but we got our deal. We were just touring the record for the first time. We had our MTV video out. Things were starting to come around our way. And that's when J.P. left to join his old band. I knew that I was having a setback, that chances were slim that I would ever be in that spot again. I'd be able to rock and roll again, but not with one of the top guitarists.

I felt pretty mixed up after the J.P. thing and it will forever be a mixed up feeling. I was a deadbeat celebrity when I was with J.P. Nobody really knew who I was, but I was staying in great hotels, going around in limousines, and I was up on stage in these places where people were going absolutely nuts. It's nice, but you know what? It isn't the end-all. It's something that's good: it's good for everybody to be a superstar for a couple of years just to see what it's all about. But then, having been a superstar for a couple of years makes it a lot easier for me to face my other jobs, whether it is working with a band at a little bar and enjoying it for what it is, or my photography work, or my cooking work. I work with some guys who decided when they were eighteen they were going to go to Culinary Institute of America and be a chef, and here they are, twenty-nine years old, and they are still working to be a sous-chef and have been in the kitchen all this time and they really have a chip on their shoulder about some of these people out front to whom they're serving food who arrived in a limousine and who are staying in the hotel! I'm really glad that I had the opportunity to be the one staying at the Sunset Marquis and getting limousine service for a few years so I can see that side of it. It makes working in the back of the house easier; it equals it all out.

In fact, I'll tell you a weird thing. I still have a lot of thinking to do about those J. P. years. During the time it was actually happening I was very depressed. For one thing I was being shoved into something overnight that I hadn't worked to achieve, so I felt I was getting something I didn't really deserve.

Well, I was pretty happily out of the music and didn't think I was going to get back into it. One day the girlfriend of the bass player in my old band called me up and said, "R. is going to sell all his equipment." I said, "Gee, that's not right." She says, "Yeah, he's had it with music. He can't find the right guys to play with. He's not going to do it anymore." So after talking to her, I thought about it and I said, "Well, it's true I haven't played and I haven't done anything, but there's been a security blanket knowing that R., a few towns over, has all that old band equipment in the garage." It was like a safety blanket to me knowing that, even though I wasn't out there playing, I still had my band around me and at a moment's notice I could throw it together. So I suddenly said, "Well, hell, let's get together and jam a little bit and see what happens." That happened about a year ago. That's why I got the old band together again.

I'm not depressed now and a lot of things are finally coming together. I've spent all these years trying to learn how to be the perfect teenager and it's finally coming together. By the time I'm forty, I should have it down!

In my rehearsal hall I've got a portrait photography setup. A lot of black and white stuff, shooting bands, shooting models, shooting actresses, shooting people who need promotional photography. When I was in California, I started buying cameras. I'm really old fashioned. I've got old

Nikons with old Nikon lenses and it's all manual. I like natural light, but most of it's with backdrops, inside. And I still draw. I was doing a comic strip for a while for one of the local music magazines.

I love the hotel kitchen. I love cooking. I've got my own little kitchen. I do a lunch every day. A "club luncheon" we call it. And I do my own specials. I have a great time. I play my music back there and I rock and roll. It's therapeutic as hell for me. It's a one man show and I have my music and my posters and my food and my specials and I just do it my own way.

For a long time I was going to open my own restaurant. But too much cooking wouldn't give me enough time for the rocking. I gotta rock too, because too much back of the house, you need that release. On the other hand, after rock and rolling for the weekend and all that craziness, it feels great to get back to work and be a regular guy.

10

Students Who Were Enrolled in Sudbury Valley For Their Last Two High School Age Years

We now turn to those people who came to Sudbury Valley for two years,[1] and completed their basic schooling here. For many of these, Sudbury Valley School was the equivalent of their "junior" and "senior" years in high school. For the rest, it was simply the last way-station before going on to adult pursuits. For every member of this group, entry into SVS involved a major readjustment from prior schooling experiences. Since they spent only a total of two years at the school, they had less time than the previous groups to effect this adjustment, and to take advantage of the educational philosophy of the school; this does not however necessarily mean that the school had less impact on their lives.

There were forty-eight people in this group, of whom forty-one were respondents in the study, for a response rate of 85%. All of the data presented in this chapter will refer to the forty-one respondents only, of whom twenty-two (54%) were male, and nineteen female.

Thirty of the forty-one (73%) received diplomas before leaving. Of the eleven who did not receive a diploma from Sudbury Valley, four went on

---

[1] We count only years actually enrolled in the school. For students who left Sudbury Valley for a time and subsequently returned, the time spent away from Sudbury Valley is not included in the calculation of the length of stay at school.

to get a GED, and one a diploma from another school. Two of these eleven received college degrees; three were involved in entrepreneurial businesses. One is an unskilled laborer; the other ten have various skilled occupations.

Basic Demographics

—— How old are they now?

Figure 10.1 shows the distribution of this group by age on January 1, 1991. The range of ages extends from twenty-one to forty. The average age of the group is thirty-one; the median age is thirty-three. This group is slightly older than the previous group (which spent three to four years at the school).

Figure 10.1

Distribution by Age, January 1, 1991

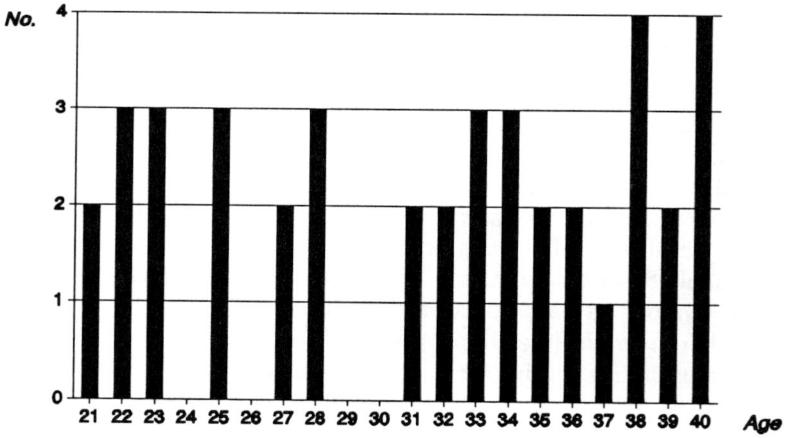

— Their marital status

Of the forty-one people in this group, fifteen were single (37%): twenty were or had been married (49%) — four of these were divorced, one of whom remarried, and two of whom were living with significant others; and six of the twenty-one who had never been married were living with significant others (14%). Six people were married ten years or longer, four for fifteen years or longer. This group of forty-one people had a total of thirty-six children, ages one to seventeen. In this group, sixteen people (39%) had children; one had five, one had four, two had three, nine had two, and the other three had one. There is a significant increase in average family size in this group relative to the earlier ones.

— Where do they live?

Table 10.1 shows where these people live. Twenty-seven of them (66%) live in Massachusetts; twenty-one of these live in towns that are considered to be in the school's catchment area.

Table 10.1

Current Geographical Distribution of the Group

No.	*Town*	*State*
1	Islamorada	Florida
1	Acton	Massachusetts
1	Brighton	Massachusetts
1	Cohasset	Massachusetts
1	Eastham	Massachusetts
2	Framingham	Massachusetts
1	Hingham	Massachusetts
1	Holliston	Massachusetts
1	Hopkinton	Massachusetts
1	Hudson	Massachusetts
1	Marlboro	Massachusetts
1	Medway	Massachusetts
1	Middleboro	Massachusetts

No.	*Town*	*State*
1	Nantucket	Massachusetts
3	Natick	Massachusetts
1	Needham	Massachusetts
1	Newburyport	Massachusetts
1	Northboro	Massachusetts
1	Quincy	Massachusetts
1	Sherborn	Massachusetts
1	Somerville	Massachusetts
1	Walpole	Massachusetts
1	Watertown	Massachusetts
1	Weston	Massachusetts
1	Winchendon	Massachusetts
1	Casco	Maine
1	Blue Hill	Maine
1	Norway	Maine
1	Stockton Spring	Maine
1		New Hampshire
1	Yellow Springs	Ohio
1	Friendswood	Texas
1	Burlington	Vermont
1	Rochester	Vermont
1	Eatonville	Washington
1	Tacoma	Washington
1	Jackson	Wyoming
1		Malaysia

— How old were they when they enrolled?

Figure 10.2 shows the ages at which this group entered the school. The ages range from thirteen to nineteen, with both the average and the median age being sixteen — again slightly higher than the previous group.

Figure 10.2

Distribution by Age of Entry

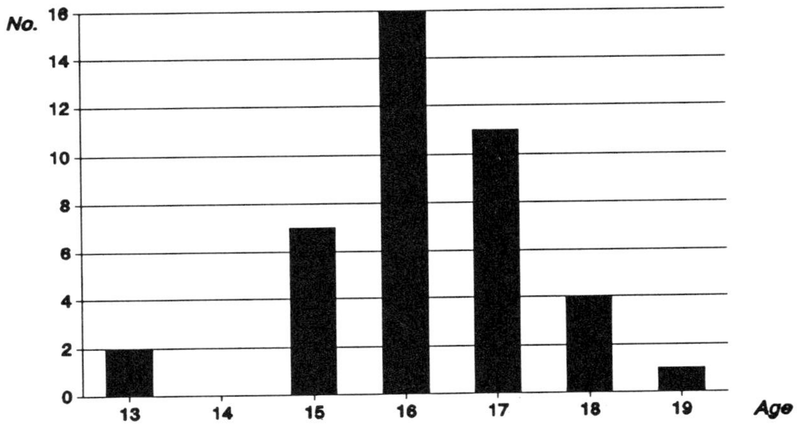

— What was their prior schooling?

Every member of this group had extensive exposure to more traditional schooling before entering Sudbury Valley. Figure 10.3 details the number who went to various categories of schools prior to SVS. We distinguish between private and public schools. Since a person may have gone to both private and public schools at any level, the total number at each level is higher than the actual number of individuals who went to school at each level.

Figure 10.3

Schooling Prior to Sudbury Valley

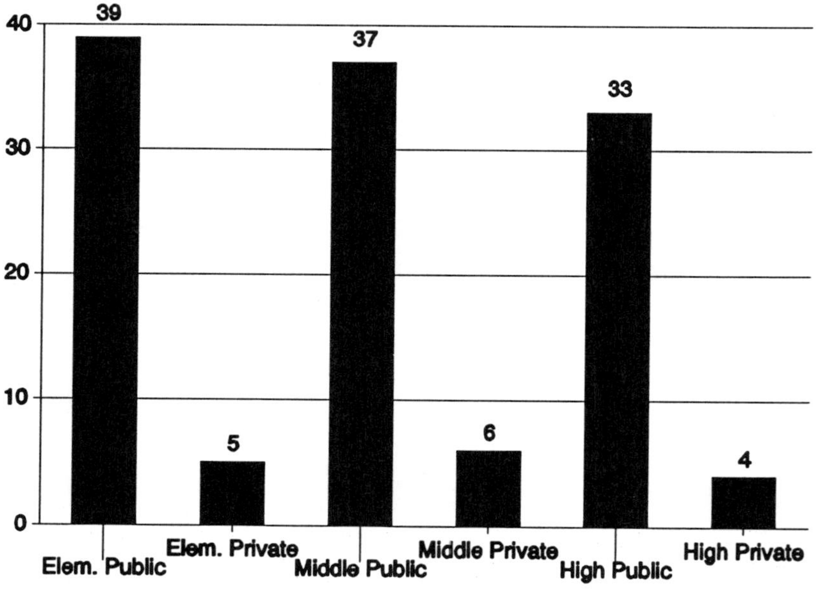

Of the forty-one, all attended elementary school. One of these went on to be home-schooled before coming to Sudbury Valley — our first home-schooler in this study. The other forty (98%) all went to middle school. Thirty six (88%) also attended high school. Two people attended only private school at the elementary level; three people attended only private school at the middle level; three people attended only private school at the high school level. Out of the entire group of forty-one, eight different people (20%) attended a private school at some time before entering Sudbury Valley; only one of these eight attended private school exclusively. Thus, thirty-three people (80%) had attended only public schools, and forty (98%) had attended public schools at some time. Once again, these figures show conclusively that this particular population was not drawn from among families who traditionally send their children to private schools, and that such families were very much the exception.

— How old were they when they left school?

Figure 10.4 shows the ages at which members of this group left the school. Both the average age of leaving and the median age of leaving is eighteen.

Figure 10.4

Distribution by Age at Leaving

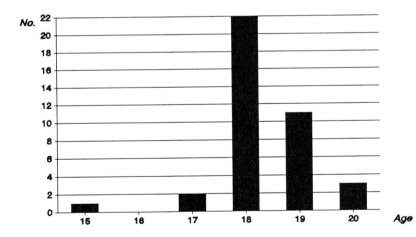

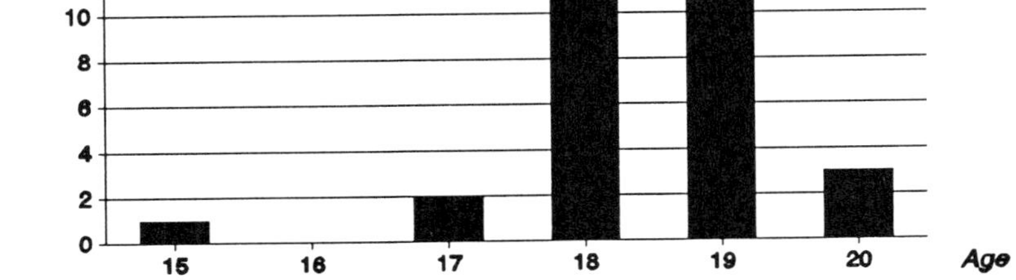

— Where did they live?

Table 10.2 shows the geographical distribution of this population at the time that they were students here. The number of towns from which this group was drawn, and the radius of commute, are similar to the prior group.

Table 10.2

Geographical Distribution While in School

No.	*Town*
3	Acton
1	Ashland
2	Boston
1	Brookline
1	Concord
1	Framingham
4	Hingham
2	Holliston
1	Hopkinton
1	Hudson
1	Lexington
2	Marlboro
1	Medfield
2	Milford
6	Natick
2	Needham
1	Newburyport
1	Sherborn
2	Southboro
1	Stow
1	Sudbury
1	Walpole
1	Waltham
1	Wayland
1	Worcester

Occupations

— What are they doing now?

Table 10.3 summarizes by category the variety of occupations presently engaged in by members of this group. Occupations marked with an asterisk denote entrepreneurial or self-employed situations. Any individual can appear in more than one category of occupation.

Table 10.3

Present Occupations
(Arranged by Categories of Occupation)

Category	*Number in Category*	*Specific Occupations*
Business Management	7	administrator in aerospace company food broker manager, wine department *international public relations for Boston businesses *video business *car cleaning business *owner, health insurance agency
Office Manager/ Executive Assistant	2	treasurer of a credit union bookkeeper
High Tech	3	technician in a multi-media company computer systems manager *freelance computer programmer
Professional	4	*lawyer therapist EMT nurse
Law Enforcement	1	court specialist in child and spousal abuse
Parent	4	parent (4)

Category	*Number in Category*	*Specific Occupations*
Education	5	college and graduate school teacher of tourist development drama coach and teacher pre-school teacher (2) missionary
Marketing	2	network marketing art gallery representative for corporate sales
Trades	14	carpenter auto mechanic machinist truck dispatcher *house painter *construction (2) *cookie baker *freelance copy editor nutrition counselor (2) caterer (2) bartender engineering technician armed forces serviceman
Design	3	*graphic artist (2) *jewelry maker pattern engineer in a shoe company
Creative Arts	2	*artist *playwright
Performing Arts	1	*musician in group
Unskilled Labor	2	kitchen worker estate caretaker
Student	3	psychology fine arts accounting

Table 10.4 lists the occupations in which each of the people in this sample are currently engaged. The list is in ascending order of age. There is no predominance of any category of work in either the younger or the older part of the group.

In this group of forty-one people, only one person who is not a student is an unskilled laborer — the youngest member of the group, twenty-one years old.

Table 10.4

Present Occupations (Arranged in Order of Age)

Age	*Present Occupations*
21	kitchen worker
21	missionary
22	carpenter
22	technician in a multi-media company
22	fine arts student, *artist, caterer
23	*freelance computer programmer
23	accounting student, estate caretaker
23	*musician, manager of a wine department
25	truck dispatcher
25	auto mechanic
25	film student
27	*house painter, *cookie baker
27	treasurer of credit union
28	pre-school teacher
28	administrator in aerospace company
28	*graphic artist
31	computer systems manager
31	*construction
32	*video business
32	US Army serviceman
33	*graphic artist, *jewelry maker
33	engineering technician
33	nurse
34	drama coach and teacher, playwright

Age	*Present Occupations*
34	*lawyer
34	bartender, *car cleaning business
35	*owner of health insurance agency
35	parent, *freelance copy editor
36	parent, pre-school teacher
36	psychology student, bookkeeper, nutritional counselor
37	parent
38	parent, network marketing
38	pattern engineer in shoe company
38	art gallery representative for corporate sales
38	machinist
39	therapist
39	*international public relations for Boston businesses, college and graduate school teacher of tourist development
40	*construction, EMT
40	food broker
40	nutritional counselor, caterer
40	court specialist in child and spousal abuse

— Range of occupations

Table 10.5 presents as complete a list as we have available of all the occupations engaged in by members of this group after they left school (including those in the above table of present occupations). As in Table 10.3, occupations marked with an asterisk denote either entrepreneurial or self-employed situations. The category of "student" shown in Table 10.3 has been dropped since a subsequent section will take up in greater detail the education pursued by members of this group.

Table 10.5

Occupations Engaged in Since Leaving Sudbury Valley (Arranged by Categories of Occupation)

Category	*Number in Category*	*Specific Occupations*
Business Management	16	administrator in aerospace company
		food broker
		manager, wine department
		*international public relations for Boston businesses
		*video business
		*car cleaning business
		*owner, health insurance agency
		retail department manager
		coffee house manager
		*used car business
		*restaurant owner (2)
		antique store manager (2)
		building manager
		stereo store manager
		art store manager
		jewelry wholesale business manager
Office Manager/ Executive Assistant	7	treasurer of a credit union
		bookkeeper (4)
		secretary
		research assistant
		city planning assistant
High Tech	3	technician in a multi-media company
		computer systems manager
		*freelance computer programmer
Professional	6	*lawyer
		therapist
		EMT (2)
		nurse
		city planner
		advocate for disabled
		manager of a mental retardation program
Law Enforcement	1	court specialist in child and spousal abuse
		policeman
Parent	4	parent (4)

Category	*Number in Category*	*Specific Occupations*
Education	11	college and graduate school teacher of tourist development
		teacher of nursing
		drama coach and teacher
		pre-school teacher (2)
		missionary
		music teacher
		English tutor
		aerobics teacher
		child care
		youth counselor
Marketing	4	network marketing
		art gallery representative for corporate sales
		carpet salesperson
		car salesperson
Trades	27	auto mechanic
		machinist (2)
		welder
		truck dispatcher
		*house painter (2)
		*construction (2)
		carpenter (3)
		electrician
		*cookie baker
		*freelance copy editor
		nutrition counselor (2)
		caterer (2)
		chef (4)
		bartender
		engineering technician
		armed forces serviceman (2)
		farmer
		arborist
		blacksmith
		horse trainer
		bus driver
		trucker (2)

Category	*Number in Category*	*Specific Occupations*
Trades *(cont'd)*		printer (2) proofreader nurse's aide (2) custom photoprocessor
Media	1	*video producer
Design	5	*graphic artist (3) layout designer *jewelry maker pattern engineer in a shoe company
Creative Arts	3	*artist (2) *playwright
Performing Arts	3	*musician in group (2) drama producer, director, actor
Unskilled Labor	26	kitchen worker (3) estate caretaker museum aide veterinary1031Xassistant retail clerk (7) stockperson security guard (2) chambermaid (2) house cleaner delivery person (3) custodian (2) gas station attendant hotel clerk carpet installer waitperson (2) grocery clerk (3) mail clerk warehouse worker electronic assembly technician archaeological assistant factory worker bank teller cab driver chauffeur

While they were attending school at Sudbury Valley, twenty-six of the forty-one (63%) held jobs. Some of the jobs were relatively advanced, such as carpenter, store manager, freelance computer programmer, chef, kitchen supervisor, auto mechanic, gymnastics coach, and caterer. One was an apprentice chef in a Boston gourmet restaurant. The other jobs were more routine, typical of those held by high school students: kitchen worker, waitperson, resort clerk, pizza deliverer, hostess, florist's assistant, nurse's aide, retail clerk, day care assistant, fast food clerk, factory worker, gal Friday, library clerk, gas station attendant, guard, chauffeur.

— Where have they worked?

Table 10.6 lists some of the places where members of this group have worked or currently work. The table is arranged by job category and contains only a sampling; we have included it to give an idea of the kind of work environments this group has chosen.

Table 10.6

Places of Work
(Arranged by Categories of Occupation)

Category	*Company or Institution*
Business Management	David Erlich
	Antioch College
	Ava Boteille
	Mayo's Car Care Service
	River House Cafe
	Kennedy Associates
	Art Asia Boston
	Bernheimer's Antique Arts
	Chase Brokerage
	Tech HiFi

Category	*Company or Institution*
Office Manager/ Executive Assistant	Federal Credit Union
	WGBH
	Hill Construction
	Alma Desk Company
	Knoll International
	City of Burlington (VT)
	Goodwill Industries
High Tech	Lincoln Labs
	Digital Equipment Corporation
	ASA Inc.
Professional	Colby and Frye, Attornies
	Harvard University
	Town of Milton
	Delta Mental Health Projects
Education	Kiddie Lodge
	South Natick Children's Center
	Latino Youth Lab
	Sudbury Valley School
	Children's Theater of Newburyport
	Pingree School
	American School in Switzerland
	Salem State College
	YMCA
	Boston University
Law Enforcement	Quincy Court
	Hingham Police Department
	Hull Police Department
Marketing	NuSkin
	Bay View Gallery
Trades	King's Guard (Norwegian Army)
	US Army
	US Navy
	Ro-Mar Terminals
	Bay State Shippers
	AutoSport Engineering
	Whittier Rehabilitation Hospital
	Cape Cod Cookie Corporation
	Lamy's Lower Cape Painters

Category	*Company or Institution*
Trades *(cont'd)*	Prime Computer
	Union House Retaurant
	NutriSystems
	Dom's of Boston
	Chanticleer, Nantucket
	Obediah's, Nantucket
	Hampshire College
Design	Collins and Drew
	Input/Output Computer Services, Inc.
	Propaganda
	Carlson Type and Design
	Federal Research Press
	Wellington Management Company
	Iverson Design

— Personal comments on employment

The spontaneous comments offered by the respondents during the interviews often dealt with how they felt about their work. Many were proud of what they were doing: "My supervisors are pleased with my work, and several times I got the employee of the month award," said the only person in a non-skilled job who was not primarily a student. Another person, highly skilled, commented: "Freelance programming gives me pride in the products that I develop that appear in the market."

Over and over again, members of this group stressed the joy and satisfaction they got out of what they were doing, occasionally stressing the special benefits of self-employment. Here are some samples:

> *I am very satisfied with my life. I have changed work drastically several times, but I have been satisfied with many jobs, as long as I am able to be creative and show some ingenuity and initiative. I like projects I can sink into for more than full time hours, and then I enjoy time off when the project ends.*

> *I am very content with my present situation. My self-motivation at work is greatly appreciated by my boss. I was one of a few survivors of massive layoffs.*

I enjoy carpentry because I like to see the results of what I do, and I like to make pretty things.

I am happy trying to make it with music. I have turned down lucrative job offers in order to have time for music. I also like working at jobs where I can learn about the product.

I like being able to make a living on my own terms, dealing with people, and being with my family. My kids are the biggest joy of my life.

I love working hard, earning my own living, being independent. I have been self-employed for five years, and enjoy being good at my profession, as well as the opportunity to be outdoors. Being self-employed lets me schedule my time to spend plenty of time with my children.

I like being the boss, not having people tell me what to do.

I love fly fishing. I love to have my own business. I am happy working two days a week and fishing.

I like painting [fine arts] because it is independent and challenging.

I enjoy working in shoe manufacturing, where I have worked my way up through the ranks to a position that includes management, product development, liaison with production. I continue to be challenged, and I am pleased to be doing work that is personally satisfying, helps me be financially secure, and allows me to constantly learn new things and to produce an excellent product.

I am very content with my work.

I enjoy helping people. I liked being a waiter. I liked dealing with motorcycles. I like self-employment. I have liked most of my work. I am happy with my accomplishments and with challenging work.

I find computers mentally challenging and enjoy my work.

Most all of my work has given me satisfaction — financial benefit, team membership, pride in quality of workmanship, self-expression, and contribution to society.

Further Formal Education

— Where did they continue their schooling?

Out of the forty-one members of this group, thirty-three (80%) have at some time or another attended formal classes somewhere in order to further their education. Thirteen (32%) completed the requirements for one or more degrees. Table 10.7 lists the schools attended after Sudbury Valley; however, our list of these institutions is incomplete. Schools marked with an asterisk are those from which degrees have been received. In several categories, there are more school names than the number attending. This is because several students attended more than one school.

Table 10.7

Schools Attended After S.V.S.

Type of School	*Number Attending*	*Number Completing Degrees*	*Names of Schools*
art schools	3	n/a	Boston Museum of Fine Arts School (2) DeCordova Museum School
trade schools	3	n/a	Cordon Bleu Cooking School, London Boston Architectural Center C.E.T.A.
miscellaneous	3	n/a	Keefe Technical School New Hampshire Vocational Tech. National Mountaineering School
community college	7	AA (3)	*Mass Bay Community Coll. (4) *Mount Wachusett Community Coll. Massasoit Community College *Greenfield Community College
junior college	5		Ricks College Dean Junior College Graham Junior College (2) Quincy Junior College

Type of School	*Number Attending*	*Number Completing Degrees*	*Names of Schools*
college	28	AA (1) BS (2) BA (7) BSW (1) Cert. of Design (1)	Antioch College Berklee College of Music Boston College Boston State College *Boston University (3) Bradford College California School of Professional Psychology *Castleton State College Central New England College (2) *Emerson College Framingham State University (4) Harvard University Extension (4) Mass College of Art New England Conservatory New Hampshire College *Northeastern University (4) Phoenix College *Rhode Island School of Design *Roger Williams College Tufts University UMass Amherst *UMass Boston (2) University of Maine University of Montana Western Washington State Coll. *Wheelock College
graduate school	4	MSW (1) LLD (1) MA (1) MEd (1) MFT (1)	*University of Colorado *Suffolk University Law School *West Virginia University *Kantor Family Institute *Cambridge College

—— Education vs. occupation

In Table 10.8 we look at the relationship between what the members of this group chose to study in their further formal education, and the occupations they are currently engaged in. We did not include in this Table the seventeen people who were either primarily students or who had not pursued any further formal education in a serious manner. The table is arranged in ascending order of age of the remaining twenty-four people.

Table 10.8 shows a strong correlation between subjects studied in formal schooling and current occupations. Members of this group generally seem to have used formal schooling as a tool of vocational education, and probably also to explore career possibilities that they are not currently pursuing.

Table 10.8

Relationship of Formal Education to Occupation

Age	*Type of School*	*Degrees*	*Area of Study Concentration*	*Most Recent Occupation*
22	college		business	carpenter
23	college	BA	creative writing	freelance computer programmer
23	college		music composition	musician, manager of wine department
25	junior college		business adm., law enforcem't	truck dispatcher
27	college		computer science	house painter, cookie baker
28	college	AA, BA	early childhood education	pre-school teacher
28	college	AA	communications	administrator in aerospace company
28	college		graphic design	graphic artist
31	college		business	computer systems manager

Age	*Type of School*	*Degrees*	*Area of Study Concentration*	*Most Recent Occupation*
32	college	BS	political science	video business
33	college	cert. design	art and design	graphic artist, jewelry maker
33	college		music, psych., electronics,	engineering technician
33	college	BS	nursing, bus. management	nurse
34	college, graduate school	BA, MA	theater, theater education	drama coach and teacher, playwright
34	college, graduate school	BA, LLD	anthropology, law	lawyer
35	college		business, management	owner of health insurance agency
35	college		English literature	parent, freelance copy editor
36	community college		early childhood education	parent, pre-school teacher
	trade school		cooking	parent, network marketing
38	college, trade school		psychology, mountaineering	pattern engineer in shoe company
38	college	BA	art history	art gallery representative for corporate sales
39	college, graduate school	BSW, MSW, AAMFT	social work	therapist
39	college		city planning	int'l p.r. for Boston businesses, college teacher
40	college, graduate school	MEd	counseling	court specialist in child and spousal abuse

— Personal comments on education

Many of the remarks made by members of this group about their further schooling were quite interesting:

> *In college I was self-directed and studied on my own. I was prepared to be self-directed and had no trouble getting into any school.*
>
> *I worked the graveyard shift at a department store and realized I could work super hard doing a man's job. I could push myself and work through the night. This made me realize I could put all this energy into an education.*
>
> *Sudbury Valley's open campus made my college experience comfortable and easy.*
>
> *College was what I was interested in, and when you are interested, it is easy.*
>
> *After SVS I decided not to go to college unless I had a reason to go. I never regretted not finishing college.*
>
> *School after SVS was a waste of money. I should have stayed at SVS. I love books — anything to do with print is a lot of fun.*

A couple of people pursued somewhat unorthodox paths relative to their education. "I got into a Master's program without a BA based on exams," noted one. Another said, "Not having a college degree didn't harm my career. The irony is that I teach courses at the graduate and undergraduate level in tourism and in marketing and promoting the city. I learn through teaching, not by taking courses."

Several members of this group expressed the intention of doing more formal schooling. Two of the people who already have degrees plan to continue in graduate school. Four others are planning to complete the requirements for degrees. Six more have plans to continue formal education without necessarily receiving certification of any kind. Thus a total of twelve people (29%) planned to continue their formal education in some manner.

Travel

This group, like the other groups, appears to display a distinct interest in travel. Table 10.9 lists some of the places they have visited. It is organized by age and is based on incomplete information. Seventeen of the forty-one members of the group are not included, either because we lack information or because they actually have not traveled extensively.

Table 10.9

Travel Experiences

Age	*Places Visited*
21	cross country USA
21	Idaho, Arizona, Texas
22	Scandinavia, Greece, East Coast USA, cross country USA, sailed across the Atlantic
22	cross country USA
23	Japan, Mexico, Czechoslovakia, Spain, Western Europe
23	extensively in USA
23	extensively in Europe (including Hungary and Czechoslovakia), North Canadian wilderness, Caribbean
25	Mexico, Canada, Germany
28	England, Ireland, extensively in USA
32	Holland, Germany, France, Sinai
33	extensively in Europe and USA, Mexico
33	extensively in USA
34	extensively in Europe
35	Hawaii, Caribbean, Eastern USA
36	England, Europe
38	England, Caribbean
38	El Salvador, Costa Rica, Mexico, Dominican Republic, India
39	Germany, world wide with Navy
39	all of continental USA
39	Austria, France, Germany, England, Japan, Tahiti
40	extensively throughout North American and South Pacific
40	Europe, cross country USA several times
40	extensively in USA, Canada, Bahamas, Europe

Personal Perspectives

Many members of this group made a point of discussing their roles in social or political activities in the community. These comments were far more prevalent in this group than in all the others combined, although it is difficult to draw any conclusions from this observation, since all such comments were unsolicited and off the cuff. Here is some of what they said:

> *My long term plan is to be able to travel with my wife on our own in a Peace Corps type way — I as an EMT, and she as a forester, on a volunteer basis.*
>
> *I am active in politics as a precinct captain. I am also a community organizer of an alternative PTO for Hispanic parents, and I am a board member of a holistic health clinic. I like to foster participant democracy.*
>
> *I enjoy working in left-wing, radical organizations.*
>
> *I am active in organizations for the self-employed.*
>
> *I have always been interested in working with children. I run training programs all over the country relating to battered spouses.*
>
> *I enjoy public speaking and organizing people.*
>
> *I am involved in Jewish/Quaker studies. I work in ward politics, and was elected to work on the allocation of federal funds. I worked for Vermont's Socialist Congressional Representative. I wrote a guidebook for planning boards about legal obligations to the handicaps, and won an award for it from the American Planners Association. At one time I was also resident in a shelter which I helped to start.*

The general comments offered by members of this group about their lives and about Sudbury Valley are extremely upbeat, and in many cases reflect a strong sense of the deep positive changes in their lives that they feel were brought about by their Sudbury Valley experience. This group as a whole seems much more aware of the internal processes that they underwent during their stay at the school, even though — or perhaps because — it lasted only two years.

Sudbury Valley helped me to be myself and grow up earlier. It helped me stay in school and not drop out.

Sudbury Valley taught me how to get along with people of all ages, and to exercise initiative in learning. It was a happy time in my life.

Sudbury Valley changed my whole life. It gave me a chance to become me, to grow. I couldn't be married, couldn't have a child, couldn't do anything without it. I had to find out I could accomplish something. I learned to read people better and be streetwise.

I am very happy, challenged, and busy. Sudbury Valley gave me a new and better way of relating to friends and living together responsibly with friends.

I loved the school and had a great time there. I met lots of wonderful people whom I still know.

Sudbury Valley was critical in my development. I came worn down by personal problems. The school instilled in me a powerful sense of self-worth which was never totally erased during a long period afterward of tremendous personal problems. Somehow, I held on to a sense of identity. I got lots of support and affection at SVS; it lessened the conflict and guilt about maintaining a sense of self.

It was wonderful being at Sudbury Valley. It was a real life saver.

Sudbury Valley was a totally positive experience. It showed me how to get along and I learned a lot about life from talking about different subjects — from using pantyhose as a fan belt, to how to go to college and have confidence in oneself. I realized more about my rights, which is hard to realize as a kid.

Sudbury Valley was a big help because I refused to go to public school, and it was my springboard to becoming a citizen of the world.

Sudbury Valley was wonderful and allowed me to find myself.

When I came to Sudbury Valley I was in bad shape. I liked it a lot. I probably wouldn't be living now if I hadn't come.

Sudbury Valley was the best thing that ever happened to me in my life.

Sudbury Valley saved me. It gave me room to find out who I was and what I wanted to do.

Sudbury Valley helped me to liberate my concepts. I read more and problem solved more than in public school. I learned what and when I wanted to without pressure. It helped me a lot.

Sudbury Valley gave me space and some stability. It gave me a nice secure place — everyone treating everyone else as equals, caring about each other, nurturing. Sudbury Valley was a miracle for me.

11

Students Who Were Enrolled in Sudbury Valley for Their Last High School Age Year

In this chapter we examine the group of people who enrolled in Sudbury Valley for one year and then went on to what are generally considered to be "post high school" activities. A few of these people came with the intention of staying only one year, to organize their lives before going out to the adult world. Others came without necessarily having a definite time span in mind, and left after a year for a variety of personal reasons. For all members of this group, Sudbury Valley was a brief interlude, which nevertheless had the potential of making an impact on their evolving attitudes toward education and life.

There were thirty-nine people in this group, of whom twenty-four were respondents in this study, for a response rate of 62%. All of the data presented in this chapter will refer to the twenty-four respondents only, of whom five (21%) were male, and nineteen female. (Even if the non-respondents are included, the number of females is still an unusually high 64% of the whole group.) We have no explanation for the preponderance of females in this group relative to all the other groups.

Eight of the twenty-four (33%) received diplomas before leaving. We would not necessarily expect any members of this group to have received diplomas, since it is the school's expressed preference to consider for diplomas only students who have been enrolled for at least two years. In fact, during the time between the school's first diploma awards, in June

1970, and June 1991, a total of only twelve people received diplomas after attending one year. Over time the school has become progressively more reluctant to consider one-year enrollees for a diploma; this evolution is reflected in the fact that during the years 1970 - 1981, nine of these twelve diplomas were awarded, whereas only three were awarded during the next ten years, even though there were many more graduates in the second period, and more students who stayed for only one year.

Basic Demographics

—— How old are they now?

Figure 11.1 shows the distribution of this group by age on January 1, 1991. The range of ages extends from twenty-one to forty, as with the group in Chapter 10. The average age is 31.5 and the median age is 32.5; both figures are not significantly different from that group.

Figure 11.1

Distribution by Age, January 1, 1991

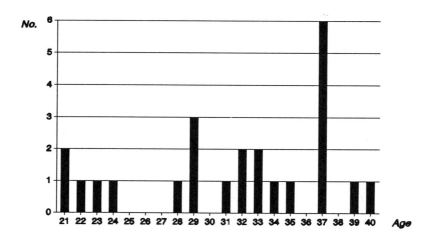

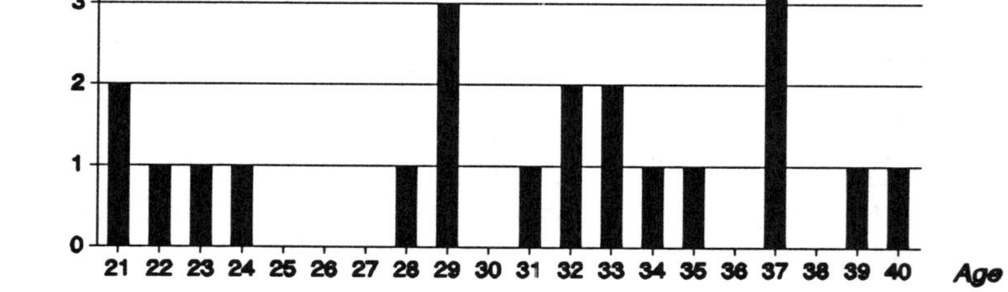

— Their marital status

Of the twenty-four people in this group, nine were single (38%); eleven were or had been married (46%) — three of these were divorced, one of whom was living with a significant other; and four of those who had never been married were living with significant others (17%). Four people were married ten years or longer, two for sixteen years. This group of twenty-four people had a total of seventeen children, ages one to sixteen. In this group, nine people (38%) had children; one had four, one had three, three had two, and the other four had one. The average family size in this group is similar to that of the group examined in Chapter 10.

— Where do they live?

Table 11.1 shows where these people live. Thirteen of them (54%) live in Massachusetts, all in towns that are considered to be in the school's catchment area.

Table 11.1

Current Geographical Distribution of the Group

No.	*Town*	*State*
1	Concord	California
1	San Francisco	California
1	Boulder	Colorado
1	Telluride	Colorado
1	Bethany	Connecticut
1	Decatur	Georgia
1	Chicago	Illinois
1	Beverly	Massachusetts
1	Bolton	Massachusetts
1	Canton	Massachusetts
2	Framingham	Massachusetts
1	Jamaica Plain	Massachusetts
1	Lunenburg	Massachusetts
1	Marlboro	Massachusetts
1	Medway	Massachusetts

No.	*Town*	*State*
1	Reading	Massachusetts
1	Wayland	Massachusetts
2	Worcester	Massachusetts
1	Hollis	New Hampshire
1	Guilderland	New York
1	New York	New York
1	Austin	Texas

—— How old were they when they enrolled?

Figure 11.2 shows the ages at which this group entered the school. The ages range from fifteen to twenty, with both the aveage and the median age being seventeen — one year older than the group in Chapter 10.

Figure 11.2

Distribution by Age of Entry

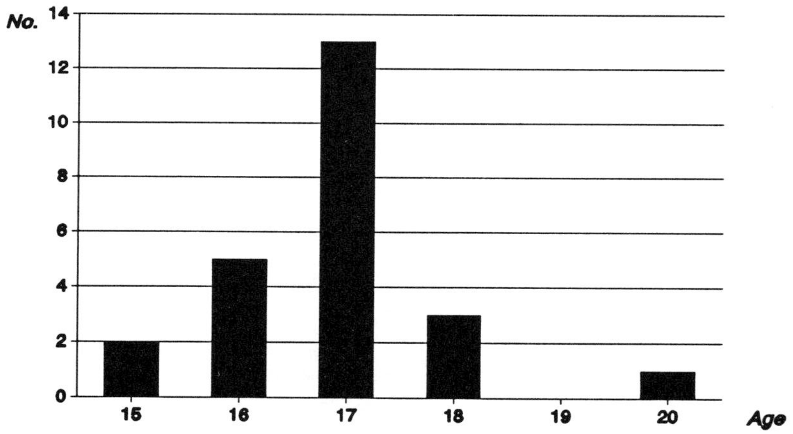

— What was their prior schooling?

We have information on only twenty-two of the twenty-four people in this group concerning their schooling before entering Sudbury Valley. Figure 11.3 details the number who went to various categories of schools prior to SVS. We distinguish between private and public schools. Since a person may have gone to both private and public schools at any level, the total number at each level is higher than the actual number of individuals who went to school at each level.

Figure 11.3

Schooling Prior to Sudbury Valley

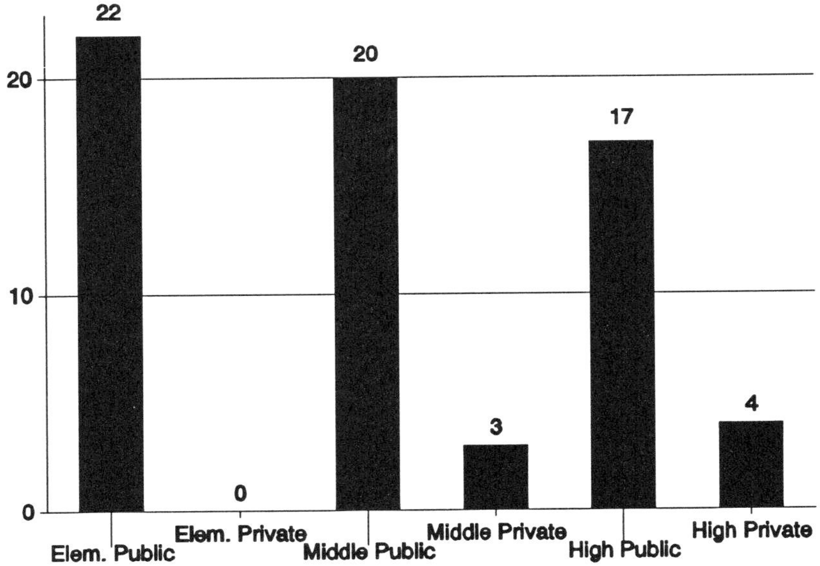

All of the twenty-two about whom we have information attended elementary and middle schools. Twenty (91%) also attended high school. One person attended college before coming to Sudbury Valley. Two people attended only private school at the middle level; three attended only private school at the high school level. Out of the twenty-two, six different people (27%) attended a private school at some time before entering Sudbury

Valley; no one attended private school exclusively. Thus, fourteen people (73%) had attended only public schools, and all had attended public schools at some time. These figures repeat the findings in earlier groups that these students were not drawn from among families who traditionally send their children to private schools.

—— How old were they when they left school?

Figure 11.4 shows the ages at which members of this group left the school. Both the average age of leaving and the median age of leaving is eighteen.

Figure 11.4

Distribution by Age at Leaving

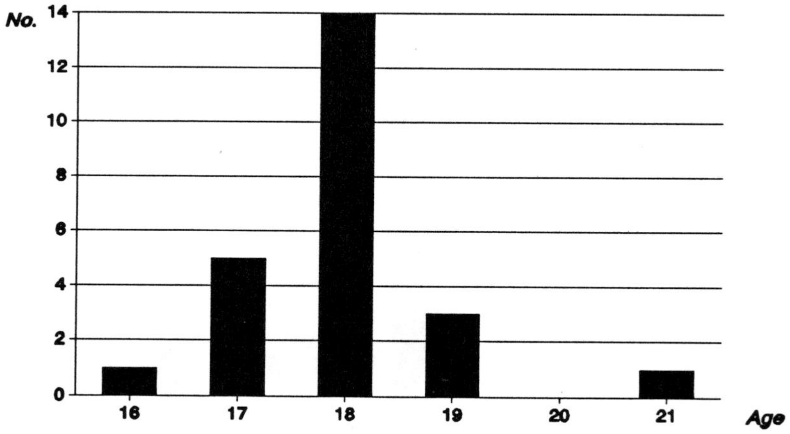

—— Where did they live?

Table 11.2 shows the geographical distribution of this population at the time that they were students here. The number of towns from which this group was drawn, and the radius of commute, are similar to the other groups in Part IV of this study. The person who came from Fair Haven, New Jersey, lived in Framingham while attending Sudbury Valley. We have no explanation for the exceptionally high percentage of Framingham residents in this group; other towns in the immediate vicinity are not disproportionately represented.

Table 11.2

Geographical Distribution While in School

No.	*Town*
1	Bolton
1	Canton
1	Clinton
8	Framingham
1	Harwich
1	Hingham
1	Holliston
1	Marlboro
1	Mattapan
1	Natick
1	Northboro
1	Wayland
4	Worcester
1	Fair Haven, NJ

Occupations

—— What are they doing now?

Table 11.3 summarizes by category the variety of occupations presently engaged in by members of this group. Occupations marked with an asterisk denote entrepreneurial or self-employed situations. Any individual can appear in more than one category of occupation.

Table 11.3

Present Occupations (Arranged by Categories of Occupation)

Category	*Number in Category*	*Specific Occupations*
Business Management	5	manager of eye care center director of operations of national medical supplies company *musicians management agency *stager of gala celebrations restaurant manager
Office Manager/ Executive Assistant	3	office manager o office furniture store personnel training coordinator in a computer company head teller
High Tech	1	computer product designer
Professional	1	*acupuncturist
Parent	2	parent (2)
Education	6	special ed teacher equestrian arts teacher *music school director teacher of massage and Chinese medicine aerobics teacher Buddhist monk
Marketing	1	advertising account executive

Category	*Number in Category*	*Specific Occupations*
Trades	5	*house painter construction worker chef hospital technician organic farmer
Creative Arts	2	*stained glass crafts *artist
Unskilled Labor	2	retail clerk security officer
Student	2	occupational therapy nursing

Table 11.4 lists the occupations of the twenty-three people in this set for whom we have information. The list is in ascending order of age. There is no predominance of any category of work in either the older or the younger part of the group. The oldest unskilled laborer is twenty-three.

Table 11.4

Present Occupations (Arranged in Order of Age)

Age	*Present Occupations*
21	retail clerk
21	*house painter
22	student of occupational therapy
23	security officer
24	special education teacher
28	equestrian arts teacher
29	office manager of office furniture store
29	personnel training coordinator in a computer co.
29	manager of eye care center
31	director of operations of national medical supplies co.

Age	*Present Occupations*
32	construction worker
32	computer product designer
33	*music school director
33	*acupuncturist, teacher of massage and Chinese medicine
34	head teller, *stained glass crafts
35	*musicians management agency
37	advertising account executive
37	*stager of gala celebrations, *artist
37	chef and manager of two restaurants
37	parent, student of nursing
37	hospital technician
39	parent, aerobics teacher
40	Buddhist monk, organic farmer

— Range of occupations

Table 11.5 presents as complete a list as we have available of all the occupations the twenty-three members of this group for whom we have information engaged in after they left school (including those in the above table of present occupations). As in Table 11.3, occupations marked with an asterisk denote either entrepreneurial or self-employed situations. The category of "student" shown in Table 11.3 has been dropped since a subsequent section will take up in greater detail the education pursued by members of this group.

Table 11.5

Occupations Engaged in Since Leaving Sudbury Valley (Arranged by Categories of Occupation)

Category	*Number in Category*	*Specific Occupations*
Business Management	8	manager of eye care center director of operations of national medical supplies company *musicians management agency *stager of gala celebrations restaurant manager assistant manager record store manager of cinema manager of jewelry store manager of leather store antique dealer ski resort food director *owner, restaurant
Office Manager/ Executive Assistant	8	office manager (2) personnel training coordinator in a computer company head teller supervisor of security insurance claims representative (2) secretary (2) trade school admissions officer
High Tech	2	computer product designer production planner for computer company
Professional	3	mechanical engineer army medic psychotherapist *acupuncturist
Parent	2	parent (2)

Category	*Number in Category*	*Specific Occupations*
Education	9	special ed teacher assistant special ed teacher nursery teacher equestrian arts teacher *music school director teacher of massage and Chinese medicine yoga teacher Buddhist monk Hare Krishna minister counselor aerobics teacher
Media	1	disc jockey
Marketing	1	advertising account executive
Trades	9	*free lance photographer *house painter (2) construction worker chef (3) caterer hospital technician lab technician horse trainer oil exploration crew member organic farmer (2) boat building apprentice white water rafting guide leather worker
Performing Arts	1	stage manager theater and film makeup, set design, lighting, wardrobe
Design	2	graphics artist jewelry maker
Creative Arts	3	*stained glass crafts *artist (2)

Category	*Number in Category*	*Specific Occupations*
Unskilled Labor	12	retail clerk (5) security officer (2) pizza delivery waitress balloon delivery soliciting for charity teacher's aide (2) day care worker (2) nurse's assistant receptionist stock person landscaping factory worker mover

While they were attending school at Sudbury Valley, twelve of the twenty-four (50%) held jobs. Some were of an advanced nature, such as cook, music teacher, court translator and stable manager. The other jobs were of the more routine kind usually held by high school students: veterinary assistant, retail clerk, fast food clerk, kennel hand, warehouseman, security guard, pizza deliverer, and assistant in a radio station.

— Where have they worked?

Table 11.6 lists some of the places where members of this group have worked or currently work. The table is arranged by job category and contains only a sampling; we have included it to give an idea of the kind of work environments this group has chosen.

Table 11.6

Places of Work (Arranged by Categories of Occupation)

Category	*Company or Institution*
Business Management	International Music Network
	Eye Care Center
	Suburban Ostomy
	Gladstone's Restaurant
	The Seafood Place
Office Manager/ Executive Assistant	FloridaPirg
	Nollman\Horrow Office Furniture
	Amica Insurance
	Prime Computer
	Stores Technical Corportion
	Buddy Dog
	Katherine Gibbs School
	YKK Zipper Company
	South Shore Bank
	Amoskeag Bank
High Tech	Hewlett Packard
	Digital Equipment Corporation
Professional	US Army Medical Corps
Education	Justice Resource Institution
	Marlboro Public Schools
	Fitchburg Public Schools
	Shrewsbury Public Schools
	New Haven Public Schools
	Hudson Public Schools
	Framingham Public Schools
	Marlboro Equestrian Center
	Head Start Framingham
	Bethwood Suzuki Music School
Media	WICN
Marketing	Marsh & Donohue Advertising Agency

Category	*Company or Institution*
Trades	Galadriel of Provincetown St. Margaret's Hospital Kaiser Permanente Telluride Ski Resort Holland America Cruise Lines Radisson Hotels
Performing Arts	Chateau de Ville

—— Personal comments on employment

These respondents, too, offered spontaneous comments during the interviews that dealt with how they felt about their work. Several were proud of what they had achieved. One noted that she was "the first woman executive chef in the Radisson hotel chain." Another was proud to have "worked my way up from crew member to a management position on a 'portable crew' for oil exploration which specialized in inaccessible areas only reachable by helicopter or by 10 to 20 mile daily hikes. I also worked every department of the pharmaceutical distribution business, then ran a major distribution center, and then was in charge of opening two new regional centers before becoming Director of National Operations."

Once again the theme of work satisfaction repeated itself:

> *I find engineering intellectually satisfying, massage emotionally satisfying, and Chinese medicine — including herbology — both intellectually and emotionally satisfying. I love teaching.*

> *I find health care fulfilling.*

> *I like working for myself and producing quality work.*

> *I like my work in engineering documentation because it is lucrative and leaves time to take care of myself and my family.*

Further Formal Education

— Where did they continue their schooling?

Twenty of the twenty-four members of this group (83%) have at some time or another attended formal classes in order to further their education. Ten (42%) completed the requirements for one or more degrees. Table 11.7 lists the schools attended after Sudbury Valley; however, our list of these institutions is incomplete. Schools marked with an asterisk are those from which degrees have been received. In several categories, there are more school names than the number attending. This is because several students attended more than one school.

Table 11.7

Schools Attended After S.V.S.

Type of School	*Number Attending*	*Number Completing Degrees*	*Names of Schools*
trade schools	3	Cert. of Ther. Massage (1) Cert. of Horsemanship (1)	*Shiatsu Massage School Culinary Institute of America *British Horse Society
miscellaneous	2	n/a	Digital Equipment Corporation Philadelphia Assn. (London)
community college	6	AA (1)	*Mass Bay Community College (2) Quinsigamond Community College (2) Allen Hancock (California) Cape Cod Community College

Type of School	*Number Attending*	*Number Completing Degrees*	*Names of Schools*
college	15	BA (7) BFA (1)	Assumption College Bentley College *Boston University Champlain College *Earlham College *Fitchburg State College Framingham State College (2) Northeastern Illinois University *Pratt Institute Roger Williams College *University of Illinois *UMass Amherst (4) UMass Boston University of Southern Florida *Yale University
graduate school	3	MS (2)	*San Francisco College of Acupuncture University of Chicago *Wheelock College

—— Education vs. occupation

In Table 11.8 we look at the relationship between what the members of this group chose to study in their further formal education, and the occupations they are currently engaged in. We did not include in the Table the eight people who were either primarily students or who had not pursued any further formal education in a serious manner. The table is arranged in ascending order of age of the remaining sixteen people.

With some notable exceptions, Table 11.8 shows a strong correlation between subjects studied in formal schooling and current occupations.

Table 11.8

Relationship of Formal Education to Occupation

Age	*Type of School*	*Degrees*	*Area of Study Concentration*	*Most Recent Occupation*
21	college		literature	house painter
24	college	BA	education	special ed teacher
28	college, trade school	cert	art, horsemastership	equestrian arts teacher
29	college	BA	human services	office manager of office furniture store
29	college, graduate school	BA, MS	political science elementary education	personnel training coordinator in a computer company
31	college		business	director of operations of national medical supplies company
32	misc.		computer science	computer product designer
33	college	BA	psychology	music school director
33	college, graduate school	BA, MS, cert.	mechanical engineering, massage, acupuncture	teacher of massage and Chinese medicine
34	community college		crafts	stained glass crafts-person, head teller
35	college	BFA	theatrical design	musicians management agent
37	college		biology, anthropology, nursing	advertising account executive
37	college	BA	fine arts	artist, stager of gala celebrations

Age	*Type of School*	*Degrees*	*Area of Study Concentration*	*Most Recent Occupation*
37	trade school		restaurant management	chef and manager of two restaurants
39	college		design, paralegal work	aerobics teacher, parent
40	misc.		psychotherapy	Buddhist monk, organic farmer

Personal comments on education

Only a couple of comments were offered by members of this group about their educational experience after Sudbury Valley. One mentioned that when he applied to college, the admissions office "gave me a hard time. They didn't normally give interviews. But I was persistent, and I got an interview and was accepted." Another person, who received a bachelor's degree from Yale, commented that "I spent my year at Sudbury Valley getting myself into college. I was admitted to Yale, Harvard and Columbia, but I didn't seek or get a high school diploma."

Several members of this group expressed the intention of doing more formal schooling. Five of the people who have already obtained degrees plan to continue in graduate school or its equivalent. Six others are planning to complete the requirements for degrees, and two more have plans for continuing formal education without necessarily receiving certification of any kind. Thus a total of thirteen people (54%) planned to continue their formal education in some manner.

Travel

We have information about the travel history of twelve out of the twenty-four people in this group. These twelve seem to be as well-traveled as the members of the other groups. Table 11.9 lists some of the places they have visited. It is organized by age.

Table 11.9

Travel Experiences

Age	*Places Visited*
21	Florida, California
21	extensively throughout Canada and USA
24	Atlantic coast and cross country USA
28	Ireland, England, all over USA
29	Switzerland, Great Britain, California, and extensively in northeast USA
29	Great Britain, western USA
31	Egypt, Israel, Mexico, all over USA and Canada
33	extensively in Europe
34	Bahamas, Puerto Rico, Florida, Texas, California
35	Mexico, Brazil, throughout Europe, USA and Canada
37	from Germany to India by land, Ozarks and far west
40	India, Nepal, Indonesia, Malaysia, Afghanistan, Great Britain, Europe

Personal Perspectives

Several members of this group, like those of the two year group in Chapter 10, mentioned their roles in social or political activities in the community. Here is some of what they said:

> *I am health conscious, heavily into distance running, and vegetarian. I am politically active in town, and formed a Citizens for Education group.*

It's important to me to improve both myself and the environment.

I love working with my own company. It deals with music that I feel has a positive effect on the planet.

I am currently working on a program to get female prisoners with AIDS alternative treatment.

I love Boulder because people are into recycling, conservation, and the outdoorsy life. I enjoyed working with Head Start; it was difficult but rewarding work, and I may go back to it.

Because of "nuclear nightmares" at the age of eleven, I became involved in work for a nuclear freeze. Later, I became very active in Florida/PIRG and then in Mass/PIRG. I hope to become politically active in the education field. I have gotten a great deal of satisfaction from political organizing and working with special need students.

Although the members of this group had only attended Sudbury Valley for one year, it was remarkable to see how many of these students offered comments indicating that the school had a profound effect on their lives.

Sudbury Valley gave me a chance to focus on myself for a year and to really grow. I used the time to learn to be a grown-up without full adult responsibilities. I used my understanding of Sudbury Valley as a model for two music schools that I founded, which were run by students and parents together with the staff.

Sudbury Valley gave me "permission" to work with my hands. School before that didn't because I was a girl. I also loved playing with little kids and working with little kids.

I appreciate the Sudbury Valley experience and would like to have a similar school near me now that my oldest child is five. I am very happy and satisfied; I enjoy my family and family activities.

Sudbury Valley showed me that I had a lot more control over myself, my situation, my life and goals, than I had previously thought. I learned that decisions are up to the individual, and that if you make a poor decision you must deal realistically with the consequences. Sudbury Valley taught me responsibility and the importance of self-control. These issues apply to my interest in criminal justice.

The open environment at Sudbury Valley School got my self-motivation going.

Sudbury Valley was a very positive experience. I learned more there than I ever did in public schools. The surroundings and the attitudes of people made a great deal of difference.

Sudbury Valley gave me self-confidence.

Sudbury Valley gave me the space that I needed to be able to express myself. I am very happy with my life.

Sudbury Valley both influenced my views on educational philosophy, and helped me get out of a bad cycle personally. I came filled with hatred and found I could let go of it at Sudbury Valley; and then I figured out what to do with my life.

Sudbury Valley allowed me to find out about myself and learn what I wanted, but did not change my life in a major way I guess.

Sudbury Valley was the beginning of a process of eliminating misery and confusion from my life. The opportunity to do what I wanted, when I wanted, at Sudbury Valley restored that basic human necessity. Sudbury Valley began a process of empowerment which has continued.

I try to be a good human being and often draw on my experiences at Sudbury Valley in the unfolding of life. I feel Sudbury Valley sets a wonderful foundation for dealing with life and all its ups and downs. I am glad SVS existed and continues to exist as an example that truly works for people.

Sudbury Valley changed my attitude towards education. I became excited about learning again at SVS. I wouldn't have gone to any school if it weren't for SVS. I am happy with my present situation and love having my own practice.

Dealings at Sudbury Valley made me much more socially aware and I could communicate better. I became brave enough to go to a foreign country alone. I didn't realize the extent of my own problems until SVS set me on the path to solving them. I love teaching.

Sudbury Valley gave me a chance to slow down, talk to different people, get my priorities straight, and find out what I want to do in life. I got over my writer's block at SVS.

Two people made particular reference to the fact that they had been at the school for a short time:

Sudbury Valley saved my life. I wish I had been able to start younger so that I could have gotten more out of it.

Sudbury Valley helped me to want to learn. I realized that I had choices, and it made me want to educate myself. One year made all the difference.

Part V

Students Who Finished Their Schooling Elsewhere

12

Students Who Were Enrolled in Sudbury Valley Two Years or Longer and Left Before Their Last High School Age Year

The two chapters of this section deal with students who left Sudbury Valley before they felt ready to move on to adult pursuits. Due to the criteria discussed in Chapter 3, all of the people in these chapters were at least ten years old when they left. There is an extremely wide range of ages at which the students studied in these two chapters began, a large variation in the number of years spent at the school, and a wide range of ages at which they left. The school has no mechanism for ascertaining why students withdraw before they feel ready to take their place in the outside community as adults. There are many possibilities: the family leaves the area; economic difficulties make it impossible to pay tuition; the student, or one or both of the parents, are unhappy with some aspect of the school; the student is expressly seeking resources (such as intermural competitive sports) that cannot be provided at Sudbury Valley but can be found elsewhere; or any combination of these factors. We are not in a position to correlate any of these factors with individual students, nor can we speculate on the relationship, if any, between a student's reasons for leaving and the future unfolding of their lives.

This chapter deals with people who attended for two years or more. There were twenty-two people in this group, of whom seventeen were respondents in this study, for a response rate of 77%. All of the data presented in this chapter will refer to the seventeen respondents only, of whom seven (41%) were male, and ten female.

Basic Demographics

—— How old are they now?

Figure 12.1 shows the distribution of this group by age on January 1, 1991. The range of ages extends from twenty-one to thirty-six. The average age is twenty-six and the median age is twenty-four. This is the youngest of all the groups.

Figure 12.1

Distribution by Age, January 1, 1991

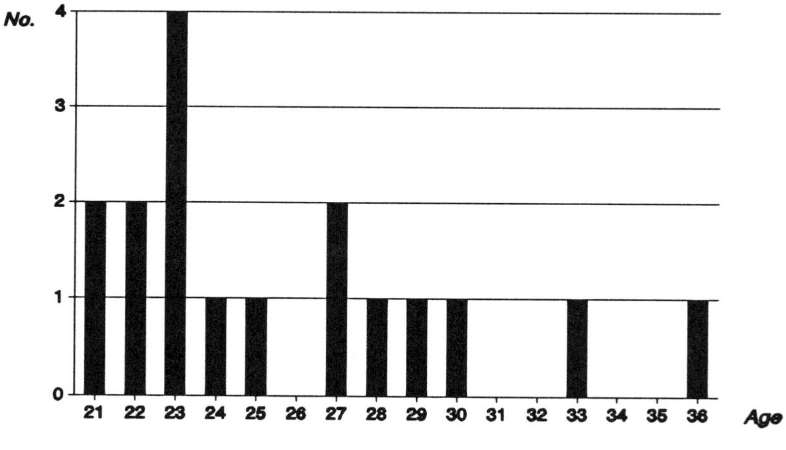

—— Their marital status

Of the seventeen people in this group, eight were single (47%); seven were married (41%); and two were living with significant others (12%). None had been divorced. Only one person was married as long as ten years, and that person had four children ages one to eight. One other person had a child, age one. Thus out of the entire group, two people (12%) had a total of five children. Clearly most people in this group had not yet gotten to the point of establishing families.

— Where do they live?

Table 12.1 shows where these people live. Twelve of them (71%) live in Massachusetts, ten in towns that are considered to be in the school's catchment area.

Table 12.1

Current Geographical Distribution of the Group

No.	*Town*	*State*
1	Culver City	California
1	Laguna Nigel	California
1	Colorado Springs	Colorado
2	Ashland	Massachusetts
1	Boylston	Massachusetts
1	Cohasset	Massachusetts
1	Everett	Massachusetts
1	Haverhill	Massachusetts
2	Marlboro	Massachusetts
1	Milford	Massachusetts
2	Stow	Massachusetts
1	Sudbury	Massachusetts
1	Waterford	Maine
1	Yonkers	New York

— How old were they when they enrolled, how long did they remain, and how old were they when they left school?

Figures 12.2, 12.3, and 12.4 show respectively the distribution of this group by age of entry into the school, the distribution of the length of stay at school,[1] and the distribution by age of leaving. A more coherent picture of

[1] We count only years actually enrolled in the school. For students who left Sudbury Valley for a time and subsequently returned, the time spent away from Sudbury Valley is not included in the calculation of the length of stay at school.

these three factors — age of entry, length of stay, and age of leaving — is displayed in Figure 12.5, in which each individual member of the group is represented by a line spanning their stay at the school. Figure 12.5 shows graphically the extremely heterogenous nature of this group.

Figure 12.2

Distribution by Age of Entry

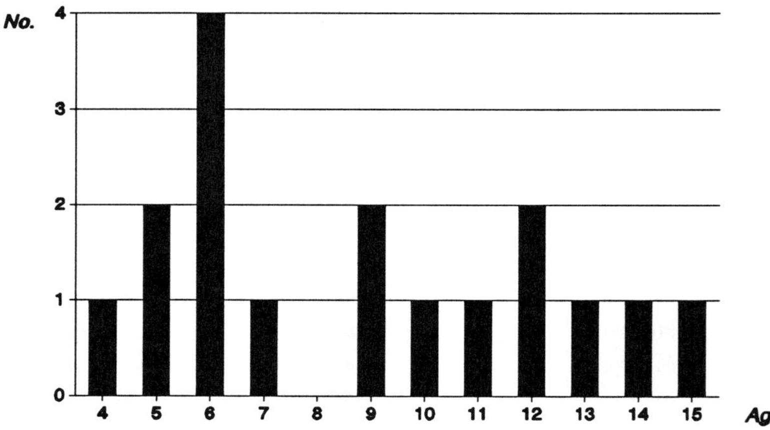

The average age of entry into the school for this group is nine years old; the median age of entry is eight years old.

Figure 12.3

Distribution of Length of Stay at the School

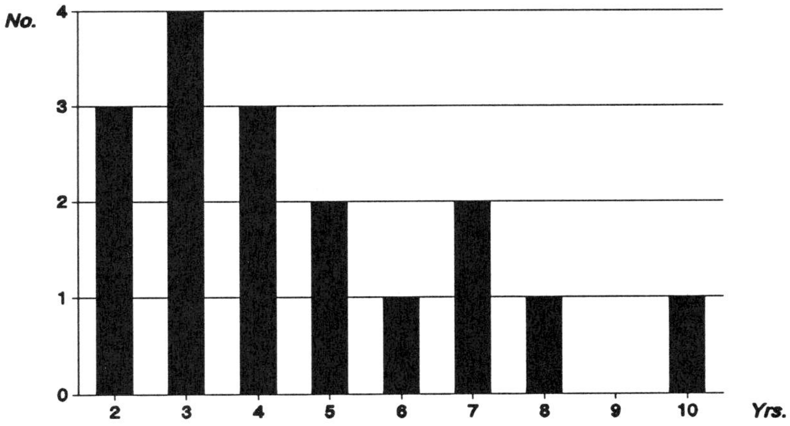

The average length of stay at the school for this group is five years; the median length of stay is four years.

Figure 12.4

Distribution by Age at Leaving

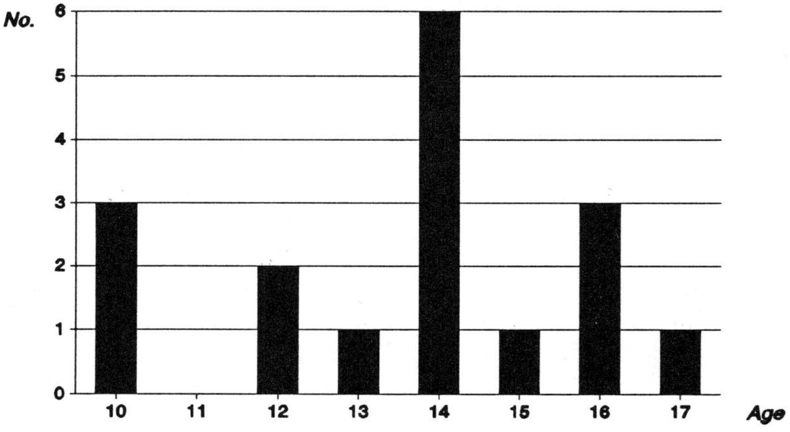

The average age at leaving school for this group is thirteen years old; the median age is fourteen years old.

Figure 12.5

Years of Enrollment, by Individual
(Arranged in Ascending Order by Age of Entry)

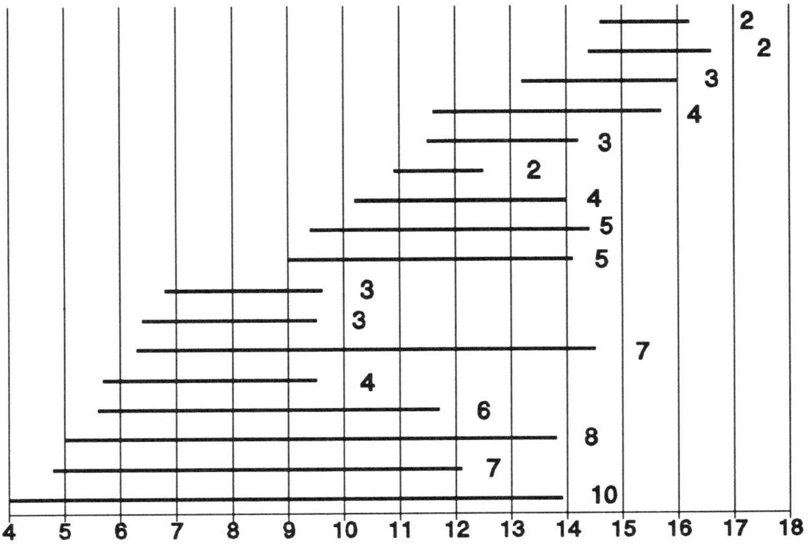

— What was their prior schooling?

For six of the members in this group (35%), Sudbury Valley was the first school attended. The other eleven all attended elementary schools — one for several weeks only — before coming to Sudbury Valley. Of these eleven, one attended public and private school, and one (6%) attended only private elementary school. Three of the seventeen (18%) went to middle school before Sudbury Valley, all three to public schools only.

— Where did they live?

Table 12.2 shows the geographical distribution of this population at the time that they were students at the school.

Table 12.2

Geographical Distribution While in School

No.	*Town*
1	Ashland
2	Framingham
1	Hingham
5	Marlboro
1	Needham
1	Rockland
1	Southboro
2	Stow
2	Sudbury
1	Walpole

Occupations

Because none of the members of this group finished their basic schooling at Sudbury Valley, we felt that we could not attach as much significance, vis a vis Sudbury Valley, to the occupational history of members of this group as we had to the prior groups. Nevertheless we decided to present a precis of this group's experiences in Table 12.3. The Table is organized in ascending order by the age of the members of the group. Occupations marked with an asterisk denote entrepreneurial or self-employed situations.

Table 12.3

Occupations Engaged in Since Leaving Sudbury Valley (Arranged in Order of Age)

Age	*Years at SVS*	*Age at Leaving SVS*	*Present Occupation*	*Previous Occupations*
21	5	14	child care worker with disturbed teens	ballet dancer
21	4	10	student of education	secretary
22	2	17	unemployed	waitress, maid, cashier
22	3	10	parent	cashier, fast food clerk, welfare office volunteer, breastfeeding counselor
23	3	10	student of humanities	retail food clerk, short order cook
23	4	14	*housepainter	
23	2	16	secretary	retail clerk, fast food clerk
23	7	12	dog officer	security guard, parking control officer
24	6	12	engineer, *prototype vehicle design company	automotive mechanic, car racing crew member
25	10	14	software engineer	warehouseman
27	7	15	day care worker	office worker, dental assistant
27	8	14	*custom business forms company	sales representative and regional marketing mgr.
28	3	14	customer services eng'r in computer co.	janitor, office coordinator, computer operator
30	4	16	back hoe operator	veterinary asst., plumber, electronics assembly
30	5	14	administrative assistant for movie production co.	waitress, bank teller, office manager, bookkeeper
33	2	13	*international art wholesale and retail	kitchen hand, car mechanic
36	3	16	president of food brokerage firm	food broker

Other Personal Information and Perspectives

After leaving Sudbury Valley, sixteen of the seventeen members of this group went on to public schools, and ultimately obtained high school diplomas; the other completed her education as a home schooler. All reported satisfactory performance in their subsequent schools, whether or not they enjoyed being there. Ten of the seventeen (59%) went on to study at the college level: one of these received an Associate of Arts degree, two received Bachelor's degrees, and six reported plans to complete work for degrees. We have not included information on the names of the schools these people attended after high school because we felt the lack of continuity between Sudbury Valley and their post-graduate schools rendered such information of doubtful relevance to our survey.

Every one of the people in this group offered some revealing comments on their lives and/or their experiences at Sudbury Valley. We have arranged them by the number of years each person spent at the school, and that number is shown at the end of each comment in square brackets along with their age at leaving.

> *I run my company as a self-governing entity because of Sudbury Valley. A percentage of me is because of that school. [2; 13 years old]*

> *I have no regrets about going to Sudbury Valley even though I didn't complete high school there. I enjoyed it very much. [2; 16 years old]*

> *I like Sudbury Valley because everyone was so nice there, and I loved the freedom. [2; 17 years old]*

> *I enjoy counseling work. The most important things in my life are welfare rights, breast feeding, and counseling other mothers. [3; 10 years old]*

> *My college work is always interfered with by my side interests and by the books that I am reading. I don't like to do things that I am not interested in. Sudbury Valley breeds people who go their own way. My attitudes about people came from Sudbury Valley and have stayed with me. [3; 10 years old]*

Sudbury Valley did the trick for me in discovering a lot about myself. One thing I learned was that I love to read. I hope when I have kids there will be some place nearby to send them like Sudbury Valley. [3; 14 years old]

My family is really important and is what makes me really happy. [3; 16 years old]

When I first went to public school I had trouble with cursive but excelled at everything else. I still tell all my friends about Sudbury Valley and remember it fondly. I feel I got a lot out of it. [4; 10 years old]

I had a disappointing experience at Sudbury Valley because I felt I couldn't learn what I wanted to from the staff. Hockey and music are what is most important to me. [4; 14 years old]

After Sudbury Valley I found high school easy because I chose to go. I had left public school on shaky grounds and wanted to prove that I could do okay there. I feel that if students went to public school before SVS for a bit, they would know what they have and appreciate Sudbury Valley more. [4; 16 years old]

I left Sudbury Valley for public high school, did perfectly, finished early, but I hated other kids' attitudes toward school and became very bored. [5; 14 years old]

I like new people, places and perspectives. I think Sudbury Valley attracts adventurers. I enjoy reaching people in dance and in human services. The work is strengthening and character building and full of struggle. It involves lots of self-analysis, self-awareness and risk-taking. [5; 14 years old]

Sudbury Valley allowed me to learn what I am. At Sudbury Valley there is no need for a shell. At public school you had to be tough, have a shell. It took me time to learn. I am still learning.

I started my own company with a friend to design vehicles. I get satisfaction out of being given a problem, and coming up with a nice, clean, simple solution that works.

Bicycle racing is a passion and a growing experience. I ride my bicycle as a T'ai Chi form. [6; 12 years old]

Dealing with the public is rewarding. I am looking forward to marriage and children. [7; 12 years old]

I am very happy with my life. Family is very important to me. I feel like Sudbury Valley didn't prepare me academically, but it taught me to think. [7; 15 years old]

I got a different perspective — openmindedness — from Sudbury Valley. College was a joke; it was a pressure cooker instead of learning. I started my own business. I am learning about the real world, and I can do what I want with my time. [8; 14 years old]

What is important to me is being happy in life and my family. Everything about my software job is a challenge to my creativity. [10; 15 years old]

13

Students Who Were Enrolled in Sudbury Valley One Year and Left Before Their Last High School Age Year

Finally, we look at some members of a group of former students who came to Sudbury Valley for only one year and then moved on to complete their basic schooling elsewhere. Since their exposure was the briefest and least complete of all, we expended the least effort in obtaining responses from members of this group. Out of a total of twenty-six possible respondents, we were able to survey eight, for a response rate of 31%. Of these eight, six were female (75%) and two were male. In the entire group, sixteen were female (62%) and ten were male. This group continues the trend of a preponderance of females among short term or transient enrollees at the school, as opposed to the situation with longer term enrollees. We have no explanation for this phenomenon.

Basic Demographics

—— How old are they now?

Figure 13.1 shows the distribution of this group by age on January 1, 1991. The range of ages extends from twenty-one to thirty-eight. The average age is thirty-one, and the median age is thirty-four.

Figure 13.1

Distribution by Age, January 1, 1991

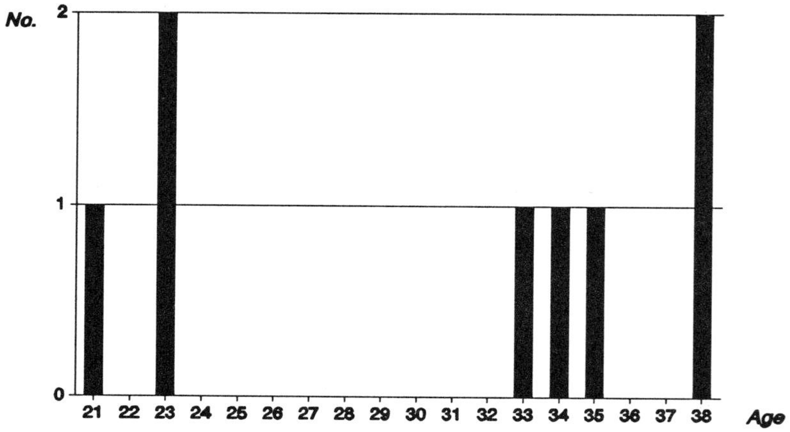

—— Their marital status

Three of the eight people in this group were single (38%); four were married (50%), one of whom was divorced; and one was living with a significant other (12%). One person was married fifteen years, the others five years or less. Five people (63%) had a total of eleven children. One had four; one had three; one had two; and two had one. The ages of the children range from one to twenty-one.

— Where do they live?

Table 13.1 shows where the people in this group live. Seven of them (88%) live in Massachusetts, five in towns that are considered to be in the school's catchment area.

Table 13.1

Current Geographical Distribution of the Group

No.	*Town*	*State*
1	Cambridge	Massachusetts
1	Framingham	Massachusetts
1	Holliston	Massachusetts
1	Orange	Massachusetts
1	Turner's Falls	Massachusetts
1	Upton	Massachusetts
1	Waltham	Massachusetts
1	Spokane	Washington

— How old were they when they enrolled?

Figure 13.2 shows the distribution of this group by age of entry into the school. With one exception, the year these people spent at the school occurred during "high school" age.

Figure 13.2

Distribution by Age of Entry

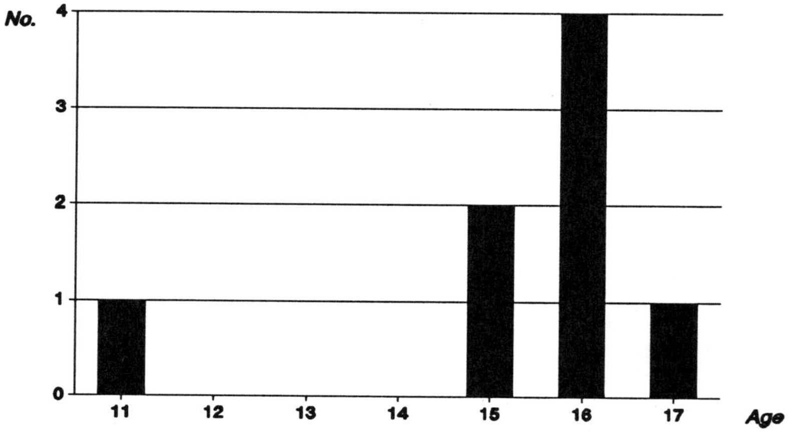

—— What was their prior schooling?

Before entering Sudbury Valley, all eight members of this group went to public elementary school. Seven of the eight went to public middle schools, and one of these seven also went to a private middle school. Seven of the eight also went to public high school; one of these also went to a private high school (not the same person who went to a private middle school).

—— Where did they live?

Table 13.2 shows the geographical distribution of this population at the time that they were students at Sudbury Valley School. The person who came from Spokane, Washington, boarded with a family in Marlboro while attending Sudbury Valley.

Table 13.2

Geographical Distribution While in School

No.	*Town*
1	Dracut
3	Framingham
1	Sudbury
1	Upton
1	Wayland
1	Spokane, WA

Occupations

Because none of the members of this group finished their basic schooling at Sudbury Valley and because, in addition, all attended for only one year, we felt that we could not attach much significance vis a vis Sudbury Valley to the occupational history of this group. Nevertheless we are presenting a precis of this group's experiences in Table 13.3. The Table is organized in ascending order by the age of the members of the group. Occupations marked with an asterisk denote entrepreneurial or self-employed situations. Note the high percentage of entrepreneurs in this particular sample.

Table 13.3

Occupations Engaged in Since Leaving Sudbury Valley (Arranged in Order of Age)

Age	*Age at Leaving SVS*	*Present Occupation*	*Previous Occupations*
21	17	*mural painter, singing telegram deliverer	*jewelry maker, bicycle assembler
23	12	student of business management	waitress, bank clerk
23	16	retail clerk	waitress
33	17	*architectural preservation carpentry	carpenter, highway worker
34	17	manager of real estate company	aerobics teacher, karate teacher, animal cardiac research asst.
35	16	*midwife	waitress, gardener, nurse's aide, *partner in restaurant
38	16	*tool manufacturing & distribution co.	quality control, prototype eng'r'g design, sales exec.
38	18	*owner, manager of real estate company	waitress, office clerk

Further Education

After leaving Sudbury Valley, seven of the eight members of this group went on to high schools, and all eight ultimately received high school diplomas. All but one reported satisfactory performance in their subsequent schools, whether or not they enjoyed being there. Six of the eight (75%) went on to study at the college level: two of them received an Associate of Arts degree, two received Bachelor's degrees, and one reported plans to complete work for a more advanced degree. We have not included information on the names of the schools these people attended after high school because we felt the lack of continuity between Sudbury Valley and their post-graduate schools rendered such information of doubtful relevance to our survey.

Personal Perspectives

All of the people who left Sudbury Valley in their later teens offered comments on their lives and/or their experiences at school:

> *I am interested in New Age matters. I have studied survival, homeopathy, Akaido, karate, T'ai Chi, yoga, African dance, modern dance, Native American studies, herbology, and ceramics. I like different kinds of jobs. I have a lot of trouble with schools. I found SVS difficult and not stimulating or guiding enough. I feel I need a form of teaching where the instructor leads you up to a point, and then leaves you to figure out the rest, but I can't find this anywhere.*

> *The earning potential and the variety of work in real estate is satisfying, as is matching people with homes. I have a six year old child who I am considering sending to Sudbury Valley because it was such a wonderful experience for me.*
>
> *My time at Sudbury Valley started me thinking about a career in midwifery, and I decided to go into it then.*

> *Sudbury Valley helped me during a difficult period of my life. It gave me time and space to do a lot of "identity growing." I figured out who I was, where I was going, and what was important to me.*

> *Sudbury Valley gave me the freedom to discover that I like to learn. It showed me that if I am interested in learning I can do it. It planted the seed and then I figured it out on my own.*

> *Sudbury Valley influenced my whole life. I learned it is not necessary to kowtow to the system — that you can do things on your own. You need an unstructured period of time in adolescence. I graduated community college with all sorts of honors and awards even though I was a poor student before I came to Sudbury Valley.*

I left public school because it was like the Gestapo there. The transition to Sudbury Valley was tough for me. It was hard for me to realize that no one else was going to direct me, the biggest lesson of SVS. I did not go to college because I didn't feel I needed it. If you are focussed and need further training you should go, otherwise not. Now I love having my own business. I do everything from garbage to banking. The reward comes from completing what I start.

Part VI

Concluding Remarks

14

Some Comparisons and Summaries

For some of the data that was collected and presented for separate groups in the preceding chapters, we thought it would be useful to provide tables and figures that show comparisons and totals for various combinations of groups. All of the data presented here refers to the 188 respondents only.

For the purposes of this chapter and the next, we will adopt the following nomenclature in referring to the groups:

"SVS ONLY" — students who spent virtually all their school years at Sudbury Valley (Chapters 4 and 5);

"SVS 5+HS" — students who spent a major portion of their school lives (five years or more) at Sudbury Valley, including their high school age years (Chapters 6 and 7);

"SVS 3-4HS" — students who were enrolled in Sudbury Valley during their high school age years (Chapters 8 and 9);

"SVS 2HS" — students who were enrolled in Sudbury Valley during their last two high school age years (Chapter 10);

"SVS 1HS" — students who were enrolled in Sudbury Valley during their last high school age year (Chapter 11);

"SVS LONG" — students who were enrolled in Sudbury Valley two years or longer and left before completing their high school age years (Chapter 12);

"SVS ONE" — students who were enrolled in Sudbury Valley one year at some time before completing their high school age years (Chapter 13).

Table 14.1

General Information

Item	*SVS ONLY*	*SVS 5+HS*	*SVS 3-4HS*	*SVS 2HS*	*SVS 1HS*	*SVS LONG*	*SVS ONE*	*Total*
Number in group	27	21	50	41	24	17	8	188
Number males	15	12	30	22	5	7	2	93
percent males	56%	57%	60%	54%	21%	41%	25%	49%
Number females	12	9	20	19	19	10	6	95
percent females	44%	43%	40%	46%	79%	59%	75%	51%
No. with SVS dipl	26	19	37	31	*	n/a	n/a	113**
% with diploma	96%	90%	74%	73%	*	n/a	n/a	81%**

* See Chapter 11.

** Totals for the first four groups only.

Basic Demographics

Figure 14.1

Distribution by Age, January 1, 1991
Totals for the Entire Group

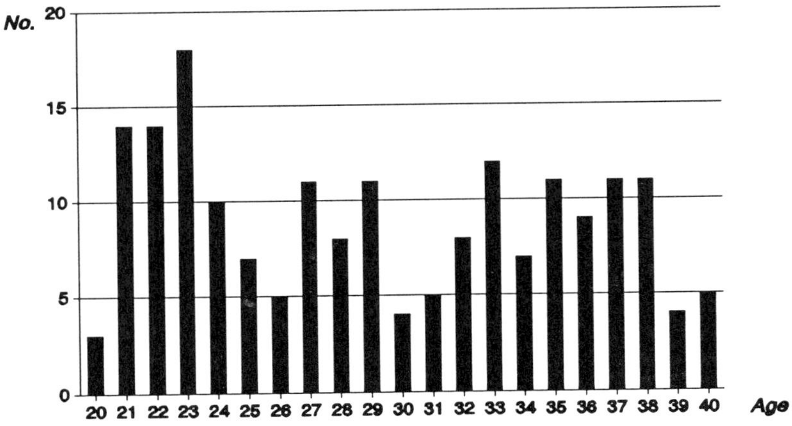

Figure 14.2

Distribution by Age of Entry
Totals for the Entire Group

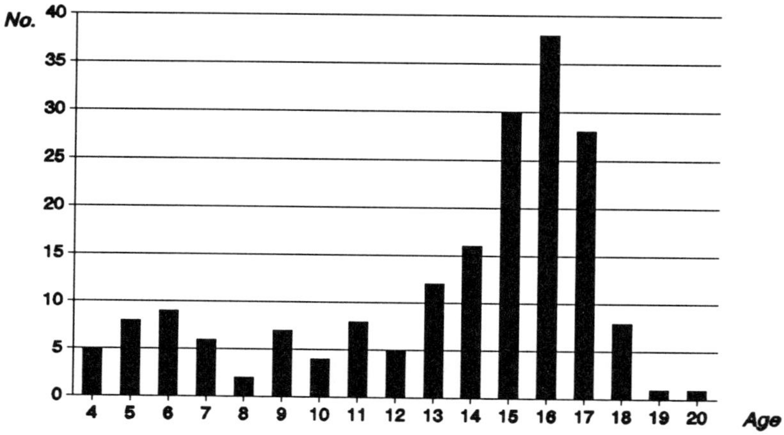

Figure 14.3

**Distribution by Age at Leaving
Totals for the Entire Group**

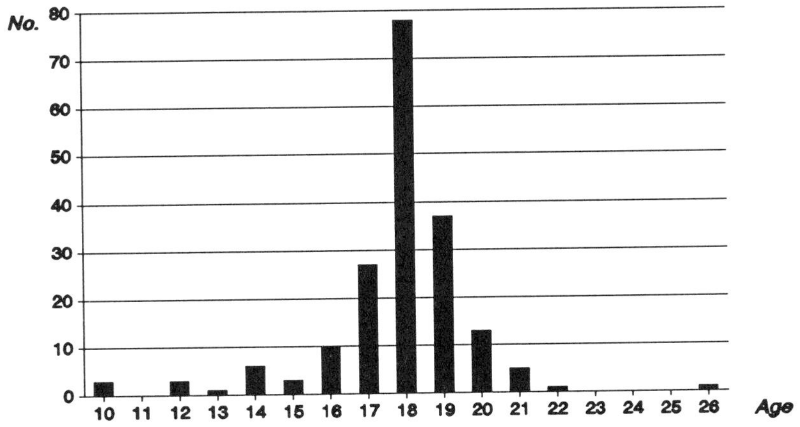

Figure 14.4

Distribution of Length of Stay at the School
Totals for the Entire Group

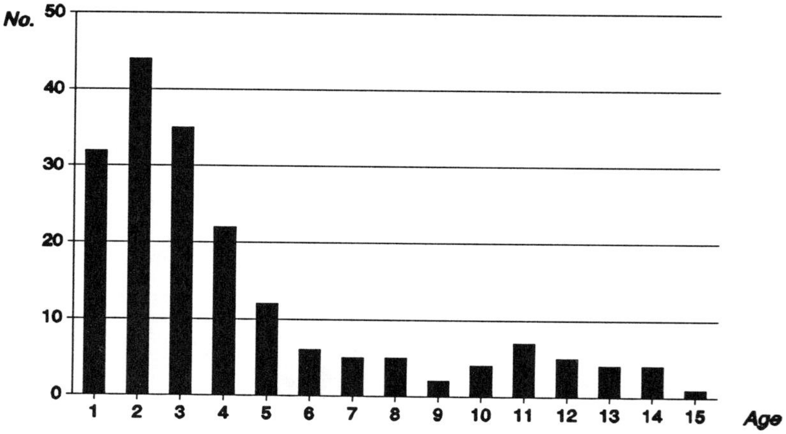

We count only years actually enrolled in the school. For students who left Sudbury Valley for a time and subsequently returned, the time spent away from Sudbury Valley is not included in the calculation of the length of stay at the school.

Table 14.2

Comparative Average and Median Ages

Item	*SVS ONLY*	*SVS 5+HS*	*SVS 3-4HS*	*SVS 2HS*	*SVS 1HS*	*SVS LONG*	*SVS ONE*	*Total*
Average Current Age	27	27	30	32	31.5	26	31	30
Median Current Age	26	26	32	33	32.5	24	34	29
Average Age at Entry	6	12	15	16	17	9	15	13
Median Age at Entry	6	12	15	16	17	8	16	15
Average Age at Leaving	18	18.5	18.5	18	18	13	16	18
Median Age at Leaving	18	18	18.5	18	18	14	17	18
Average Years at SVS	12	6	3.5	2	1	5	1	4
Median Years at SVS	12	6	3	2	1	4	1	3

Table 14.3

Marital and Family Status

Item	*SVS ONLY*	*SVS 5+HS*	*SVS 3-4HS*	*SVS 2HS*	*SVS 1HS*	*SVS LONG*	*SVS ONE*	*Total*
No. in group	27	21	50	41	24	17	8	188
No. (%) single	17 (63%)	12 (57%)	21 (42%)	15 (37%)	9 (38%)	8 (47%)	3 (38%)	85 45%)
No. (%) ever married	6 (22%)	5 (24%)	23 (46%)	20 (49%)	11 (46%)	7 (41%)	4 (50%)	76 (40%)
No. (% of ever married) divorced	0	1 (20%)	8 (35%)	4 (20%)	3 (27%)	0	1 (25%)	17 (22%)
No. (%) never married, living with someone	4 (15%)	4 (19%)	6 (12%)	6 (14%)	4 (17%)	2 (12%)	1 (13%)	27 (14%)
No. (%) with children	1 (4%)	4 (19%)	14 (28%)	16 (39%)	9 (38%)	2 (12%)	5 (63%)	51 (27%)
Avg. # children per family with children	1	1.3	1.7	2.3	1.9	2.5	2.2	1.9

Table 14.4

Current Geographical Distribution

Item	*SVS ONLY*	*SVS 5+HS*	*SVS 3-4HS*	*SVS 2HS*	*SVS 1HS*	*SVS LONG*	*SVS ONE*	*Total*
No. in group	27	21	50	41	24	17	8	188
Massachusetts	15	13	28	27	13	12	7	115
California	1	2	7		2	2		14
Colorado			1		2	1		4
Connecticut					1			1
D. C.			1					1
Florida			1	1				2
Georgia			1		1			2
Idaho			1					1
Illinois	1				1			2
Indiana		1						1
Maine		1		4		1		6
Maryland	1							1
Minnesota	2		1					3
Montana			1					1
N.H.			1	1	1			3
New York	2	1	2		2	1		8
Ohio				1				1
Oregon		1						1
Pennsylvania	1							1
Rhode Island			1					1
Tennessee		2						2
Texas				1	1			2
Vermont				2				2
Washington	2		1	2			1	6
Wyoming				1				1
Canada	1		2					3
England	1							1
Malaysia				1				1
Hong Kong			1					1

Table 14.5

Geographical Distribution While in School

No.	*Town*	*No.*	*Town*
6	Acton	2	Milford
5	Ashland	9	Natick
1	Bolton	5	Needham
3	Boston	1	Newburyport
1	Brookline	7	Newton
1	Canton	2	Northboro
2	Chelmsford	2	Randolph
1	Clinton	1	Rockland
2	Concord	1	Roslindale
1	Dracut	1	Sherborn
35	Framingham	8	Southboro
1	Franklin	4	Stow
2	Harvard	13	Sudbury
1	Harwich	1	Upton
8	Hingham	3	Walpole
12	Holliston	1	Waltham
3	Hopkinton	4	Wayland
3	Hudson	1	Wellesley
1	Lexington	2	Westboro
2	Lincoln	1	Woodville
14	Marlboro	9	Worcester
1	Mattapan		
1	Medfield	1	Fair Haven, NJ
1	Medway	1	Spokane, WA

Figure 14.5

Schooling Prior to Sudbury Valley For the Entire Group

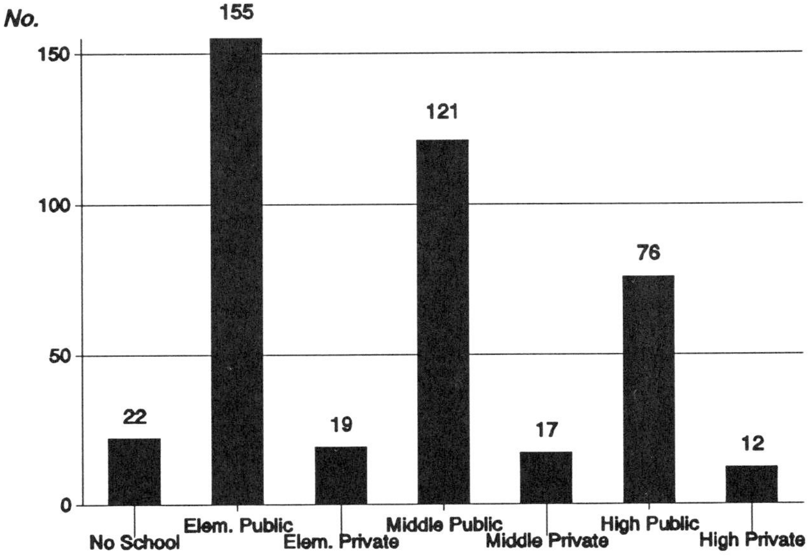

Table 14.6

Comparison of Schooling Prior to Sudbury Valley

Item	*SVS ONLY*	*SVS 5+HS*	*SVS 3-4HS*	*SVS 2HS*	*SVS 1HS*	*SVS LONG*	*SVS ONE*	*Total*
No. in group	27	21	50	41	22*	17	8	186
No. (%) with no prior school	16 59%					6 35%		22 12%
No. (%) public elementary only	9 33%	17 81%	43 86%	36 88%	22 100%	9 53%	8 100%	144 77%
No (%) public & private elem.		3 14%	3 6%	3 7%		1 6%		10 5%
No. (%) private elementary only	2 7%	1 5%	4 8%	2 5%		1 6%		10 5%
No. (%) public middle only		9 43%	41 82%	34 83%	19 86%	3 18%	6 75%	112 60%
No. (%) public & private middle		1 5%	3 6%	3 7%	1 5%		1 13%	9 5%
No. (%) private middle only			3 6%	3 7%	2 9%			8 4%
No. (%) public high only		1 5%	17 34%	32 78%	16 73%		6 75%	72 49%
No. (%) public & private high			1 2%	1 2%	1 5%		1 13%	4 2%
No. (%) private high only			2 4%	3 7%	3 14%			8 4%
Other				1** 2%	1*** 5%			2 1%
No. (%) only private schools	2 7%	1 5%	3 6%	1 2%		1 6%		8 4%

* We have no information on two members of this group; see Ch. 11.
** Home schooled after some attendance at public elementary school.
*** Attended college classes.

Occupations

Table 14.7 refers exclusively to the groups considered in Parts II, III, and IV of this book (Chapters 4 through 11), which studied people who considered their basic education complete at the time that they left Sudbury Valley.

The sum of all the category totals comes to 362. Thus, for the group as a whole, each person worked in an average of 2.2 categories since leaving Sudbury Valley.

Table 14.7

Number of Former Students Who Engaged in Various Categories of Occupations Since Leaving SVS

Item	*SVS ONLY*	*SVS 5+HS*	*SVS 3-4HS*	*SVS 2HS*	*SVS 1HS*	*Total*
No. in group	27	21	50	41	24	163
Business Mgmt.	8	11	22	16	8	65 (40%)
Office Manager	8	2	14	7	8	39 (24%)
High Tech	5	4	6	3	2	20 (12%)
Professional	3	2	13	6	3	27 (17%)
R & D	2	2				4 (2%)
Parent			2	4	2	8 (5%)
Education	6	3	8	11	9	37 (23%)
Marketing		4	3	4	1	12 (7%)
Law Enforcem't	1		2	1		4 (2%)
Trades	10	10	24	27	9	80 (49%)
Media			4	1	1	6 (4%)
Design	4	6	1	5	2	18 (11%)
Creative Arts	5	1	7	3	3	19 (12%)
Performing Arts	5	4	10	3	1	23 (14%)
Entrepreneurial Occupations (Any Category)	7	12	20	20	9	68 (42%)

Further Formal Education

All of the Tables in this section refer exclusively to the groups considered in Parts II, III, and IV of this book (Chapters 4 through 11), which studied people who considered their basic education complete at the time that they left Sudbury Valley.

Table 14.8

Number Who Attended Post-secondary Schools (By Type of School)

Item	*SVS ONLY*	*SVS 5+HS*	*SVS 3-4HS*	*SVS 2HS*	*SVS 1HS*	*Total*
No. in group	27	21	50	41	24	163
Attended <u>any</u> post-secondary school	25 (93%)	19 (90%)	45 (90%)	33 (80%)	20 (83%)	142 (87%)
Attended art schools	4	2	5	3		14 (9%)
Attended trade schools	3	2	9	3	3	20 (12%)
Attended misc. schools			5	3	2	10 (6%)
Attended community coll.	1	2	6	7	6	22 (13%)
Attended junior college			7	5		12 (7%)
Attended 4-yr. college	24	16	31	28	15	114 (70%)
Attended graduate school	3		8	4	3	18 (11%)

Table 14.9

Number Receiving College and University Degrees

Item	*SVS ONLY*	*SVS 5+HS*	*SVS 3-4HS*	*SVS 2HS*	*SVS 1HS*	*Total*
Number in group	27	21	50	41	24	163
Received *any* degrees	14 (52%)	7 (33%)	20 (40%)	13 (32%)	10 (42%)	64 (39%)
Received Associate's degrees	1	2	5	4	1	13
Received Bachelor's degrees	13	5	12	10	8	48
Received Master's degrees	2		6	4	2	14
Received Legal, Doctoral, or Medical degrees	1		2	1		4

Table 14.10

Schools Granting Undergraduate Degrees to Former SVS Students

American College in London
Babson College
Bard College
Berkshire Community College
Boston College
Boston University
Brandeis University
Castleton State College
Catherine Laboure College
Colorado Institute of Art
Earlham Colege
Emerson College
Fitchburg State College
Framingham State College
Framingham Union Hospital School of Nursing
Greenfield Community College
Hampshire College
Johnson & Wales University
LaSalle Junior College
Macalester College
Mass Bay Community College
Mt. Ida College
Mt. Wachusett Community College
Newbury Junior College
Northeastern University
Park College
Pratt Institute
Rhode Island School of Design
Roger Williams College
Smith College
University of California (Berkeley)
University of California (Los Angeles)
University of California (Santa Barbara)
University of Denver
University of Illinois
University of Maine (Machias)
University of Massachusetts (Amherst)

University of Massachusetts (Boston)
University of Rochester
University of Victoria, British Columbia
University of Wisconsin
Wesleyan University
Wheelock College
Worcester State College
Yale University

Table 14.11

Schools Granting Graduate Degrees to Former SVS Students

Cambridge College
Catholic University
Columbia University
Harvard University Business School
Johns Hopkins University
Kantor Family Institute
Massachusetts Institute of Technology
Palmer College
San Francisco College of Acupuncture
Suffolk University Law School
University of California (San Diego)
University of Colorado
University of Connecticut
University of Southern California School of Medicine
University of Wisconsin
West Virginia University
Wheelock College

15

Some Final Thoughts

Throughout the body of the study we have commented about different aspects of the material presented. Here we would like to add some further remarks.[1]

We were fortunate to be able to include a relatively large number of people in our study. During the twenty-one years spanned by the study, the school varied in size from about sixty to about one hundred and twenty students, who in turn varied widely in their lengths of stay. The total number of people meeting our study's criteria was 237, of whom we were able to gather data on 188. This sizable group represented a very high (79%) overall response rate. Of the people who had been enrolled at SVS for more than one year, during any part of their educational lives, fully 91% were respondents. Both the size of the group and the high response rate give us confidence that the material presented here is a valid representation of the experiences of former students at the school.

Throughout the school's history, there has usually been a majority of male enrollees in any given year. Table 14.1 shows such a majority for the first four groups studied, which consist of people who finished their basic schooling at Sudbury Valley ("Finishers") and were enrolled for two years or

[1] Some reflections on the data and analysis used in this study can be found in Appendix D.

more. On the other hand, the groups that did not complete their education at Sudbury Valley ("Non-finishers"), or who completed it and stayed only one year, show a marked predominance of females. We have no way of accounting for this difference or attaching any significance to it, but we think it is worth noting and keeping in mind for future studies.

Of the people who might be expected to become candidates for a diploma — "Finishers" who spent two or more years at the school — 81% did so, all successfully. All but three of the forty-eight people who spent five or more years at the school received diplomas. On the one hand, these statistics reveal a very high percentage of people who take their education to some identifiable finishing point at Sudbury Valley. On the other hand, as we discussed in the various chapters, the lives of the nineteen percent who decided not to seek a diploma from Sudbury Valley do not seem to have been adversely affected by this decision at all. Both sides of this seeming paradox are what one would expect from students at Sudbury Valley, whose focus is on what they want to do with their lives rather than on any particular certification procedure; and, indeed, during the diploma procedure it is common to hear students expound on why the decision to pursue a Sudbury Valley diploma is an integral part of their life plan rather than just the expected and automatic outcome of a "high school education."

From Figure 14.1 and Table 14.2 it is clear that on the whole we are dealing with a very young group of people. When we discuss people who have spent five or more years at the school, the group becomes even younger. This is a demographic limitation of the study which is due entirely to the age of the school and is beyond our control. Hopefully studies will continue to be conducted every decade or so and will yield increasingly rich quantities of data both latitudinally, in the size of the sample studied, and longitudinally, in the spans of years of each individual that are covered.

From Figures 14.2, 14.4, and Table 14.2, we see that during the span of time covered by the study the majority of students entered the school in their teen years — sixteen being the predominant age — and remained on the average three or four years — a two year stay being the predominant length of stay. These demographic facts place some limitations on the conclusions one might try to draw from this study about the effects of a Sudbury Valley education, the more so since the group of "finishers" who stayed more than four years totals only forty-eight individuals. Once again, future studies will improve on the situation by including larger numbers of students who have entered at a young age and stayed at school a long time. It is worth noting that from 1988 on, there has been a shift towards younger enrollment and longer stays at the school.

At the time of the study, none of the five children of former students who had been at the school five years or longer were of school age, and three of these children live in other parts of the country. Thus, we do not yet know if the people who spent the most time at Sudbury Valley will choose the same education for their own children. Of the former students who were enrolled for a shorter time, and who live within the school's catchment area, several have enrolled their children at the school at one time or another. Again, many factors are at work here, and we are dealing with a group that is too young and has too few children for any statistically significant conclusions to be reached.

Figure 14.5 and Table 14.6 together demonstrate conclusively that parents who send their children to Sudbury Valley do not come from that segment of the population for whom private schooling is the norm. There can be little doubt that parents choose to send their children to Sudbury Valley for reasons related to the specific nature of the school, and that virtually all of the families would have preferred public schooling if public schools had filled their perceived needs for their children.

From Table 14.7, as well as from the detailed data presented in the various chapters, it is clear that former students are engaged in an extraordinarily wide range of occupations. The data suggests several observations. Virtually no one who is not primarily a student is employed at an unskilled job. A surprisingly large percentage has been seriously engaged in management activities. A surprisingly large percentage has at one time or another been employed in one of the trades. Almost a quarter of the group has been engaged in occupations involving teaching; in fact, two of them returned to be staff members at Sudbury Valley. It is also striking as one reads through the various chapters to discover the large number of people who are professionally involved in the arts. All these disparate interests thrive in the same small school, a result probably attributable to the open enrollment policy and the lack of any tracking or preferential treatment for particular pursuits. Perhaps most remarkable of all — but most understandable in light of the school's educational philosophy — is the fact that 42% of these former students have been involved in entrepreneurial or self-employed situations. One could hardly ask for a more vivid demonstration of the primacy given to individual initiative and personal responsibility in every aspect of Sudbury Valley's operation.

One former student, now a physician, summed up her impression of her fellow alumni as follows:

> *When I look around, people who went to Sudbury Valley are doing lots of interesting things. A lot of people who*

> *went to some kind of college preparatory type school are going to college and maybe some of them are doing interesting things. But when I look at the people who went to Sudbury Valley, they're doing much more of a variety of things. They're not all just in college, or something like that. A lot of them are teaching dancing or they're photographers, or they're living out in the wilderness, or they're pursuing all different kinds of interests, being very individual.*

Tables 14.10 and 14.11 put to rest once and for all any doubts raised about the ability of people who have attended Sudbury Valley to matriculate in a wide variety of colleges and universities despite the complete absence of the usual documentation that entering such institutions is reputed to necessitate. It is also interesting that this applies equally to people who did not receive a diploma from Sudbury Valley and to those who did.

In fact, the processes by which Sudbury Valley's former students determine their desire or need to go to college makes the issue of college admissions almost irrelevant. They often approach institutions of higher learning in ways, and at times in their lives, that make it obvious that they are working in fields they are committed to, that they understand the fields they wish to study, and that they have already demonstrated maturity, responsibility, and the ability to learn complicated material. The trend also seems to be to take formal education at a more leisurely pace than customary — it is not a dose of medicine to be finished by the age of twenty-two. It is an organic part of the stream of their lives, and may or may not culminate in a degree.

We have already noted that there is no way for this or any similar study to provide a definitive answer to the question of how a Sudbury Valley education influences the future course of a student's life. But it is possible to answer the more limited question we set at the beginning: does a person's attendance at Sudbury Valley, whether for a short or long time, have an adverse affect on the options available to that person? The data presented in the study leaves no doubt that the answer is "No": former students at Sudbury Valley enjoy, at the very least, the full range of life choices available to every other group of young people going out into the world.

And they enjoy a childhood of freedom, respect, and trust.

Appendices

Appendix A

Questionnaire and Cover Letter

Attached is a blank copy of the questionnaire used in this survey. The latest information available in the school's files for each former student surveyed was printed on the form. Either during the interview or as part of the process of locating the interviewee, names, phones, and addresses were updated. Each interviewer was also sent a cover letter, a copy of which is also attached. The interviewer received a master list of the people assigned to them, and forms for each person.

Sudbury Valley School
2 Winch Street
Framingham, MA 01701

[Date]

Hello Interviewer,

Here are your questionnaires and some other documents which may make your work a little easier. What we did not say on the questionnaire is that you must explain to each alum why you are calling: that this is a survey the school is doing, in order to update its information. You must also explain that the conversation will take a few minutes, and make sure it is a convenient time for them to talk; otherwise, try to arrange a time to call them back that is convenient for both of you. Please read a questionnaire through before you make the first call, and note the questions on the bottom of the last page.

Included in your folder are questionnaires for the people on your list. In the front is a total former student list and a list of your people with some notes about ways you might locate their phone numbers. If it seemed like there might be anything in their file here which would help you locate them, we attached such papers to the questionnaire. There is an "F" on your master list for people who have papers attached.

Also, please keep track of the amount of time you spend working on this and of the long distance charges you amass. The school will pay for the phone charges and $10/hour for the time.

Please ask Mimsy or Danny if you have any questions.

Sudbury Valley School

<u>FORMER STUDENT QUESTIONNAIRE (1991)</u>
For Telephone Interviews

Date of interview: ______________________________

Interview conducted by: _________________________

Name:
(first name, nickname, formerly, last name)

Phone:
Address:
Birth date: Current age:
Date of graduation, if a diplomate:
First date of enrollment: Age at enrollment:
End of enrollment: Age at end of enrollment:
Number years attended:

Have you been getting our mailings to former students? _____

Here is how you are listed in our files: [read name, address, from above]
Are there any corrections to this? [correct above, if necessary]

Please give us another contact address, if you have one (parents, family etc.)

____

Parent's status: Alive? Names and addresses if possible, unless already listed above:

____

____

Marital status: _________________ Living with significant other? _____________

How long married/ significant other/ divorced: _____________________________

Children? (names, sex, and ages, if possible): _____________________________

____

____

____

<u>EDUCATION</u>: <u>What was your educational background before SVS</u>?

____

____

All schools attended after SVS (any schools, just attended, or took courses at, not necessarily to earn a degree or certificate):

Names of Schools Dates, if remembered Majors, Concentrations Degrees

How did you get into other schools?

How was adjustment to other schools?

Did you get what you wanted out of your other schooling?

As of now, any future plans for additional education?

WORK EXPERIENCE:

Work while at SVS: ____

____

Work since school (all you can recall, in as much detail as possible; e.g., what job was, how long, promotions, difficulties):

____

____

____

____

____

____

____

____

Any work changes contemplated? ___________________________________

____

____

What work has given you satisfaction? (and why):

____

____

____

____

TRAVEL

Has travel been important in your life (where, why, when, how)? __________

____

____

____

____

____

LIFE: Is there anything else important in your life, past or present, that we have not asked you about?

____

____

____

____

____

____

OTHER SUDBURY VALLEY CONTACTS? Are there other former students that you are still close to, or still know, and/or have been in touch with recently? Who? Where are they?

____

____

____

____

____

Questions not to ask, but we would love to know the answers, and you may accidentally find out:

Are they happy with present situation (work, personal, educational)?

What did schooling at SVS do or not do for them?

Have they encountered any problems relating to their unusual educational background?

Do they want to visit?

____

____

____

____

____

____

____

____

Appendix B

Information on the Respondents in the Study

The attached table presents complete information on the age, length of stay at SVS, age of enrollment in SVS, date of first enrollment, and status of diploma of each of the former students who were respondents in this study. The table is arranged in ascending order of age of the former students at the time the study began.

Information on the Respondents in the Study

Age on 1/1/91	Years at SVS	Age at Entry	Date of Entry	Diplomate?
20.0	3	14.7	09/01/85	Yes
20.2	3	14.6	05/28/85	Yes
20.2	9	8.8	09/01/79	Yes
20.5	2	16.2	09/29/86	No
20.5	5	9.4	11/23/79	No
20.5	1	16.2	09/01/86	No
20.5	3	15.3	10/28/85	Yes
20.6	8	10.2	09/01/80	Yes
20.8	1	16.7	12/02/86	No
20.9	11	6.5	09/01/76	Yes
21.0	4	5.7	09/01/75	No
21.1	2	16.4	05/19/86	No
21.1	3	15.8	09/12/85	Yes
21.1	3	15.4	04/08/85	Yes
21.3	3	13.0	09/01/82	Yes
21.4	1	16.1	09/01/85	No
21.4	7	11.1	09/26/80	Yes
21.6	8	10.3	09/01/79	Yes
21.6	2	14.4	09/27/83	No
21.6	14	4.3	09/01/73	Yes
21.8	2	17.5	09/01/86	Yes
21.8	13	5.4	09/01/74	Yes
21.8	4	15.5	09/01/84	Yes
21.9	12	6.6	09/01/75	Yes
22.0	4	13.9	12/13/82	Yes
22.0	2	17.7	09/01/86	Yes
22.0	14	4.6	09/01/73	Yes
22.1	3	6.8	09/01/75	No
22.2	2	16.3	01/11/85	Yes
22.2	1	17.6	05/14/86	No
22.3	5	11.0	09/21/79	No
22.5	12	5.1	09/01/73	Yes
22.5	3	13.7	03/09/82	Yes
22.5	1	11.1	09/01/79	No
22.6	1	15.3	09/01/83	No
22.6	3	6.4	11/01/74	No
22.6	4	10.2	09/01/78	No
22.6	2	17.3	09/01/85	Yes
22.7	2	14.6	11/29/82	No
22.8	4	14.0	02/26/82	Yes
23.0	6	12.6	09/01/80	Yes
23.0	2	16.9	10/26/84	Yes
23.1	6	11.7	09/01/79	Yes
23.2	2	15.3	02/17/83	Yes
23.2	3	16.9	09/01/84	Yes

Age on 1/1/91	Years at SVS	Age at Entry	Date of Entry	Diplomate?
23.2	1	17.5	05/21/85	Yes
23.2	7	4.8	09/01/72	No
23.4	5	14.4	01/04/82	Yes
23.4	5	13.4	01/15/81	Yes
23.5	13	6.2	09/01/73	Yes
23.9	12	7.5	09/01/74	Yes
24.0	3	14.6	09/01/81	No
24.1	13	4.8	09/01/71	Yes
24.1	14	4.1	01/18/71	Yes
24.2	6	5.6	06/04/72	No
24.2	6	12.9	09/01/79	Yes
24.2	5	12.8	09/01/79	Yes
24.2	1	14.5	04/27/81	No
24.3	3	16.3	01/19/83	No
24.8	3	14.4	09/01/80	No
24.9	2	15.5	09/01/81	No
24.9	12	7.0	01/22/73	Yes
25.0	2	15.7	09/01/81	Yes
25.0	2	15.6	09/01/81	Yes
25.0	4	14.7	09/22/80	Yes
25.4	11	3.0	09/01/68	No
25.8	10	5.5	09/01/70	No
25.8	3	14.5	09/21/79	No
26.0	4	14.7	09/01/79	Yes
26.0	15	3.6	09/01/68	Yes
26.3	5	11.0	09/01/75	Yes
26.7	7	11.3	09/01/75	Yes
26.7	7	6.3	09/01/70	No
26.7	9	9.4	09/01/73	Yes
26.7	2	16.4	09/01/80	Yes
26.8	14	4.4	09/01/68	Yes
26.8	8	10.6	11/25/74	Yes
26.9	13	5.1	03/17/69	Yes
27.1	4	14.8	09/01/78	No
27.3	8	5.0	09/01/68	No
27.4	2	16.4	01/30/80	No
27.4	3	16.0	09/01/79	No
27.5	11	5.2	09/01/68	Yes
27.6	2	16.7	02/01/80	Yes
27.7	3	11.5	10/29/74	No
27.8	10	6.4	09/01/69	Yes
27.8	2	15.4	09/01/78	Yes
27.9	12	5.6	09/01/68	Yes
28.1	1	16.8	09/01/79	No
28.2	2	12.8	09/01/75	Yes
28.5	11	6.1	09/01/68	Yes
28.7	11	8.6	12/09/70	Yes
28.9	1	17.2	04/06/79	Yes

Age on 1/1/91	Years at SVS	Age at Entry	Date of Entry	Diplomate?
29.0	3	13.8	09/22/75	Yes
29.0	3	13.7	09/01/75	Yes
29.1	5	14.7	09/01/76	Yes
29.1	11	6.7	09/01/68	Yes
29.1	1	16.8	09/01/78	No
29.2	5	10.5	04/21/72	No
29.2	4	11.6	06/04/73	No
29.4	1	16.4	01/10/78	No
29.7	5	9.0	05/04/70	No
29.7	10	7.4	09/01/68	Yes
30.2	3	14.9	09/01/75	No
30.2	4	15.0	10/15/75	Yes
30.5	2	16.5	01/03/77	No
30.6	11	8.3	09/01/68	Yes
31.0	1	16.8	10/04/76	Yes
31.0	3	14.6	09/01/74	Yes
31.3	2	15.3	01/10/75	Yes
31.6	11	9.3	09/01/68	Yes
31.8	2	13.2	05/10/72	No
31.8	4	13.1	04/21/72	No
31.8	1	16.5	09/01/75	No
31.8	7	9.5	09/01/68	Yes
32.2	1	16.9	09/01/75	No
32.2	4	14.9	10/10/73	No
32.4	2	16.7	04/07/75	Yes
32.5	5	10.1	09/01/68	Yes
32.8	1	17.5	09/01/75	No
32.8	2	15.0	02/22/73	Yes
32.8	4	13.7	11/30/71	Yes
32.9	1	14.8	12/05/72	Yes
32.9	4	15.6	09/01/73	No
33.1	6	13.3	03/29/71	Yes
33.1	1	15.7	09/01/73	No
33.2	2	15.9	10/15/73	Yes
33.2	3	14.3	03/06/72	Yes
33.3	2	10.9	09/01/68	No
33.3	2	15.5	02/26/73	Yes
33.7	2	15.4	09/25/72	Yes
33.8	2	16.5	09/27/73	Yes
33.8	2	18.5	09/01/75	Yes
34.0	1	16.0	01/08/73	No
34.1	1	16.8	09/01/73	No
34.2	4	14.8	09/01/71	Yes
34.4	3	12.7	05/05/69	Yes
34.5	1	17.1	09/01/73	Yes
34.5	5	12.2	09/01/68	Yes
34.5	8	12.1	09/01/68	Yes
34.8	4	13.8	01/19/70	Yes

Age on 1/1/91	Years at SVS	Age at Entry	Date of Entry	Diplomate?
34.8	2	16.0	03/06/72	Yes
34.9	1	15.5	09/01/71	No
35.0	2	16.6	09/01/72	Yes
35.0	3	17.7	09/01/73	No
35.1	6	15.2	03/08/71	Yes
35.1	3	17.1	01/01/73	No
35.2	5	13.2	01/25/69	Yes
35.5	3	13.2	09/01/68	No
35.5	2	15.1	09/01/70	Yes
35.7	2	16.4	09/28/71	No
35.8	3	15.5	09/01/70	Yes
35.8	3	15.7	12/01/70	Yes
35.9	4	13.5	09/01/68	Yes
35.9	4	13.6	09/01/68	Yes
36.0	3	14.2	03/23/69	Yes
36.3	4	13.9	09/01/68	Yes
36.6	3	14.8	03/27/69	Yes
36.6	3	16.3	09/01/70	Yes
36.6	1	15.7	02/28/70	Yes
36.7	4	14.3	09/01/68	Yes
36.8	1	16.8	01/05/71	No
36.9	3	16.8	12/09/70	Yes
37.1	1	16.3	03/18/70	Yes
37.1	1	16.8	09/01/70	No
37.1	1	16.4	04/23/70	No
37.1	1	17.2	03/01/71	No
37.2	2	16.1	11/30/69	No
37.5	2	16.6	02/01/70	Yes
37.6	4	15.3	09/01/68	Yes
37.6	2	15.2	09/01/68	Yes
37.7	1	15.4	09/01/68	No
37.8	1	16.6	10/22/69	No
37.9	3	15.5	09/01/68	Yes
38.0	3	15.9	09/01/68	Yes
38.2	3	15.8	09/01/68	Yes
38.3	2	15.9	09/01/68	Yes
38.4	2	16.0	09/01/68	No
38.4	4	16.0	09/01/68	Yes
38.5	2	16.2	09/01/68	Yes
38.7	3	16.4	09/01/68	No
38.9	2	16.5	09/01/68	No
39.0	1	17.2	03/19/69	Yes
39.6	2	17.2	09/01/68	Yes
39.7	1	20.4	09/27/71	No
39.8	2	17.4	09/01/68	Yes
39.9	2	17.6	09/01/68	No
40.4	2	18.0	09/01/68	Yes

Appendix C

Structure of the Data Bases

Below are the structures of the basic data file of the study, alumques.dbf, and the comment file, alumcomm.dbf. Both are defined in dBase III Plus, which was the program used to analyze all the material.

ALUMQUES.DBF

Field	*Type*
ENTERED	Logical
CODE	Character
LASTNAME	Character
FIRSTNAME	Character
DIPLOMA	Logical
THESIS	Logical
BIRTHDATE	Date
ENTRYDATE	Date
ENTRYAGE	Numeric
DATEDIPL	Date
ADDRESS	Character
TOWN	Character
STATE	Character
ZIP	Character
PHONE	Character
NICKNAME	Character
FORMERLY	Character
UNCNTIGENR	Numeric
REALYRSHER	Numeric
YEARSHERE	Numeric
ENDENROLL	Date
ENDAGE	Numeric
TOWNORIGIN	Character
CURRENTAGE	Numeric
SVSCONTCTS	Character
NMBRCONTCT	Numeric
INTERVUER	Character
INTERVUDONE	Logical
RESPUSED	Logical
BATCH	Character
MARTALSTAT	Character
HOWLONGMAR	Numeric
NOCHILDREN	Numberic
AGECHILD1	Numeric
AGECHILD2	Numeric
AGECHILD3	Numeric
AGECHILD4	Numeric
PRESVSSCHL	Character
POSTSVSCHL	Character
POSTSVSMJR	Character
DEGREES	Character
POSTSVSNAM	Character
FUTEDUCPLN	Character
EDUCADJSTM	Character
EDUCSATISF	Logical
WORKATSVS	Character
WRKSVSPLAC	Character
WRKPOSTSVS	Character
WRKPOSTPLC	Character

WORKCHANGE	Logical
TRAVLVALUE	Logical
TRAVLWHERE	Character
TRAVELCONT	Character
RESP85	Logical
RESP86	Logical
RESP87	Logical
RESP88	Logical
RESP89	Logical
CONTACT89	Logical
RESP90	Logical
CONTACT90	Logical
ORALHISTRY	Logical
ADHOC	Character

ALUMCOMM.DBF

ENTERED	Logical
CODE	Character
LASTNAME	Character
FIRSTNAME	Character
FORMERLY	Character
RESPUSED	Logical
BATCH	Character
COMMENTS	Memo
ADHOC	Character

Notes on the structure of alumques.dbf:

Most of the fields are self-explanatory, especially when compared to the questionnaire. The exceptions are the following:

UNCNTIGENR is a field to store the number of uncontiguous enrollments for students who came, left, and returned again, and is important for calculating the actual number of years a student attended the school, and is found by direct reference to the school's files.

REALYRSHER is the number of actual years spent at school taking into account uncontiguous enrollments, leaves of absence, etc.

RESPUSED refers to instances where written responses were used in place of interviews in person or on the telephone.

BATCH is a label for the various groupings.

The fields from RESP85 on are supplementary fields used to locate additional information available in the files from earlier contacts with these students.

Appendix D

Additional Remarks on the Data and the Analysis

The questionnaire used to collect the data, reproduced in Appendix 1, contains some items that were not meant to be, or did not turn out to be, subject to analysis for this study. Thus, for example, the query about our mailings to former students, and that relating to the former student's parents, were designed to elicit information that could be useful in maintaining contact with these students. The question about other Sudbury Valley contacts was included to provide possible leads to students with whom we had lost continuous contact. As it turned out this question did help us find several people we might not otherwise have located. The other items on Page 4 of the questionnaire were designed to open lines of communication for casual conversation and, where they succeeded in doing so, they often provided the text for the comments included in this study. We would like to note that the reason we did not include the questions at the bottom of Page 4 in our set of questions methodically put to everybody was to avoid turning this into a survey on the attitudes of these students towards their experience at the school. In general, questions relating to why people did things, or how people felt about things, were avoided in favorable of more "objective" questions that were as value-free as possible.

It turns out that the three questions on Page 2 (after the listing of schools attended after SVS) were only occasionally answered, and then with answers that were not readily categorizable. As a result, only occasional use was made of them in the text, mostly by quoting them in the comments. No one who responded to these questions indicated any difficulty in getting accepted into other schools or successfully meeting the requirements of other schools, although some people who left before completing their high school age years expressed difficulty with their adjustment to their next school. If information of this sort is ever wanted in a future study, the questions relating to it will have to be phrased in a more pointed manner so that the answers will be readily categorizable.

The questions related to work change and work satisfaction, on Page 3 of the questionnaire, posed similar problems, and were used in a similar way. We discovered (too late to change it) that the question "Any work changes contemplated?" had an inherent design defect. We designed it to elicit information about the degree to which the respondents were comfortable in their work situations, whereas we should have realized that for many people a change in job signifies progress in their current vocation — continued growth — rather than dissatisfaction with their current situation. Change in itself had no significance.

The chief problem encountered in this study was a methodological one that arose directly from the budgetary constraints within which we operated. Ideally, we should have had the survey carried out by one person carefully trained to collect the data in a uniform, consistent and complete manner. This would have required sufficient funds to hire a qualified researcher full-time for about half a year to trace respondents, to interview them, and to sort and enter the data. We feel that future studies should be conducted in this manner with due consideration given to the ever-increasing size of the data base.

The question of when the next comprehensive study should be scheduled can be answered with some degree of confidence based on the experience of the four studies made to date. In order to develop greater depth of understanding of the unfolding of former students' lives, at least ten more years should pass, bringing the ages of the oldest respondents into the mid and late forties. Allowing a decade to pass will also probably serve to double the size of the data base, thus opening the possibility of some significant new findings. It would therefore seem to make sense for the school to make preparations for a fifth survey of former students around the year 2000.

Appendix E

FORMER STUDENTS-WHAT ARE THEY DOING NOW?
(A Trustees Study)

1972

Hanna Greenberg
(Chairman, Trustees' Committee for the Study)

Contents

Published by the Sudbury Valley School Press, S.C.
Reprinted from The Sudbury Valley School NEWSLETTER, v. 1, no. 9

FORMER STUDENTS-WHAT ARE THEY DOING NOW?
(A Trustees Study)

I. The Purposes of the Survey

As the fourth year of the school was getting under way, it became apparent that quite a number of students had already come and gone and that we really did not know what they were doing. Many people, such as prospective parents, educators, evaluators, and other asked us: how do former students adjust to life in the outside world? — or to public school, in case of transfer? — or to college, with its required courses and exams? — or to work, with its bosses and drudgery? We could not answer these questions, so we decided to ask our students directly.

Many people who come into contact with our school seem to believe that knowing what our alumni are doing would provide them with a measure of our success or failure, and they feel that in the statistics collected from our responses to the above questions lies the measure of the validity of our approach. I would not accept this view; for, while I think that the material is fascinating, it does not hold in any way the simple answer to whether the Sudbury Valley School is good or bad. Apart from the fact that this is a philosophical question that really can never be solved by data and statistics, it seems to me that the small number of students involved, and the short time that they spent at The Sudbury Valley School, should give us pause before we reach conclusions of any kind. Any prejudice that one brings with him can surely be validated by such skimpy data. In addition, and more important, it is not at all clear whether "success" for The Sudbury Valley School means good college and good jobs or whatnot for its alumni. We have not addressed ourselves to the meaning of "success" for the school as yet, and surely not in this particular study.

We also wanted to know how people heard about us, so that we might improve our publicity and reach more people.

Lastly, we wanted to find out what our alumni want from the school after they leave.

II. How the Study was Done

We contacted by phone all former students who left us in good standing and on good terms. Out of thirty-three, nine had moved out of the area or could not be reached. Two others said they would come but did not do so in time for this report. All the rest, twenty-two in total, came to the school and were interviewed on tape by some six or seven people associated with the school. The tapes were then summarized by three Assembly members, Hara Bouganim, Michael Sadofsky, and Phyllis Toback.

The following guidelines for the interviewers contain the questions that were asked as well as the limitations we imposed on ourselves — in particular, not to delve into personal matters:

<u>Guidelines for Interviewing Former Students</u>

(1) Be sure not to ask personal questions of the kind we never ask at the school — about personal attitudes, problems, history, relationships — and remember that the material will go into the open files.
(2) Do not solicit testimonials for the school — this is not a p.r. job.
(3) Try to elicit full, relaxed answers, with anecdotal detail if possible. If details and examples are not spontaneously forthcoming, try to pry some out of the interviewee, gently.
(4) Don't ask leading questions. If the interviewee doesn't talk, even in response to requests for more details, drop the subject.

The three main categories of information we seek to obtain from the interviewee are:

(1) How he first got to the school.
(2) What he has been doing since leaving the school.
(3) What kind of relationship, if any, would he like to have with the school in the future.

Under each category, the following questions interest us (in addition to any others suggested to the interviewer by the course of the conversation):

(1) How did you first get to the school?
How did you hear about the School?
How long after you heard about it did you make contact?
Describe your first contacts.
When did you decide to enroll?
Did your parents think it was a good idea for you to enroll?
(2) What have you been doing since leaving the school?
Tell in detail what kinds of things you have been doing since you left school; e.g., jobs, travel, further schooling, other similar things.
(For those who went to another school:
How did you adjust to the different type of environment?
How did you fit in academically?)
(For those who got a job:
Describe how you heard about the job, and got yourself hired.
How long did you stay? If you left, why?)
(3) What kind of relationship, if any, would you like to have with the school in the future? Probe whether the interviewee wants to keep in touch; to be informed about school developments; to be in contact with others who went to the school with him; etc.)

Some answers were then tabulated, but we think that the most interesting and illuminating material is in the words of the students themselves. So we edited the summaries to remove all personal references and redundancies, and we are printing them here, otherwise unchanged.

We would like to thank all the students who came to the school for the interviews.

III. Tabulation of the Replies

(1) How did you hear about SVS?

	Personal contact	Public School Guidance Dept.	Public Media (Newspaper, TV...)	Public Lecture by SVS
# of students	16	2	3	11

NOTE: Many students indicate multiple exposure to SVS — e.g., heard from a friend and read the Globe article; but the table indicates the first awareness of the school.

How long after you heard about SVS did you make contact?

	Fast	1/2 year or more
# of students	20	2

Did your parents think it was a good idea to enroll?

	Both parents approved	One parent approved; one did not	Both parents did not approve
# of students	13	4	5

(2) What have you been doing since leaving SVS?

	School	College	Work	Other
# of students	6*	3**	12***	1 (music study on his own)

* All but one are in their appropriate grade level.
** Two are full time students, one a part time student.
*** Ten work full time and are essentially self-supporting; one is working part time. Three of these are planning to continue their studies in college next year and have actually started or been accepted, as of May, 1972.

NOTE: The answers to this question show that after leaving school these people are far from settling down, but are instead constantly experimenting, evaluating, and changing their situations, from work to study to travel, etc.

How did you adjust to your regular school after leaving SVS?

Of the nine who are now studying in school or college, two adjusted poorly — they dislike their situation, are not applying themselves and are getting bad grades. Four are doing well, as far as academic standing and grades; of these, one likes the school, while two tolerate or fight the administration (they view it as a bad situation that they must put up with). The other three are in college and are doing fine academically and otherwise because, they say, they are really interested in the material and they want to be there.

How you got a job, etc.

The responses to this question are really impossible to tabulate and actually are the meat of most of the interview summaries printed below.

(3) What kind of relationship, if any, would you like to have with the school in the future?

Again, it is not really pertinent to tabulate the answers to this question. Most of the respondents want to be able to visit the school from time to time, want to know that it is still going, and some would like to keep abreast of the major developments: and a few want to come back as public members or as students.

IV. Summaries of the Interviews

Former students with an SVS diploma

(1) L.B.

L.B. got to the school as follows: A neighbor had a brochure. After L.B. read it, she went to hear one of the staff members speak at the local Unitarian Church and convinced her parents to accompany her. She had already decided that she wanted to attend the school. Her mother was sympathetic but unsure. The interview at school was difficult. They decided to have a second one. This time her parents were favorably impressed and decided to let her enroll for one year.

She got a job in the middle of her third year at Sudbury Valley. Her brother and a friend had jobs at a hospital. She asked about what kind of jobs were available there. She got a job by contacting the director, rather than going through the personnel office, and by pursuing the position rather than waiting for them to call her. She remained at the job for eight months, but left it to travel abroad. She has thought about what she wants to do abroad, but has not fixed plans or schedule. She would like to become a translator.

L.B. would like to keep in touch with the school, would like to know more about the major things happening at the school. She would also like to do some work publicizing the school. She thinks the Newsletter is an excellent idea. She has had thoughts about coming back to the school for a year at some point in the future — perhaps ten years later.

(2) N.C.

He was told about the school by Q.D., his friend from high school, who was then attending SVS. After reading the literature, he came to the school for an interview. He decided after the interview to enroll for the fall. Both parents favored his attendance at the school. Neither he nor his parents understood the nature of the school at the time, assuming he would take the same six courses as in high school.

Since leaving the school, most of his time has been taken up with the management of and performing in a rock band. He plays guitar, does the hiring and firing in the eight man band, arranges the music, makes the business arrangements. The group has been building up a repertoire and playing skills. N.C. has a real need to play, to entertain, to perform. He sums it up, "I'd be playing guitar even if I saw no financial gain in it ... to my dying day. That's how it is right now."

He maintains a warm relationship with the school, visiting often, reading the School Meeting Record, waiting for his diploma to be approved by the Assembly (as it was two weeks after the interview). He is considering becoming a public members (which he did), but doesn't have that much time for a regular schedule. At this point he feels he has no direct need for the school, but he can't "dismiss it". Short of a "statue of me put up on the front lawn," he wants only not to have to sign out a visitor's slip.

(3) D.C.

A friend told him about the school when it was about to begin. He wrote for the literature, read it, discussed it with his parents, applied for an interview. After the interview, he decided to try it out for one year. His parents both had reservations about it. His father was more interested, and his mother decided to go along with their views.

While he was at school he got an apprenticeship in the pathology department of a hospital. He also worked there full-time for a summer. He rotated from lab to lab as a technician, being trained on the job, and staying as long as he felt he was learning. After leaving SVS, he worked three months in an antique shop on Cape Cod. He ran the shop, attended auctions, picked up furniture. Toward the end of that summer the hospital called, said they desperately needed someone to do cytology work for one week. He took the job, then stayed at the hospital on a permanent basis in another lab. One of the things he also does at the hospital is assist at autopsies. During his apprenticeship, he had been permitted to watch. He gained this opportunity only after a year and a half of talking to them about it — it took him that long to convince the hospital staff of his seriousness. He feels that they were testing to see whether he could put up with whatever they could dish out. Yet he found most of the work interesting and his involvement increased. He decided to apply to a medical school, and visited one. He told them what he had been doing for the past few years, and they offered to admit him as a student. He is not sure now if he wants to attend.

He definitely wants to keep in touch and know what is going on. He has subscribed to the Newsletter. He wants to know about new policies. He likes to visit and see for himself how things are running. He thinks reunions might be amusing, enjoyable.

(4) Q.D.

His parents saw an ad in the paper and told him about it. He had an interview and enrolled the following fall. His parents thought it was a very good idea at first, then changed their feelings; they are indifferent at this point.

While he was in school he became interested in the field of psychology. He found out about a school that trains professional psychologists, applied, and was accepted on the basis of his application (which included essays, an autobiography, letters of recommendation, and an interview). He convinced them that he would be able to tolerate a more structured school because it was clear to him what he wanted to do. He felt that the pressure and responsibility would all come from within. He has adjusted to the school very well.

He had several jobs before he enrolled in the professional school, mostly of a menial nature, such as construction, factory work. He couldn't do the kinds of things he wanted to do, such as working in hospitals and schools. It was this handicap, plus a great deal of curiosity, that made him decide to get professional training.

He likes to know what is going on at SVS. He wants to receive the Newsletter. He has though about becoming a staff member, or possibly starting a similar school.

(5) C.D.

C.D. had been looking for a school and heard of SVS from his mother, who in turn heard about it at an art class in Boston. Within 24 hours, he called and set up an appointment for an interview. At the interview he listened while his parents talked. His mind had already been made up and the interview confirmed his decision. Of parental approval, he hesitantly says, yes; they went along with it.

In terms of his interest in SVS, D.C. says he would like to come by occasionally and see how the school is doing. In contrast to some others, he says, "once I'd left I couldn't come back" as a student.

(6) D.D.

She first heard about the school from a student who knew of it in May, before it opened. Her brother started attending. She started after Christmas of the first year. She had started the year at another school, but didn't like it. She visited SVS during Thanksgiving and Christmas, and then decided to attend. Both parents thought SVS was the best thing for her, because she was so unhappy at her other school.

She was interested in becoming a cook after she left school. She got a job at a restaurant working on salads and baking. She still holds that job. She took a six week course in the Fall at a restaurant in Boston, and was accepted at an internationally-known cooking school in Europe, which she will attend next year. There is a job at the Boston restaurant waiting for her when she returns. She got her present job by walking into the restaurant and telling the hostess she would do anything in the kitchen, and didn't care about the salary. She got to talk to the chef even though the hostess said she didn't think a job was available, since the restaurant had only men in the kitchen.

D.D. likes to visit the school, has thought of coming back as a student. She would like to help the school if she can, perhaps with speaking engagements.

(7) D.E.

D.E. heard about SVS from his mother, and an interview was set up with a staff member in response to his expressed interest in further information. Present were he, his parents, and his brother. Their attitude included astonishment at the physical appearance of the school, as well as curiosity and shyness of the unknown. D.E. indicates that he wanted to try SVS; in retrospect he realizes that he didn't understand the school at the time. The decision to attend was made during the summer with parental approval.

Since leaving the school last Spring, his activities included teaching sailing for the summer, approximately three months of cross-country travel, and a return to music study while residing in Brookline for four months and since returning to his parents' home. He travelled to get away, to find himself; he returned when he had determined that music was "the most important thing in my life." His jobs have been part time, casual labor.

His relationship with SVS is restricted to an interest in certain individuals on a personal level. He evidences no interest in the institution.

(8) U.E.

U.E. heard about the school through two students who were there when it first opened. He got the catalog and made several visits to the school during the first summer and the first year. He wanted to enroll immediately but it took one year to convince his parents. They didn't, and still don't, think it was a good idea.

He is attending a junior college and working part time. He chose that college because it offered the technical program and approach to grades and courses that he wanted. He wrote an explanatory letter to the Admissions Office about his lack of a transcript. He went for several interviews until he convinced the Dean of Admissions to accept him. It was the only college he "really tried to get into." His part-time work, at a radio station, is closely related to his interest in technical work. He took a three-week training course in preparation for the job. He found no difficulty in adjusting to the college because he is doing what he wants to do. He makes a strong distinction between the courses he really cares about and those he just wants to get by in. He did not find himself academically behind because of his year at SVS. On the contrary, he feels that he is ahead of his classmates because he is more interested in what he is doing than the other students are. He doesn't feel the pressure of grades the way they do because he is mainly interested in the material. He plans to transfer to a four-year school with a similar technical orientation.

He would like to keep in touch, would like to help out people at the school. He would like to receive the Newsletter, and thinks it should perhaps contain reflections by former students. He is interested in knowing how other former students feel about the school. He thinks reunions would be good if they were for an interchange of ideas.

(9) N.G.

N.G. heard of SVS from three sources within a two week span: (1) a guidance counselor suggested he look into SVS; (2) another student at the public high school he was attending mentioned SVS; (3) a friend talked about SVS. Within two weeks of his first awareness of the school, he and his friend drove out in May 1968 and met a staff member. N.G. speaks of his reaction to SVS this way: he couldn't get over the concept of being his "own boss" and when school started in the fall, he says, "I was pushy, testing." His decision to enroll occurred on the day of his visit — his parents, however, did not like the idea of SVS; they wanted to know what it would do for him. N.G. goes on to indicate that SVS imposed his first responsibility when it required him to pay for his own schooling.

Since leaving SVS, he has been "adventuring. I've lived in extremes, seen the world, and met people." This means lots of travel, hitchhiking predominantly, picking up jobs, and return to home when the money runs out. He indicates that he is settling down now for about a year — this appears to be a gathering of financial resources for a trip to Europe.

N.G. indicates an explicit interest in SVS — he indicates, very strongly, an inclination to return as a student and pursue his academic interests in theater (and perhaps other areas) in the SVS environment, where he can "address truth."

(10) D.G.

D.G. had left both public and private schools and for a two month period since Christmas vacation had been living in Boston. He heard about SVS from "some people on the street." After two weeks passed, he telephoned SVS and apparently engaged someone in conversation about the school. Two months later he visited for two weeks. During this period, his mother visited and spoke with a staff member; "but I was all set." Speaking of his initial reaction he says, "I didn't think it was a school." He describes it as a completely different concept from what he had been told on the phone; "but I liked it just as much." It is difficult to determine parental attitude toward SVS. Apparently the relationship between parents and son was pretty strained prior to his SVS enrollment. His counselor's approval of SVS apparently gained some measure of parental ok.

Since he left SVS, he has "just been enjoying life." He skied for three months, and then registered with the Massachusetts Division of Unemployment Security for a job dealing with animals or children. After waiting through job offers in the general labor categories, he was hired as a veterinary assistant in the Spring; he is still at this job. He indicates that he is learning more now out of school than when in school. He reads more and groups material on like subjects to read together. He says he "makes mini-courses for myself." He has also signed up for child psychology and philosophy courses at a local university. D.G. indicates an interest in living in England. He apparently contacted the British equivalent of our Chamber of Commerce and in terms of their negativism on the availability of jobs in a casual labor category, he is saving money to attend a British Trade School in cycle mechanics, and then maybe get a shop — stay 30-40 years he says.

D.G. indicates some interest in SVS. He says, almost casually and in obvious contradiction to his U.K. residency plans, that he'd like to be on the staff. He indicates that his interest is in the school's development and he'd like to receive the leaflets that he has seen in other students' homes.

(11) L.H.

She heard about SVS through friends of a staff member. Her father was very much opposed to her enrolling. Her mother suggested that she go for the summer. After the summer, her mother asked her if she wanted to attend for the whole year.

She decided before she left the school that she wanted to work in a museum. She did volunteer work at the photo lab in the Museum of Fine Arts for the summer. Towards the end of the summer she was given a paying permanent job there. She left this job in January because she found the work frustrating. She felt she couldn't get anywhere with that job. She did not work for one month; then she found a job in a small corporation in Boston. She started as a file clerk, got a higher position when someone else quit. She stayed at that job for five months, then left to take courses because she decided that she wanted to go to college. She took two courses and found no difficulty with them because she was really interested. In the Fall she enrolled in two night courses and got a job as a salesgirl. She is attending college because she wants to get a better job, and also finds it relaxing and enjoyable. She would like to work in a museum and needs a degree. She expects the courses she has been taking to give her a better chance of admission as a full time student.

L.H. would not like to be completely cut off and have absolutely no information about the school. She would like to know that it hasn't closed, or completely changed.

(12) Q.I.

Q.I. heard about SVS from her ninth grade guidance counselor who had received literature apparently via a SVS mailing. She discussed it with her parents and an interview was set up with a staff member. This sequence of events extended over 2-3 weeks during which time she saw the available SVS literature. The interview was ok. Her father liked the school; her mother couldn't tolerate it. After visiting an open house — of which she says, "No desks, no blackboards; this is a school?" — Q.I. decided to enroll. She subsequently indicates that the final decision to enroll was made by her father along with her; "I hated public school — I just came — figured I'd give it a try."

Since leaving SVS she has been working as a nursing assistant at a hospital. She heard about the job from another student whose father is associated with the hospital. She was interviewed and hired for a job whose requirements she describes as only a chest x-ray and a high school diploma. She likes her job, learns something new every day, and plans on wrking there for many years.

She keeps in contact with a few people who are still at SVS.

(13) F.S.

F.S. was uncertain about enrolling at first because of financial difficulties. She was not sure until the interview. Her parents believed in the school wholeheartedly. It coincided with her mother's philosophy.

After leaving school, she got a job through an agency as a clerk underwriting life insurance. She left because she had mastered the job quickly and found it boring. She got another job through a friend as assistant manager at a health spa. But she left the job after she discovered that she was really a clerk to the manager. She spent some time travelling, camping. She was interested in going into business with a friend but that didn't work out. She returned to her first job in a position of greater responsibility. Her present job there is more involved, more difficult, takes more intelligence. But she expects to be bored in another year. She is frustrated because there is no way to move up the administrative ladder in jobs such as these. She attributes this to discrimination against women and against people without college degrees. She is thinking of going to college for a degree in Business Administration. She is presently preparing to get accepted to college.

She wants to stay in touch with SVS, wants to make sure the school will continue. She wants to know about major changes in the school before they occur. She is a public member. She likes to be able to participate, vote, and visit. She would definitely want her own children to attend the school. She would like to keep in contact with former students but doesn't think that this should be the school's responsibility.

Former students who left aged sixteen and over (no diploma):

(14) D.F.

His mother learned about the school and told him about it. They visited and he decided to come. He heard about it in the middle of the summer and enrolled in the fall. His mother wanted him to attend, and his father was not sure.

Since leaving SVS, he is going to public high school. During the summer he sails, water skis. He might work this summer painting houses. He will probably stay in high school until he graduates. He didn't have much trouble adjusting to the school because all his friends go there. It was hard at first getting used to going to classes. He decided to go back to public high school for a lot of reasons. His father did not want him to return to SVS; it was a long trip to commute, and all of his friends were in the public high school.

He would like to be able to visit, talk to people, and have friends at SVS.

(15) C.E.

C.E. was brought to the school by a graduate school instructor at Lowell State College. C.E. had quite school and was sitting in on classes there. He says from the first it was the "whole concept of the school I liked." His parents were glad to see him going to school, "any school," and paid the tuition willingly. Adjustment was slow. It was a new experience not being told what to do, yet when he wanted to start a project, the bureaucracy bothered him.

During his year at the school, C.E. read and learned to play the flute. He spent much of the time at home, at times sculpting, and at colleges, sitting in on courses. He realized by the end of the year that he didn't really need a high school or college degree. Close friendships and intellectual relationships with people provide him with the education he needs.

While at SVS, C.E. wa already working as an outreach worker in Lowell in a city-financed project, first with alcoholics, then with the drug community. The program was successful and became Federally supported. C.E. left when he realized that he couldn't guarantee the addicts' safety and immediate help with no police surveillnce. He then took a job doing community team work with teenagers, focussing on ecology along the Merrimac River. The project was a success. After SVS, he travelled in Canada and the United States for a year. On his return, he got a job as an educational intern doing remedial reading with elementary school kids. He is now home temporarily, doing construction work. He got the job through a relative, and plans to use his new skills soon. He and some friends are establishing a community in Nova Scotia on land they have bought. Although he doesn't envision the community in Canada as a lifetime venture, he welcomes the structured situation, wants to live with people, so that "when something is on my back, I won't walk away. We'll have to go through some sort of confrontation ... we're all going to be dependent on each other to be self-sufficient." C.E. says he wants to see if he can live with it, if it will "make me better, and bring me closer to people I like."

C.E. plans to stay in contact with SVS, in contact with people like some of the original staff members "because it's definitely a commitment on your part and it's an amazingly constructive thing." He wants to see the school continue and will help when called upon.

(16) X.E.

X.E. first heard about the school from two friends who were SVS students. He had an interview with a staff member. His sophomore year at high school had ended in severe conflict with the administration, and he had "cut out." He enrolled in SVS for the next year, feeling, "it must be a good idea, not so much academically, for me anyhow, but just so I could learn how to learn." His father, who had already heard of the school, supported his decision; he ignored his mother's opposition.

X.E. had been working while at SVS at a store. The promotion did not mean much of a pay increase, so he left and found another job as a concrete inspector. This job paid well, but was highly dangerous. When the building he had been working on collapsed, he found some of his reports had been thrown out. Since September he is back in public high school as a senior. Although he finds the work incredibly easy, he resents the "college or bust" attitude. The public school system, he feels, has you very much by the throat. An accredited high school diploma is necessary for college and graduate school, two steps toward his goal, a career as a lawyer. He now fits into the school routine better than before, noting that it's a matter of listening and self-discipline, learned at SVS and on the job. Thus the next seven years are mapped out; he is optimistic. "I just gained interest, motivation, I never had before ... I have the capacity to do anything I want to do and I found something I want to do, and that's how I'm going to be happy. That's what I must do, quite basically, and this is the way I must do it."

As a former SVS student, X.E. is interested in hearing about the school, wants to see it continue, but does not want to specify the relationship he expects.

(17) G.I.

A "teacher friend," after seeing the Globe article about the school, visited and suggested investigating it. G.I. wrote and was told he must pay to enroll. He decided immediately to attend and got a part time job. His parents preferred his remaining in public high school, with its excellent academic reputation, but they "went along for love of me." They did not understand the radical nature of the school and originally opposed it on grounds of cost.

In the year and a half since he left the school, G.I. has held two jobs, the first for the state, the other as a salesman in a department store. He had no difficulty obtaining either job.

The real focus of his life has been his community, combined with personal growth. He had been instrumental in directing the aims of a local coffee house toward community involvement. His experience at SVS led naturally to this work: "I had just come down from the school, the glorious endeavor ... was looking ... for that kind of work ... right here in my neighborhood ... I was accused in the beginning of having a 'hidden agenda' because I came in with full-blown ideas and knew ways to handle meetings." Later he says, "The school gives you a different ... footing for operating in any kind of organization. You come in already knowing the hard, cruel facts of meetings, of political stratagems."

On the day of the interview G.I. re-enrolled in SVS in order to have a position in the school to do things in the School Meeting and the Corporation. He feels that there are things in the school that put the student at a disadvantage in the learning experience, so that "unless political changes are made, the student will be further and further from this." He feels that there should definitely be a relationship between alumni and the school. The school should encourage the connection and have an attitude of receptiveness. Since alumni should have fully achieved the idea of the school, being out from the base, they will be "wrapped up in the learning experience because they're in the community, they are the resources."

(18) M.N.

M.N. heard about the school through a friend in January 1968, and saw a catalogue before the school opened. He decided to enroll before the interview in the Spring, which was just a formality. He came the first summer. His parents were not happy about his enrollment at first.

He did part time jobs before he left the school — painting, carpentry. Then he did these things full time for a summer. He moved to Maine where he held a variety of jobs. He returned to Boston, didn't work for a while, then got a job as a general maintenance worker at a motel. He decided that he wanted a job involving signs or interior design or displays. He looked in the Yellow Pages for listings. He found a sign company, walked in and asked for a job. He feels that the only way to get a job is to present yourself personally, talk to the people you might be working for, and convince them that you want the job. He remained at this job for eight months. He found some of the work interesting, other aspects repetitive and worthless. He left the job for personal reasons. He has been out of school for 1 1/2 years and has been self-supporting. He has enough money now to live without a job for a while and to do some travelling. His future plans are uncertain because of his draft status. He would like to travel, and study various kinds of architecture.

He would like to keep in touch, and would like to be able to visit the school. He would like to hear about people he knew at the school, about physical changes in the school, and about new publications. He would like to know about the possibility of coming back just to get a diploma.

(19) U.T.

U.T. heard about SVS from a friend who was about to enroll. He had been seeking an alternative to public high school and describes herself as "fed up ... had to get out." She visited SVS and apparently gave her parents an ultimatum: SVS or quit school. She says her parents accepted this in order to keep her in school.he had decided to enroll even before visiting. The interval from initial awareness to enrollment encompassed about one month. U.T. makes an interesting comment about her initial reactions: "I found (SVS) almost cold. People here were doing their thing. I came in not knowing what I wanted to do." This resulted in her spending a lot of time in the smoking lounge reading and thinking.

Her activities since leaving SVS do not fit any simple pattern. She worked for the summer, she travelled; sometime in this scheme she left her parents' home and moved to New York. For an indefinite time she stayed in her New York apartment reading and doing little else. She eventually got a job on Wall Street and enrolled in a night school program. This job may have been a turning point; she describes it as changing her into "another person" in terms of dress and appearance as well as introducing visions of a career. However, she did not complete her night school program and left her job. She subsequently married and moved to Boston. She indicated she wanted to return to SVS but did not have the money and so enrolled in a public high school; she says she wants an SVS diploma. U.T. is considering going on to college, perhaps without completing high school, but "I haven;t decided what I want to do in school if I get accepted into school" and in response to a query of why go to college, she replies, "what else would I do?" She desires to meet people with ideas, says this is difficult on the street and the kids at high school seem immature. She is carrying six courses at high school and is getting better grades without trying hard; but she is getting "more or less absolutely nothing out of (her) courses" and is taking them so the record will look good.

U.T. indicates that she wants more contact with SVS and with former students. Perhaps the essence of her last year is summed up in one final phrase: "I just want to come back (to SVS)."

Former students who left under age sixteen:

(20) K.B.

He first heard about SVS from his mother who had heard from a friend. This occurred in the spring of 1968. During early summer he visited the school with his parents. No formal interview took place. Attitudes and reactions are not noted. He apparently enrolled for the summer and in that interval decided to enroll for the year. He attended SVS for two years. His parents' attitude toward the school is not clear. He notes that he would rather attend SVS than his local high school, but his parents won't let him return. They "like the school" but feel it is "not for him." Whether this is a change in attitude on their part is not indicated; one may presume so, since K.B. attended SVS for two years.

After leaving, he enrolled in public high school. He is now in the second year of that environment. He describes his adjustment as difficult. He was "not used to being told what to do" and "flunked everything but didn't stay back." "Now it's ok" he says, as he has become "used to it." But he would rather attend SVS. In his words, "I think I learn a little more here (at SVS) because just 'cause I get good marks or something, which I don't though, even if I did, I'll do it and then I'll forget everything. But here I learn more about myself and everything, that I won't forget."

In terms of a relationship with SVS, within the pragmatic constraints he recognizes and apparently accepts, K.B. indicates that he likes to visit occasionally to see how everything is going.

(21) B.B.

B.B.'s family was acquainted with one of the original staff members and was aware of SVS from the time of conception and planning. B.B.'s enrollment was a foregone conclusion as far as he and his parents were concerned, although his attendance at the initial summer session in 1968 was not to his liking (he wanted to spend time with his friends from public school) but was agreed to as an attempt to find an alternative to his former "crummy school."

He left SVS in his early teens because of his father's employment abroad. He now attends a private school for English speaking children. He dislikes this school, and its structured environment, and apparently has made a poor fit academically. He is studying music with piano lessons taken outside of school. He notes that if such lessons were available within his school, he would not pursue them. His comments on the student body do not indicate a fit.

His desired relationship with SVS is summarized in his words: "I'd like to go (to SVS) ... but I can't. (SVS is the) only decent school around."

(22) Q.H.

Q.H. came to the school in search of an alternative to public school. She visited, read the literature, then for two weeks looked at other private and public schools before enrolling.

Her mother had heard about SVS at a P.T.A. meeting three years ago. The decision to enroll was made by the whole family.

The year at SVS was accompanied by a change in her feelings about herself and her ability to handle her situation. She says: "I left with much more of a better outlook on myself." Her mother says she and her husband don't understand how "this inner strength came into her last year." She describes Q.H. as a doormat, cut to the quick by other children's remarks, crying internally. Now that's gone, and "people can't hurt her now the way they did before." Q.H. has returned to public school, in the junior high of her choice. Her parents had no difficulty enrolling her in her proper grade level. Her program is tailored to her needs. She was even able to continue math, her most difficult subject, with students in her own grade, in spite of the year's time away from studying it.

She plans to continue writing while attending the public schools, and asks only to be able to visit SVS in the future. She feels the year at SVS came at just the right time in her life, gave her time to think. "When you're thinking, things develop in your mind. Just sitting there, you get ideas ... Thinking is a very good use of time — it's as good as reading a book."

V. Some Impressions of the Interviews

One of the Assembly members who summarized several of the interviews wrote the following overview:

"The initial question was designed to support recruitment efforts. In general, the group of interviewees I dealt with were actively seeking an alternative school environment. In most cases, however, the search was not in a positive direction but rather for any alternative that would enable them to stay in school and satisfy parents, while reducing the hassles of the typical public school environment.

The second question was designed to provide a documented basis for responses to the questions raised by parents of prospective enrollees — questions which relate to how well SVS students can fit into the mainstream of society. The range of impressions is vast. Some interviewees appear very articulate, rational, and 'together.' Others are elsewhere in the spectrum. Their activities, also, spread over the spectrum.

The third question evolved from a desire on the part of SVS to maintain some contact with former students for future studies of this sort when time introduces, perhaps, more significance. Responses were quite diverse. In most cases there was an indicated desire to maintain occasional contact with selected individuals. In several cases, a desire to return to SVS as a student was emphatically indicated. In only one case was an interest expressed in SVS as a developing institution."

Another of those who summarized the interviews provided the following impressions of the interviews:

"There seems to be a discernible pattern of character traits and behavior in students who leave SVS. Many of them convey the sense of a strong self image. They feel that they are pretty good, and can get what they want (if they want it enough) by convincing others of their merit. This is coupled with a realistic attitude toward their goals for either professional or personal fulfillment, or they may concentrate on a more immediate activity (even one such as 'enjoying life'), but they do not seem to be plagued by the feelings of insecurity, inadequacy, confusion, or resignation that are typical of many other people their age.

They are not troubled by the fact that they do not have the formal credentials of most high school graduates. They overcome this potential handicap for jobs or acceptance to schools by demonstrating a great deal of initiative and persistence in approaching the people who make decisions about these applications. Or else they find alternate routes to these goals, such as working as volunteers or apprentices in fields they wish to enter, or studying independently or part-time for schools they wish to enroll in.

If they are confident of success, they seem equally unafraid of failure or change. They do not hesitate to admit to themselves that a job has not turned out to be what they thought it was. They are capable of doing work which does not interest or challenge them, if they see some point in doing this, but they are not afraid to leave a position to seek another one, even in a time of high unemployment.

In short, they seem to have acquired the ability to make decisions about what they want to do with their lives, determine ways to pursue their goals, and retain confidence in themselves in spite of setbacks or errors in their course of activity."

Appendix F

Article About the 1972 Study

Reprinted from *The Sudbury Valley School Newsletter*, Vol. 3, No. 1 (Oct. 1973), pp. 4-11.

* * * * * *

REFLECTIONS ON THE TRUSTEES' STUDY ON FORMER STUDENTS

Phyllis Toback

When a school is radically different from familiar educational models, it is often very hard for people to accept it, even if they are impressed by the philosophy and organization. They may need to come and visit the school to see for themselves if it really is what it claims to be. They may want to talk to students who attend the school. Sometimes they want to know what has happened to students who have left the school, either to attend a different school, or to find their place in the adult world. How do these people fit in? How well do they do?

Ever since the Sudbury Valley School opened its doors in July 1968, people outside the school community have been wondering about the students who emerge from this radically different school. What happens when a student is entirely free to decide what he wants to do with his own education? What happens when there is no externally imposed set of values for how he spends his time? What is it like to go to a democratic school where all members have equal votes on all matters, including budgets, hiring of staff, and rules and regulations? What does it mean to leave with a high school diploma that is awarded when the student has defended, to the satisfaction of the school community, his thesis that "he is ready to assume full responsibility for himself in the community at large?"

The Trustees' Study

In the fall of 1971, the Trustees of the Sudbury Valley School established a committee to investigate some of the results of an educational experience at the school. The committee was able to contact thirty-three former students, and twenty-two of them came to the school for interviews in the fall and winter of 1971. The interviews were conducted by several staff members, enrollees and Assembly members of the school. In an informal conversational atmosphere all the former students were asked three basic questions: How did you first get to the school? What have you been doing since leaving the school? What kind of relationship, if any, would you like to have with the school in the future?

The Trustees' committee felt that the most important question was the second one, which dealt with how the students had made the transition to another environment and how they pursued various goals. But they were also interested in how the image of the school was communicated to prospective students and their parents, and what responsibilities the school might have to former students. The tape-recorded interviews were studied by the committee, and a report was produced, *Former Students — What Are They Doing Now?* (published by the Sudbury Valley School NEWSLETTER, v.1, no.9). The report contained an explanation of the study, summaries of the interviews, tabulation of some of the material and some commentary by committee members. Caution was exercised by the committee in drawing conclusions about the interviews because of the small number of former students involved in the study and the relatively short time that they spent at the school.

A Personal Interest

As one member of this committee, my orientation to the material was slightly different from the others'. Unlike them, I did not personally know any of these former students. I had first come to visit the Sudbury Valley School in the spring of 1971 with an academic interest. As a college English professor, I was struggling with a number of educational problems, particularly involving motivation and performance of students, and the relationship between student and teacher. The Sudbury Valley School seemed to provide solutions for many of these questions. As I continued to visit, I developed a strong personal interest in the school and in its students. I thought not only about my students, but also about my personal educational experience and the prospective experience of my young son. I wanted to know more about the students who had passed through the school because I saw them as providing important documentation of the school's philosophy. That is why I became involved with the Trustees' study and I continued to be interested in the interviews even after the report had been produced. Several of us, in listening to the recordings, felt that there were many places where the former students' own words were far more interesting than any summary could be. Therefore, I decided to transcribe these recordings as accurately as possible so that people who were interested could have access to them in a form closer to the original than the published summaries. These transcripts are available in the school archives for anyone who wishes to examine them. In working closely with this material I could not help but form some opinions. I had first approached these interviews with some fairly conventional notions of success and failure and with a traditional scale of values for different types of activities. But I found myself becoming more interested in how these people saw themselves, what led them to do the things they did, how they handled the situations they were in, and what made them persevere, or change their positions. In the pages that follow, I present some of my observations about these former students, accompanied in several cases by their descriptions of themselves. I think it is important to note that this group of students is not a representative sample of students currently attending the school. All of them spent a number of years at other schools, and their time at Sudbury Valley may represent a small portion of their educational experience. Nevertheless, I think they reveal in their interviews some of the effects of their stay at Sudbury Valley.

Effects of the School

Parents often express reservations about sending their child to a school that doesn't "prepare" them for particular career goals. But from the interviews it would appear that students don't need to be carefully guided along a particular path. Many of these former students have independently chosen to concern themselves with what they want to do with their lives once they achieve adulthood and independence. It is my impression, having worked with college students for the past seven years, that students who emerge from the Sudbury Valley School have gotten further with these concerns than those who have relied on the schools to take care of things for them. They seem to have reached stages of maturity that most young people don't achieve until after they graduate from college or after they have held positions of responsibility. They do not seem to be plagued by those feelings of uncertainty, confusion, or despair that characterize so many people who are on the verge of assuming adult responsibilities. They examine their motives and activities thoroughly and continually, regardless of what particular thing they are doing, and they are not afraid of obstacles or of failure. A number of the former students described effects of their experience at the Sudbury Valley School. For example, they spoke of feeling more confident, of understanding themselves better. In one interview, the parent accompanying a former student described a dramatic change in her daughter: "I don't understand, but it is very mysterious ... this inner strength ... it came to her last year. I can't put my finger on how or when ... There she was ... this doormat that let anybody walk over her and who would be cut to the quick by remarks that kids would make, just remarks, they didn't even have to touch her. And I don't think she showed much to them, but she would be crying internally and miserable at home. And that's gone. People can't hurt her now the way they did before. She has this inner something."

As she herself put it: "I had to unlearn to be frightened. I just didn't know what I was. I considered myself kind of cowardly, no-good, not-too-smart, nothing. When I left here, I wasn't feeling superior, but I just had a better outlook on myself ... I had (had) to dig out soul things and think things over. Up to then I had been thinking, 'I' this way, there's no way I can improve myself.' And after a while here it became clear that I could." This former student decided to return to public school because, as she puts it, "I think I've gotten what I needed from this school. It was really lucky. I came at the time when I really needed it." She wanted to take advantage of the programs the public school offered in connection with her interest in art and creative writing.

One former student described his relationship with the steering committee of a coffee house that was involved in community service: "I came in with a lot of full-blown ideas ... from the school ... the way to handle meetings and things. (Sudbury Valley) gives you a different footing for operation in any kind of organization. You come in already knowing the hard cruel facts of meetings, of political stratagems."

Others spoke of their ability to learn from their experiences, to act in a responsible way in the communities they were in, to impose self-discipline in completing their chosen tasks. These characteristics found expression in a very broad spectrum of activity and inclination. Since the Sudbury Valley School enrolls students regardless of their previous interests or performances, it was not surprising to find a heterogeneous group emerging from the school.

Careers

Finding meaningful jobs was a concern of many of these former students. At the time of the interviews, two of them were already working in their chosen careers — one in a business of his own, and the other in the nursing profession. Another group was pursuing a course of independent study to prepare for a specific goal. In this group were those studying music, working as a laboratory technician (and contemplating making use of an acceptance to medical school), preparing to become a translator while living abroad, and travelling and working in preparation for architecture and interior design.

A number of former students felt the need of formal training. This meant enrolling in a professional school of psychology, or a technical program at a college, or a cooking school, or returning to high school to prepare for a literary career or law school. Others planning to enter various programs — a mechanics trade school, a liberal arts college with concentration in art history (for museum work), a college degree program in business administration.

The people in this last group all chose to move into a more controlled educational environment than they had experienced at Sudbury Valley. Although some expressed disapproval or even scorn of the things they were expected to do, they were comfortable and apparently successful in their situations because they were willing to endure some things they disliked in order to reach their goals. One former student described his situation in college:

> When I went to Sudbury Valley I was ... doing what I wanted to do. When I went to G. (Junior College) I was also doing what I wanted to do. So as far as my own head goes, there was no real difference, but as far as the atmosphere goes ... there are a lot of students at G. who are there because their parents wanted them to go there ... It wasn't difficult (for me to adjust) because I did make up my mind that I was going to put with certain things. For example, my first year there, there were several courses in journalism, and in television, radio, that I really enjoyed. But they also told me that in order to be a 'well rounded person' I had to study sociology, psychology, western civilization, and so I put up with it, and I went to class enough times to get all the homework done, and I made it a point to be there during all the tests, and for two nights before each test I'd buckle down and study, and so I got by. I suppose that was the hardest adjustment to make, realizing that I'd have to make a few sacrifices, but then, even when I was here (at Sudbury Valley) I was making a few sacrifices to come out here. I was hitchhiking twenty miles a day to get out here and twenty miles to get back home, and so it was all the same ... They were different hassles, but I was hassling to do something I wanted.

Another student was more sensitive to the environment in the high school he returned to after leaving Sudbury Valley and working for a year. He returned to high school in order to get the proper credentials for college and law school.

> There was really no adjusting, because when I left here I just went to work, and I was used to working. I was used to a little bit of regimentation, and not doing exactly as I pleased. So I did that, working ,and I just did the same thing when I went back to school. So I don't see how there was any adjustment. I'm fed up with a lot of the attitudes that run around that high school. I'm fed up with the college-or-bust attitude, just like a packing crate, a packing machine, canning kids for college, and getting them out. 'This bunch is ready, send in the next one, get the machine primed and going.' This is what the high school is, a college machine, and a very inefficient one too.

Nevertheless, he achieved academic success:

> I find it incredibly easy, most of the classes, with the exception of math. I always had a hard time with math ... the A's don't come nearly as hard ... I attribute it mostly to this place and my working experience that I was able to do as well as I could. It's a matter of paying attention in class. It's a matter of being self-disciplined, which I learned here and in my working experience. I had to. You've got to. And I learned to develop an interest in the subjects that I couldn't care less about, although now I find myself thinking about all my classes and more interested than I was, and I'm sure the day I leave I'll lose the interest, until I get another class, in which I will automatically gain interest. There will be some of them that I will carry interest over to, history, French, English and so forth. But the math won't interest me too much, algebra. I'll probably dabble in it, because I'm used to it now.

Personal Goals

For a number of former students, the question of what career to pursue seemed less important than personal development. Many of them deliberately patterned their lives to advance personal goals. One of them gave her reasons for seeking jobs that provided unusual experience rather than going to college:

> I went to the University of R. to visit a friend, and stayed about a month ... I lived there. I wasn't a student or anything, I was just visiting ... I've always had friends that were in college, and whenever I went to visit them, I was sorely disappointed in their friends in college that I met. I couldn't understand why they were there. They went there because they were supposed to. I was just unimpressed. So it was a good experience going to this big university and meeting a lot of different kinds of people, a lot of the same people who didn't really want to be there. And that shaped my ideas about going to college. I didn't want to go then. And I just really severely disapproved of people going for the sake of going. I think that people should go to school when they have a reason to go, and not just because their high school guidance counselors started them on the road to filling out applications, and the applications are a lot of work, and then once you get them filled out, and you pay a lot of money, and then if you get accepted somewhere you figure you might as well go, because it cost a lot of money, it was such a pain in the ass to fill them all out, and so you go. Well, it's fun, the social life is nice, but I don't think people make the best use of school at a point like that.

This student was concerned with doing things that gave her a sense of independence and experience with different kinds of people. She felt that she was learning a lot from the various jobs that she held: "I think that in some sort of a funny way, Sudbury prepared me for the big wide world and influenced me so that I got a lot out of these working experiences, even though the first two experiences were of very short duration."

For other former students there were important personal interests: community activities, religious pursuits, observations of the psychological states of people under extreme conditions or unusual environments, living in a self-contained community and confronting difficult personal relationships. Some of these people used academic environments to further their personal goals. This involved auditing courses, or taking courses in conjunction with a personal program of readings and "mini-courses," or even using school as a place to meet people and exchange ideas.

It would appear that for many of these people the definition of learning is much broader than that generally encountered. It includes learning from life in a highly personal, conscious and self-structured way.

Orientation Problems

There were several younger former students who hadn't formulated goals or interests, and this was perhaps related to the circumstances under which they left Sudbury Valley. Their family situation caused their return to traditional educational institutions, although two of them would have preferred to remain at the school. Their dissatisfaction with the traditional schools and their apparently poor performances were contrasted with the better adjustment of those who personally elected to return to traditional schools and who were therefore more willing to tolerate conditions they did not like.

Job Hunting

Quite apart from the question of future professional or personal goals, the need or desire to find a job presented itself to many of the former students. For some of them the job was simply a means of supporting themselves while they pursued other interests. For others the job itself was more important. Many of them displayed a good deal of ingenuity in finding these jobs. And they were all able to get jobs when they needed them. One former student described lessons he had learned from job hunting:

> When you're looking for a job (except perhaps for positions I don't know anything about, professional positions) the only way to find a job is to walk in and ask for it, and to talk to exactly who you're going to be working for. Written applications are really meant to be filed away ... You want to walk in, present yourself, make a personal appearance, say you want the job, say you're really interested in the job, you're interested in learning some of their things. You could name a price at which they're afraid not to grab you because you're so cheap, or a price which infers that you do good work and are used to getting paid well for it.

I was struck by their determination to find out for themselves what kind of work they did or did not want to do, and to persist until they got what they wanted. They seemed to be undaunted by their ack of formal qualifications. Their belief in themselves enabled them to find entrances to positions that would have been closed to people with only an average amount of self-confidence and determination. Once they were in these situations, they continued to examine their actions and feelings, and did not hesitate to admit failure or disappointment, and make a change if necessary. Incidentally, this pattern of persistence and ingenuity seemed to be present also in those who were attempting to gain admission to various schools.

Relationship with the School

A number of former students reported that their initial impressions of the Sudbury Valley School were incomplete or incorrect. For example:

> The first time I came out to the school, I don't want to say I was overwhelmed, but it was really a little too much for me to stand. I got out here, and I was so used to ducking teachers from the public high school, and I was so used to trying to make myself look busy. I was in the smoking room listening to records one day, and I had my books. I was reading books on the Constitution. I was having a smoke. Dan walked in, and I grabbed one of my books and starting reading for fear that he would say something. It took me a while to realize what the story was. When I think of it now, it's ridiculous. I'm back in the public high school now, and I don't care what they see me doing. I don't care if they see me jumping off the roof. It really wouldn't make a hell of a lot of difference to me. I came here and really didn't know what the place was about. I came here with one idea and had that straightened out on me, and I went into a sort of depression about it, because I thought I was in the wrong place, and then after a while it began to dawn on me that it must be a good idea, not so much academically, for me anyhow, but just so that I could learn how to learn.

This student, incidentally, is the one who return to public high school to prepare for law school.

For some of them the school was simply an escape from a repressive educational environment:

> I wasn't so much looking for an alternative in education. I wasn't concerned with taking my own responsibility for my actions. I wasn't concerned with being a decent citizen or what I was going to do in the future. I just wanted to get out of the situation I was in, I was looking for an escape, and to be honest, if Sudbury Valley had just been another nice off-white liberal school, if I thought I could have gotten away with anything with them, I would have done it. I didn't realize what this school was all about until the middle of my second year. I knew when I heard about it and when I started visiting around here I couldn't get over the fact that I was going to be my own boss. I couldn't believe it. I kept saying, 'you mean I can really do this, I really can do that?' And of course, later on, when the school started the next year and I came here I knew — well, I had to test it out. So I was pushing, and there were a bunch of people doing the same

> thing. The first time they had ever had any freedom and the responsibility that goes with it. We all just had to push it to see how far it could go. Boy, we sure did ... There were about forty of us who were 'asked to withdraw,' that's how they phrased it. I don't really remember now how they did phrase it, but we were politely told to get out for a very good reason. We were ruining the school. We were killing it, strangling it. We completely ignored the basic concepts. We were just demanding to be speared and molded. Of course no one was about to do that for us, so when we did not get people to point the way and do things like that for us we started to fuck up, and we had no business coming here stoned on drugs. ... I went down to the Cape for about five days and sat on the beach and threw rocks and decided that — I still at that time didn't know what I had to do, but I knew that the people who were involved in this school and loved this school were a lot closer to the kind of person I wanted to be than anyone else, and that all my 'freak' friends hadn't helped me out and I sure as hell needed some help. I knew that. They weren't about to take me by the hand but they were still there. The presence of the people like Danny, and Hanna, Dennis — I was striking out at them all the time, but at the same time I knew without their presence — well, I just knew that that's where it was. In other words, I acted almost as if I hated them, but I didn't, it was just in me, I was just turning it outwards. I was hating what was in me. This may sound like the psychology of a twenty-five cent novel, but I really think that's what it was.

This student remained at Sudbury Valley for two years and left with strong positive feelings. As he put it, "I am just starting to realize what an amazing influence it had on my life. I think I learned more about living in the two years that I was here than I would have learned in ten because there was just no running away, there was no getting away from it. It was very hard to fool yourself because there was no one who was going to allow you to bullshit them."

In another case, hindsight was illuminating:

> While I was at the school I really felt that I was using the school to the fullest potential that I could, and when I left it I realized that it was anything but that, that I really felt sort of half way between being embarrassed and ashamed of what I had accomplished while being there. But then I look at it in a different way and say, well, if I hadn't gone to Sudbury Valley, I wouldn't be in the position I am now to look back and realize that. ... Maybe other people have found that they didn't completely comprehend Sudbury Valley until they left, because I know I didn't. I didn't really understand the whole reality of Sudbury Valley until I left it.

But for many others the initial image of the school struck a strong responsive chord:

> I read the literature (about the school). And I knew that these people were putting into practice a lot of the ideas that I had had since some time around the first grade when I was first going to regular school. I had hated it pretty much all along, was supposed to do very well, and I tested very well, and I did very badly all the way along. I was a classic underachiever. Just all the things that I hated about regular school and that I thought were immoral — it just really wasn't a decent way of treating people. And then from reading the catalogue and from visiting, I knew I wanted to go to Sudbury.

These remarks were made by the student who had been so perceptive in her reasons for not going to college right away.

Looking back on their experience at the Sudbury Valley School the former students expressed strong positive feelings. They seemed to have an interest and a bond that is not ordinarily found in relationships to traditional schools. These ties were partly personal and partly philosophical. One former student observed:

> I think I definitely feel a kinship with the institution, but I also feel one for the people I was with. But more than I would suspect with the institution, more than one would normally suspect, I really do. More with the staff than a lot of the students. It's funny. In other schools where I've only been able to have relationships with students out of school, I've developed much stronger relationships with students who have chosen to be my friends (there haven't been that many). But here where I've been able to talk and have friends here at school, it's been a different kind of thing totally. The people that are my friends at school I don't see as much, partly because they are so far away, but it is really strange. I don't know why. I guess you can form friendships in school that are totally different. I have a lot more friendships here. A lot of people that I wouldn't have chosen to be my friends have really opened my eyes to different kinds of people, much more than I would if I was just choosing friends. Because I'm here and I'm around them, and I hear them, and something will catch my interest that normally wouldn't have.

Many of the former students expressed strong feelings about being able to visit the school and to keep in contact with people they attended with. A number of them also wanted to help the school in some specific way, or were already doing so. And quite a few wanted to return to the school at some future date, either as students or in some teaching capacity. They did not expect the school to solicit their interest or to keep tabs on them. They felt that if there were things they wanted from the school, that they would pursue them independently. This is consistent with the overall atmosphere in the school.

In conclusion, I would like to say that after listening to these people talk about what they were doing, how they came to be doing it, and the factors and insights that went into their immediate or long-range plans, I found myself discarding my conventional expectations and looking at very different things — at qualities like self-awareness, initiative, motivation, responsibility, perseverance, patience and vision. But just as each person brings his own values, biases, and insights to what he reads and observes, it remains for each reader of these interviews to form his own observations and conclusions.

Appendix G

A STUDY OF FORMER STUDENTS

AT SUDBURY VALLEY

Done in 1975

by
Barbara Chase

(Sponsored by the Board of Trustees)

The Sudbury Valley School Press, S.C.
Winch Street
Framingham, Mass. 01701

Contents

Prefatory Note

At the meeting of February 12, 1974 it was decided that the Trustees would like to sponsor another study of former students. After Barbara Chase presented an outline of a proposed study to the Trustees' Meetings — October 8 and November 12, 1974 — the Trustees decided to sponsor the data collection phase of her work. Subsequently, at their meeting of June 11, 1975, after reading a draft of her study, including her data analysis, the Trustees voted to sponsor the study as a whole. Trustee sponsorship does not imply that the Trustees as a group necessarily endorse all of the conclusions that she has drawn in her study, but it does indicate that the study was initiated and carried out with the full official support of the Trustees.

Wallace Rubin, Secretary

Chapter I. Basic Facts About the Study

Several years ago, during the 1971-1972 school year, the Trustees sponsored a study of former students, the results of which were published by the SVS Press. At the time the Trustees expressed their intention to continue sponsoring studies from time to time in order to follow up longitudinally on the students that have already been surveyed and in order to gain new data on new students who leave in between each study. Ultimately, over a long period of years, the school hopes to accumulate data both from the development of the lives of our former students in early years and from an ever-growing number of students who leave in later years.

This is the second study and of course contains a much larger number of former students who were canvassed and a much larger number of respondents who answered.

The range of the study was defined by certain limiting dates. It tries to cover all students who were ever enrolled in the school and attended for any significant length of time, and who left (that is, whose enrollment period terminated between January 1, 1969 and December 31, 1974). Thus, the study covers a span of six years.

January 1, 1969 was picked as the early cutoff because there were very special problems associated with the students who left before that date in the early months of the school. As is well known, the school struggled with internal problems that finally were settled by the end of 1968. By January 1, 1969 all those people who had been involved in whatever controversies there were in the early days of the school and who were dissatisfied with the school had left. The terminal cutoff of December 31, 1974 was picked because the study was conducted in the winter of 1974-1975.

There were twelve persons who were technically "former students" but were not included in the data base. For each of the twelve there was a signed enrollment contract. However, three neither paid tuition nor ever attended; two attended at most a few days and were suspended for lack of attendance; one had her enrollment terminated by School Meeting for lack of attendance; five attended school no more than eight days; and the one remaining student not included was a part-time five year old who was technically withdrawn at the end of January 1969, but actually attended very little (if at all) after December 1968. Fortunately, it turns out that there is a clear distinction in the records between those aforementioned "students" who attended at most for a few days and were excluded from this study, and other students who attended briefly perhaps, but for at least several months. The dividing line is quite sharp between those who are included in this study as former students and the twelve who, it seems obvious, did not consider themselves students in the school.

I started by going to the archives of the school. I went through each folder, year by year, and gathered information available in the folder. The information was entered on a standard data sheet (see attached copy of the blank sheet) — or at least I entered as much information as I could find. It is possible that there might be some persons missing from this study whose files have completely disappeared from the school's archives. Midway through this study I learned of one such case, which I then included. The likelihood that this happened in many other cases is very small, since the files give the appearance of being quite complete and in good order.

Some basic statistics gathered from the files are summarized in Table 1. (Note that in Table 1, as in all the tables in this study, percentages — where included — will be found in brackets after the absolute numbers to which they refer.)

Table 1. Data Base for the Study

Total number of persons covered by the study	142	
Total number who left after up to 1 year of enrollment	83	[58%]
Total number who left after 1-2 years of enrollment	34	[24%]

Total number who left after 2-3 years of enrollment	17	[12%]
Total number who left after 3-4 years of enrollment	6	[4%]
Total number who left after 4-5 years of enrollment	1	[1%]
Total number who left after 5-6 years of enrollment	1	[1%]

Meanwhile a questionnaire was prepared for the survey. I first drew up a draft and presented it for consideration at the Board of Trustees' meeting in October 1974. There was further discussion, and a few additions were made to the original draft, at the November 1974 meeting, after which it was voted that I be authorized to proceed with the interviews based on the approved questionnaire, a copy of which is included on the next four pages.

Basically the rationale for the questionnaire was as follows. There were a lot of questions that were constantly being asked about former students by people in the school and outside of the school. I consulted with people around the school (like the Enrollment Clerk, the Visitors Clerk, and people in general), and I also called on my own experience during seven years of association with the school. These questions were put together, so that the questionnaire is essentially a compilation of unrelated questions, each of which has been of interest to various other persons over the years. The questionnaire is thus obviously flawed in the sense that it is not a scientifically constructed instrument.

On the other hand, it was felt to have considerable value to the school because it sought to answer questions that for one reason or another people associated with the school wanted to have answered. In addition, I continued to operate under a self-imposed restriction that had been operating in the earlier Trustees' study and reflected general school policy: highly personal questions, and direct questions about attitudes towards the school were expressly ruled out.

Given this questionnaire, this is how I proceeded. I first started by trying to locate each and every person from the information on the data sheet that I had taken from the files. I contacted as many people as possible by telephone. I informed each one of my study and invited him or her to come to the school for an interview. To each person unable to come to the school I mailed a questionnaire to be filled out and returned to me. To those I was unable to reach initially by telephone I wrote letters, inviting each one to the school for an interview. I also gave each one the option of telephoning me for an interview at the school or of filling out the questionnaire and returning it to me. A few persons (7) answered the questions over the phone; a few more (3) filled out questionnaires at school on days I was not present. I interviewed 34 at the school and received 56 answers by mail. Thus, all in all, I did manage to interview 41 personally, while the remaining 59 respondents filled out the forms in writing. There are three of these cases where direct contact with the former student was not possible, and a parent gave me what information he or she could. In some cases, with younger students, parents assisted in preparing answers. With these exceptions, all questionnaires were responded to personally by the former students being surveyed.

I spent a lot of time searching for people. In some cases I made several phone calls to different places and wrote to more than one address in order to locate a former student. As hard as I tried, I simply could not locate seven people. In cases where I did not receive an initial response, I kept after people by phone and by mail. In most cases where necessary I reminded people at least twice, in many cases three of four times. Since each round of reminders brought forth a few more respondents, I felt it was worth pressing the matter; however, the study did have to end sometime, so I decided not to issue more reminders after May 22, 1975.

Table 2 summarizes the data on the response rate.

Table 2. Data on the Responses to the Questionnaire
Out of a Total of 142 Persons covered by the Survey

Number whose present location could not be traced	7	[5%]
Number who were reached, but did not respond	35	[25%]
Number who responded	100	[70%]
Number reached who did not respond who were enrolled up to 1 year	27	[33%]
Number reached who did not respond who were enrolled 1-2 years	7	[21%]
Number reached who did not respond who were enrolled over 2 years	1	[4%]
Number reached who did not respond who had received SVS diplomas (out of a total of 36)	2	[5%]
Number of those in former study (out of a total of 21) who responded in this study	19	[91%]

In order to analyze the data the entire group was split into two basic age ranges which were treated separately — namely, the age range of students who left before age 17 and the age range of students who left at age 17 and up. The rationale for this separation developed as the study progressed. Those who left at age 17 and up knew that they didn't have to be in school any more (even if they did choose to continue). They were more on their own, more independent, had more choice of what they could do with their lives. Some didn't go back to school, some did go to other schools, some left with diplomas, some didn't, but they had one thing in common: they were legally more or less on their own, and their behavior was influenced by that fact. By contrast, those who left under the age of 17 generally had the feeling that they were expected to go on in school even though some of them didn't. Like any other artificial divide, this one is not perfect. A few of those in the under seventeen age group had an SVS diploma or were quite independent, so they would more naturally have fit in with the older group. However, the separation by age was found to be satisfactory overall, especially since it related easily to the kinds of categorizations generally made in the world of education outside SVS.

For the sake of clarity, I should explain that when I say a person is a certain age (for instance, 17 yrs.), I mean he is anywhere between 6 months after the previous birthday (age 16) and 6 months after that specified birthday (age 17). In other words, I considered a person is 17 yrs. old any time between the exact ages of 16 1/2 and 17 1/2 years. This accords with common usage. Thus when I say I divided students into two basic age groups, those who left before the age of 17 and those who left at age 17 and up, this means those who left before and after reaching exactly age 16 1/2, the exact age to which the law refers when it specifies how long a person needs to be in school.

Table 3. Respondents in the group who left before age 17

Number of persons who left before age 17	56	
Number of persons who responded	36	[64%]

Table 4 Respondents in the group who left age 17 and up

Number of persons who left age 17 and up	86	
Number of persons who responded	64	[74%]

The succeeding chapters will treat the two age groups separately. In addition I broke down the data for those who left before age seventeen into further subgroups in order to pick up differences in the various ages I thought would be interesting. I divided them into the different subgroups that are commonly used to divide age groups in the community at large — namely, those who left when they were still pre-school age, those who left when they were of primary school age, and those who left when considered middle or high school age. In addition, I also provided comprehensive data for all three subgroups together — in other words, for all those who left before the age of 17. The tables and data will be presented in the appropriate chapters.

After having had a lot of experience with the questionnaire, I thought it may be of interest to people contemplating further studies to know how I feel about it now. I already explained how the questions were drawn up and now, after having experience using them, I have the following feeling about what was useful and what wasn't.

Under the question "1.b. What have you done since leaving SVS? (1) schooling" it would have been helpful to ask for specifications such as whether enrolled full time or for specific courses, length of time enrolled, and whether degrees were sought or received.

Under the same questions, category "(2) job" it would have been helpful to ask for specifications such as length of time employed, employed full or part time, and whether the job is considered skilled or unskilled.

The question "1.b. (3) life experience" was the most misunderstood question; or, I should say, that many did not understand what information was desired by the question. In personal interviews I explained it in relation to answers I had previously received. Some people summarized what valuable insights they had learned from life; other people told me of specific experiences they had learned from. I feel the ambiguity of this question may have been beneficial in the sense that it presented the opportunity for much of the richness and creativity that is evident in the personal comments. For this reason, I cannot recommend any specific change in this question.

Under question "1.c. Did the fact that you attended SVS affect any specific opportunity for a job or school that you desired: Did your records or credentials bring forth any reaction, positive or negative? If so, how?" it would have been helpful, I believe, to have added after "negative," "or indifferent from administrators, teachers, or employers?" In some cases a person wrote about a reaction from a school or an employer but not always both, even when the person had applied both to a school and for a job. Now, there may not have been a reaction in each case, but I feel an extension of the question may have brought forth more information.

Questions 2.a (2) and 2.a. (3) were redundant and question 2.b. (3) didn't appear of much value. Predominantly the answer was "financial" but not otherwise informative. Questions 2.b. (4) and 2.b. (5) together served the same purpose. I would, therefore, have eliminated 2.a. (2) and 2.b. (3).

Aside from these few comments and recommendations, I feel the questionnaire worked well.

My personal experience with the interviews and my opportunity to meet personally with the respondents interviewed was most rewarding and informative. Basically, all of them were more than willing to answer all my questions. Many seemed to welcome the opportunity to talk to me and inform me of more than I asked. It was obvious to me from their openness that they trusted me because of my association with SVS.

Generally, they were articulate, confident and enthusiastic about their lives. Many of their answers were not given hurriedly. They were given a great deal of thought, and it was not uncommon for the person being interviewed to ask me to read back what he had said for further thought.

I had the distinct feeling from many that they were pleased to have been contacted by someone in the name of the school. When they came to the school to be interviewed, many chose to spend some time here and asked questions about the state and progress of the school.

THE SUDBURY VALLEY SCHOOL
1974-1975 TRUSTEES STUDY OF FORMER STUDENTS

Name____

Address(es) and phone numbers of latest enrollment form (or later document, if available)

Birth Date:

Dates of enrollment at school:

Diploma: yes ( ) no ( )

Apprenticeship, or school-sponsored work, if any:

Other official information of interest in school file, if any:

Objective questions:

a. What are you doing now?

b. What have you done since leaving SVS?
   (1) schooling

   (2) job

   (3) life experience

c. Did the fact that you attended SVS affect any specific opportunity for a job or school that you desired? Did your records or credentials bring forth any reaction, positive or negative? If so, how?

d. Do you find the fact that you attended SVS a factor, positive or negative, with your personal friends? If so, how?

e. Do you ever get together with others who attended school with you?

f. Have you ever visited school since leaving? Have you visited this past year (1973-1974)?

g. What is your present family status?

2. Additional questions

a. (1) Do you like what you're doing?

(2) Do you intend to continue?

(3) Do you intend to make a change?

(4) If so, do you have any idea what you're going to do next?

b. (1) Have you travelled or do you plan to?

(2) If so, for what reason?

(3) Is there a particular reason for living where you are?

(4) Do you plan to move in the near future?

(5) If so, for what reasons?

c. (1) Are you politically active? If so, how?

(2) Do you belong to any social groups or fraternal organizations?

Chapter II. Data for Respondents Who Left Before 17

Table 5. Breakdown According to Length of Time Enrolled at School Prior to Leaving, for Respondents Who Left Before Age 17 (total of 36)

Length of Time at School	Number	Percentage
Up to 1 year	23	[64%]
1-2 years	9	[25%]
2-3 years	3	[8%]
Over 5 years	1	[3%]

Table 6. Breakdown According to Age at Time of Leaving, for Respondents Who Left Before Age 17 (total of 36)

Age at Time of Leaving	Number	Percentage
Under 7 ("pre-school age")	10	[28%]
Between 7-12 ("primary age")	8	[22%]
Between 13-16 ("secondary age")	18	[50%]

Table 7. Detailed Breakdown According to Length of Time Enrolled and Age at Time of Leaving, for Respondents Who Left Before Age 17

Length of Time Enrolled	Under 7	Age 7-12	Age 13-16	Totals
Up to 1 year	8	5	10	23
1-2 years	2	3	4	9
2-3 years	0	0	3	3
5 plus years	0	0	1	1
Totals	10	8	18	36

"Pre-School Age"

Table 8. Present Educational Status of Respondents Who Left SVS Before Age 7 (total of 10)

Type of School	Number
Public School	9
Private School	1

Note 1. The one student presently in private school attended public school after SVS and prior to enrolling in private school.

Note 2. One of the students presently in public school was enrolled in a private special-education clinic after SVS.

Table 9. External Reactions to SVS Attendance, for Respondents Who Left Before Age 7 (total of 10)

Type of Reactions	Number
Positive reaction of school(s) attended after SVS	1
Negative reaction of school(s) attended after SVS	0
Indifferent reaction of school(s) attended after SVS	9
Positive reaction of friends	1
Negative reaction of friends	0
Indifferent reaction of friends	8

Note 1. In this Table, as in many Tables, not all respondents replied; also, some respondents provided more than one entry per person, as when several schools were attended.

Table 10. Relations to SVS after Leaving, for Respondent Who Left before Age 7 (total of 10)

Type of Relationships	Number
Saw other SVS students after leaving	8
Visited SVS after leaving	5

Note 1. "Former students who saw other SVS students after leaving" includes those who saw personal friends who happened to attend SVS, and includes those who saw former or present SVS students at any time after leaving (I cannot separate those who saw people right after they left and then lost contact).

Note 2. "Former students who visited SVS after leaving" includes all those who visited at all (once or more) since leaving, <u>except</u> that a visit for the purposes of this study or the previous study is not counted.

Table 11. Change and Mobility, for Respondents Who Left Before Age 7 (total of 10)

	Number
Like what they are doing now	6
Do not like what they are doing now	4
Have travelled	7
Plan to travel	1
Plan to move	2

Note 1. One respondent said he planned to change what he is doing, and knew what he would do next.

Note 2. Five of the seven who have travelled (or plan to travel) did so for purposes of "enjoyment," a category that includes such things as touring, curiosity, visiting friends and/or family, etc.

Note 3. A person can be entered as both having travelled and planning to travel (of course, he will appear only once in each category, that is, he doesn't get counted twice if he took two trips). Also, a person can have several reasons for travelling.

Note 4. One of the two planning to move is doing so in order to change life style; the other, to return to a former home town. Persons may have more than one reason for a move.

Table 12. Miscellaneous Data, for Respondents Who Left Before Age 7 (total of 10)

	Number
Held one or more paying jobs (or out-of-home volunteer jobs) after leaving	3
Politically active	1

"Primary Age"

Table 13. Present Educational Status of Respondents Who Left SVS Between Ages 7 and 12 (total of 8)

Type of School	Number
Public School	4
Private School	4

Note 1. One of the four students presently in private school lives abroad and has to attend a private English-speaking school because he is not fluent in the native tongue of his country of residence; this same student attended public school in the U.S. after SVS (but before going abroad).

Table 14. External Reactions to SVS Attendance, for Respondents Who Left SVS Between Ages 7 and 12 (total of 8)

Type of Reaction	Number
Positive reaction of school(s) attended after SVS	1
Negative reaction of school(s) attended after SVS	2
Indifferent reaction of school(s) attended after SVS	4
Positive reaction of friends	4
Negative reaction of friends	1
Indifferent reaction of friends	3
Positive reaction of employer	0
Negative reaction of employer	0
Indifferent reaction of employer	1

Table 15. Relations to SVS After Leaving, for Students Who Left Between Ages 7 and 12 (total of 8)

	Number
Saw other SVS students after leaving	4
Visited SVS after leaving	3

Note 1. See notes to Table 10.

Table 16. Change and Mobility, for Respondents Who Left SVS Between Ages 7 and 12 (total of 8)

	Number
Like what they are doing now	7
Do not like what they are doing now	1
Have travelled	6
Plan to travel	2
Plan to move	2

Note 1. Two of those who travelled or plan to travel did so for enjoyment; three specified other reasons, one of which was because of parents' work. Also, see notes 2 and 3 of Table 11.

Note 2. One person planned to move for bigger quarters, another for reason of work.

Table 17. Miscellaneous Data, for Respondents Who Left SVS Between Ages 7 and 12 (total of 8)

	Number
Held one or more paying jobs (or out-of-home volunteer jobs) after leaving	2
Politically active	2
Belong to groups or organizations	3

"Secondary Age"

Table 18. Educational Status of Respondents Who Left SVS Between 13 and 16 (total of 18)

	Number presently 13-16 (total of 7)	Number presently over 16 (total of 11)	Total Number (18)
Attended public school after leaving SVS	2	4	6
Presently in public school	2	2	4
Attended private school after leaving SVS	1	7	8
Presently in private school	1	6	8
Received high school diploma	0	4	4

Note 1. Of the six persons presently over 16 who are enrolled in private schools, two are in college and one is in the Museum School of Fine Arts; all three of these are post-high-school programs of study.

Note 2. One of the four high school diplomates received an SVS diploma.

Table 19. External Reactions to SVS Attendance, for Respondents Who Left SVS Between Ages 13-16 (total of 18)

Type of Reaction	Number
Positive reaction of school(s) attended after SVS	5
Negative reaction of school(s) attended after SVS	3
Indifferent reaction of school(s) attended after SVS	4
Positive reaction of friends	8
Negative reaction of friends	0
Indifferent reaction of friends	7
Positive reaction of employer	1
Negative reaction of employer	0
Indifferent reaction of employer	8

Table 20. Relations to SVS After Leaving, for Respondents Who Left SVS Between Ages 13-16 (total of 18)

	Number
Saw other SVS students after leaving	12
Visited SVS after leaving	9

Note 1. See notes to Table 10.

Table 21. Change and Mobility, for Respondents Who Left SVS Between Ages 13-16 (total of 18)

	Number
Like what they are doing now	11
Do not like what they are doing now	5
Indifferent to what they are doing now	2
Intending to make a change	11
Those intending to change who know what they will do next	9
Have travelled	14
Plan to travel	9
Plan to move	4

Note 1. Of those who travelled or plan to travel, thirteen did so for enjoyment, five for study or work, six for other reasons. Travel may be for one or more reasons. See also notes 2 and 3 of Table 11.

Note 2. One of those who planned to move did so for financial reasons.

Table 22. Miscellaneous Data, for Respondents Who Left SVS between Ages 12-16 (total of 18)

	Number
Held one or more paying jobs (or out-of-home volunteer jobs) since leaving	16
Politically active	7
Belong to groups or organizations	5

Table 23. Summary Table, for Educational Status of All Respondents Who Left SVS Before Age 17 (total of 36)

	Number	
Presently in public school	18	[50%]
Presently in private school	13	[36%]
Received high school diplomas	4	

Note 1. An additional four students attended public school after leaving SVS, but prior to enrolling into private institutions.

Note 2. Three of those attending private schools attend post-high-school institutions.

Table 24. Summary Table for External Reactions to SVS Attendance of All Respondents Who Left SVS Before Age 17 (total of 36)

	Number
Positive reaction of school(s) attended after SVS	7
Negative reaction of school(s) attended after SVS	5
Indifferent reaction of school(s) attended after SVS	17
Positive reaction of friends	13
Negative reaction of friends	1
Indifferent reaction of friends	18
Positive reaction of employer	1
Negative reaction of employer	0
Indifferent reaction of employer	9

Table 25. Summary Table, Relations to SVS After Leaving, for all Respondents Who Left SVS Before Age 17 (total of 36).

	Number	
Saw other students after leaving	24	[67%]
Visited SVS after leaving	17	[49%]

Note 1. See notes to Table 10.

Table 26. Summary Table, Change and Mobility, for All Respondents Who Left SVS Before Age 17 (total of 36)

	Number	
Like what they are doing now	24	[67%]
Do not like what they are doing now	10	[28%]
Indifferent to what they are doing now	2	[5%]
Intending to make a change	11	[30%]
Those intending to change who know what they will do next	9	[25%]
Have travelled	27	[75%]
Plan to travel	12	[33%]
Plan to move	8	[22%]

Note 1. See notes 2 and 3 to Table 11.

Table 27. Miscellaneous Data, for All Respondents Who Left SVS Before Age 17 (total of 36)

	Number	
Held one or more paying jobs (or out-of-home volunteer jobs) since leaving	21	[58%]
Politically active	10	[28%]
Belong to groups or organizations	8	[22%]

Chapter III. Data for Respondents who left Age 17 and Up

Table 28. Breakdown According to Length of Time Enrolled at SVS Prior to Leaving for Respondents Who Left Age 17 and Up (total of 64)

Length of Time at School	Number	Percentage
Up to 1 year	25	[39%]
1-2 years	19	[30%]
2-3 years	13	[20%]
3-4 years	6	[9%]
4-5 years	1	[2%]

Table 29. Breakdown According to Educational Situation at Time of Leaving, for Respondents Who Left Age 17 and Up (total of 64)

Status	Number	Percentage
Received SVS diploma	33	[52%]
Left SVS without diploma, but went right on to another school	6	[9%]
Left SVS without diploma, and went on to life	22	[34%]
Came to SVS with diploma ("adult" students)	3	[5%]

Table 30. Detailed Breakdown According to Length of Time Enrolled at SVS Prior to Leaving, and Educational Situation at Time of Leaving, for Respondents Who Left Age 17 and Up

	Situation upon leaving				
Length of time enrolled	Received SVS Diploma	Left, with-out dipl., but went right on to another school	Left, w/o dipl., went on to life	Came to SVS with dipl., (adult students)	Totals
Up to 1 year	2	6	15	2	25
1-2 years	12	0	6	1	19
2-3 years	12	0	1	0	13
3-4 years	6	0	0	0	6
4-5 years	1	0	0	0	1
Totals	33	6	22	3	64

Table 31. Schooling Subsequent to Leaving SVS, for Respondents Who Left Age 17 and Up (total of 64)

	Number
Attended publicly financed high school after SVS	3
Attended private high school after SVS	2

Attended publicly financed college as full-time student	14
Attended private college as full-time student	15
Attended technical or trade school as full time student	6
Had part-time instruction at college, trade school, or evening school (includes students who went full-time later or earlier)	21
Had instruction at only one school after SVS	20
Had instruction at more than one school after SVS	21
Presently full-time student at some school	21

Note 1. Table includes study abroad.

Note 2. All five of those who attended high school after SVS had been enrolled 1 year or less at SVS prior to leaving SVS.

Note 3. It is possible for the same individual to appear in different entries — for example, a person may be a full-time student at a public college and then transfer as a full-time student at a private college, in which case this person would be entered once under each category. The totals, therefore, do not necessarily add up to the total number of different individuals who attended college; the actual number of different individuals could be smaller than the total shown, because of double entries. See Table 32 for data on the number of different individuals.

Note 4. The following is an alphabetical list of colleges, technical, and trade schools at which former SVS students have been enrolled. The number in parentheses following the name of the school designates the number of former SVS students who attended, if more than one.

1. Bennington College
2. Berklee College of Music
3. Boston Architectural Center
4. Boston University (5)
5. Brandeis University
6. California School of Professional Psychology
7. Chamberlayne Jr. College
8. Cordon Bleu, London (2)
9. Curry College
10. Graham Jr. College
11. Greenfield Community College
12. Hairdressing School
13. Institute of Plastic Arts, San Juan, P.R.
14. Ithaca State College
15. Lansing Community College, Michigan
16. Los Angeles City College
17. Massachusetts Institute of Technology (2)
18. Michigan State University
19. New England Conservatory (2)
20. Northeastern Illinois University
21. Northeastern University (2)
22. St. John's Seminary College
23. Simon Fraser University, British Columbia, Canada
24. University of California at Los Angeles
25. University of Denver
26. University of Grenoble, France
27. University of Massachusetts (4)
28. University of Minnesota
29. University of Vermont
30. Vocational School — dressmaking
31. Washington State College
32. Youville School of Nursing, Cambridge

Table 32. Breakdown of Post-SVS Education According to Length of Time Enrolled at SVS, Respondents Who Left Age 17 and Up.

Number of years enrolled at SVS	Total number of students	Attended public or private college or technical or trade school, as full-time students	Number who had any formal instruction after SVS
Up to 1 year	25	8	15
1-2 years	19	9	11
2-3 years	13	8	8
3-4 years	6	3	6
4-5 years	1	1	1

Table 33. Those Who Did or Did Not Receive a High School Diploma, for Respondents Who Left Age 17 and Up (total of 64)

	Number	
Received SVS diploma	33	[52%]
Received equivalency diploma	4	[5%]
Received diploma from another school	3	[5%]
Came to SVS with diploma	3	[5%]
Have not received a diploma	21	[33%]

Note 1. Three people went on to full time post-graduate schooling without receiving a diploma; there is little likelihood that they will ever seek a high school diploma since their subsequent schooling would supersede their high school status.

Table 34. Detailed Breakdown of Those Who Did or Did Not Receive a High School Diploma, According to Number of Years Enrolled at SVS, for Respondents Who Left Age 17 and Up (total of 64)

Diploma Status

Length of time enrl'd	(1) Rec'd SVS dipl	(2) Rec'd equiva-lency dipl	(3) Rec'd dipl from other schl	Rec'd dipl from some-where (1+2+3)	Came to SVS with dipl	Did not receive dipl from anywhere	Totals
Up to 1 yr	2	3	3	8	2	15	25
1-2 yrs	12	1	0	13	1	5	19
2-3 yrs	12	0	0	12	0	1	13
3-4 yrs	6	0	0	6	0	0	6
4-5 yrs	1	0	0	1	0	0	1
Totals	33	4	3	40	3	21	64

Table 35. Employment Situation After Leaving School, for Respondents Who Left Age 17 and Up (total of 64)

	Number	Percentage
Held full-time job for any length of time (excludes self-employed)	50	[92%]
Held full-time job for a year or more	27	[42%]
Self-employed	7	[11%]
Held part-time job for any length of time	21	[33%]
Held any skilled job	41	[64%]
Held any managerial or executive level job	14	[22%]
Held two jobs (of any type, any length of time)	14	[22%]
Held three jobs (of any type, any length of time)	7	[11%]
Held four or more jobs (of any type, any length of time)	23	[36%]

Note 1. In cases where it is not known that employment was full-time, part-time or for a period of a year or more, it is not recorded.

Note 2. Jobs that many young people commonly hold such as home maintenance, child care, cooking, selling, and clerking are not counted skilled unless I have definite knowledge that a person is highly trained or experienced in that field.

Table 36. External Reactions to SVS Attendance, for Respondents Who Left SVS Age 17 and Up (total of 64)

Type of Reaction	Number
Positive reaction of school(s) attended after SVS	14
Negative reaction of school(s) attended after SVS	9
Indifferent reaction of school(s) attended after SVS	12
Positive reaction of friends	32
Negative reaction of friends	6
Indifferent reaction of friends	24
Positive reaction of employer	11
Negative reaction of employer	2
Indifferent reaction of employer	25

Table 37. Relations to SVS After Leaving, for Respondents Who Left Age 17 and Up (total of 64)

	Number	
Saw other SVS students after leaving	44	[69%]
Visited SVS after leaving	46	[72%]

Note 1. First line includes one who kept in touch over the phone.

Note 2. See notes to Table 10.

Table 38. Breakdown of Relations to SVS After Leaving, According to Length of Time Enrolled at School, for Respondents Who Left Age 17 and Up

	Relation to SVS	
Length of time enrolled, and total size of group	Saw other SVS students after leaving	Visited SVS after leaving
Up to 1 year (25)	15 [60%]	14 [56%]
1-2 years (19)	11 [58%]	14 [74%]
2-3 years (13)	11 [85%]	11 [85%]
3-4 years (6)	6 [100%]	6 [100%]
4-5 years (1)	1 [100%]	1 [100%]
Total	44	46

Table 39. Change and Mobility, for Respondents Who Left SVS Age 17 and Up (total of 64)

	Number	Percentage
Like what they are doing now	51	[80%]
Do not like what they are doing now	6	[9%]
Indifferent to what they are doing now	4	[6%]
Intending to make a change	30	[47%]
Those intending to change who know what they will do next	25	[39%]
Have travelled	60	[94%]
Plan to travel	27	[42%]
Travel (or plan to) for pleasure	45	
Travel (or plan to) for study or work	21	
Travel (or plan to) for other reasons	19	
Plan to move	29	

Note 1. Of those intending to make a change, it may be an internal or external change. It may also be a change in one aspect of one's life an not another.

Note 2. See notes 2 and 3 to Table 11.

Table 40. Miscellaneous Data, for Respondents Who Left Age 17 and Up (total of 64)

	Number	
Politically active	24	[38%]
Belong to groups or organizations	16	[25%]
Married	13	

Chapter IV. Noteworthy Personal Comments Volunteered by Respondents

In the course of reading the questionnaires and performing the interviews I gained a lot of information that went beyond the material that could be reduced to Tables. I was careful (as in the earlier Trustees' Study) not to solicit opinions on SVS, as this could easily appear to be self-serving. However, several people on their own volunteered reflections and comments. The completed questionnaires themselves are available for inspection in the school's files. Anyone is welcome to cull them for his own set of interesting quotations and impressions, but the following are the ones I found especially noteworthy and I think will be of interest to a wider public. For obvious reasons, I haven't identified the sources by name even though all the respondents knew that their responses would be in open files and wrote with that in mind. I have arranged the comments under a few general subject headings, and identified the sources only by age and length of time at school.

Thoughts Volunteered on SVS

At SVS I used to see H. who taught gymnastics. Dress-up corner in playroom ... I remember a boy who I didn't like, a year younger, mean to me ... when we went in dressing place it was all messy, and he came out and said we had to clean it up (we didn't) with two other girls. I remember playing on tree stumps.

enrolled 1 yr., left 6 yrs. ago at age 5

(I) remember going to the Boy Scout house way up on top of hill with friends, swimming in pond, playing out in the tree at the corner.

enrolled 1 yr., left 6 yrs. ago at age 6

I remember M.B. and a fetus pig someone was dissecting. I remember the nursery. I cried leaving M.B. ... because of SVS I have more interest in anatomy.

enrolled 1 yr., left 6 yrs. ago at age 7

SVS — something I'll never forget. School Meeting ... the way people talk to each other, the way they handle themselves at meetings. Trials ... something you don't see all the time ... effective, fair way ... maybe didn't help at first, but made an impression.

enrolled 2 yrs., left 5 yrs. ago at age 13

I have gotten my head together, and am much more stable than before. I definitely would not have gotten to this high point in life if it were not for SVS. I'm very glad I attended there. I feel that SVS really helped me a lot, but I think I was mostly recuperating from public school. I really needed that.

enrolled 1 yr., left 1 yr. ago at age 17

What this school did for me was give me time to get inspired. If I hadn't come here I would have probably continued routinely and not taken time to think. You learn you're capable of much more than you thought ... stamina, courage ... joy eliminates all that fear. I know what I can do. I know what kind of working situation I'm comfortable with, the kind of people I'm comfortable with. I didn't have any discipline. I knew it. I learned the importance of it ... it's not without its merit ... I had such distaste for it. If you can do it, you can do anything.

enrolled 2 yrs., left 2 yrs. ago at age 19

After leaving here, had a better view of how to learn from life ... using that (more or less like completing my education) every experience was a learning experience.

enrolled 1 yr., left 6 yrs. ago at age 18

If I hadn't gone to SVS when I did I feel I wouldn't have been able to cope with things as well now because it would have taken me longer to have a maturer viewpoint about life.

enrolled 1 yr., left 4 yrs. ago at age 17

The self-assurance I gained at the school I am sure had much to do with my getting jobs I desired.

enrolled 2 1/2 yrs., left 3 yrs ago at age 19

Interest and information gained at SVS always worked its way into things I did.

enrolled 1 yrs, left 5 yrs. ago at age 18

SVS broadened my personality ... a big part of my growth at that age. I could have gone either way ... I needed it.

enrolled 2 yrs., left 1 yr. ago at age 18

It affected me in sense I figured what I wanted. It made me realize I had more options, so I tried more things.

enrolled 2 yrs., left 2 yrs. ago at age 19

Educating myself here, I learned to face a situation when I needed a job.

enrolled 1 yr., left 4 yrs. ago at age 17

After SVS I found myself operating on a different level of social consciousness.

enrolled 1 yr., left 1 yr. ago at age 17

Made good friendships at SVS ... saw hope for education there ... some experiences incorporated in my short stories.

enrolled 1 yr., left 5 yrs ago at age 18

The fact I went here, I met a lot of friends I wouldn't have. One thing SVS gave me a new way to look at things ... related to people better.

enrolled 1 yrs., left 1 yr. ago at age 17

I feel being in a situation (where I was) treated more fairly ... (led to) treating other people more fairly. I lost a lot of social hang-ups you tend to pick up in traditional social situation.

enrolled 2 yrs, left 1 yr. ago at age 18

At SVS we learned to get along with people.

enrolled 3 yrs., left 3 yrs. ago at age 18

I have visited this past year, but not while school was in session. I enjoy walking the school's grounds and surrounding woods.

enrolled 2.5 yrs., left 4 yrs. ago at age 18

I don't really know how much effect SVS had on my life. It seems like a million years ago now. But sometime right around then I started getting into the person I am becoming now. I've gone through a lot of changes and a lot of learning, and Sudbury (Valley) is where most of it started.

enrolled 1 yr., left 4 yrs ago at age 18

I always try to make my friends believe in themselves instead of their teachers cause I learned to at SVS.

enrolled 2 yrs., left 5 yrs. ago at age 19

Going to SVS changed my life.

enrolled 1 yr., left 3 yrs. ago at age 21

Experiences in Other Schools

The second day of first grade, kids beat up on me. They still tease me. I cried and cried and cried. Now I ignore it ... it's now just like everyday talking.

enrolled 1 yr., left 5 yrs. ago at age 7

(In answer to the question, "Do you intend to continue what you are doing now?"), if I could figure out a way out of school, I wouldn't. Outside of that, I do. Do I have a choice?

enrolled 2 yrs., left 4 yrs. ago at age 6

(In answer to the question, "What are you doing now?"), Being bored in school.

enrolled 2 yrs., left 5 yrs. ago at age 12

When entering S.M. (another school), their first reaction was determination to get transcript ... very negative, said I wasted year of life. However, because of no transcript I was able to take equivalency tests and be placed at higher level than would have coming from traditional high school.

enrolled 1 yr., left 4 yrs. ago at age 15

The absence of grades, credits, or class records prohibited my attending a public high school, in that I would have had to acquire all 4 years of credits starting the year I enrolled (until I was 20 unless I went to summer school). (My present school) was no problem ... they felt SVS was an enriching experience and were glad to sit down and turn what I'd done at SVS into credits to see what more I needed to receive a diploma from them.

enrolled 5 yrs., left 1 yr. ago at age 16

Went back to high school for one term, almost made honor roll ... wanted to prove to myself if I could do it. I took all five English courses (the school has 78 to choose from). Diploma doesn't mean that much to me. I like to write.

enrolled 1 yr., left 4 yrs. ago at age 17

My admission to the U. of M. was based on a 20 page thesis I wrote about myself. They were a little worried about my background (what did you do in high school?).

enrolled 4 yrs., left 3 yrs. ago at age 18

Other schools' reaction positive because of other records and impressed because I knew what I was there for (directly because of SVS and thinking more about what I do).

enrolled 2 yrs., left 4 yrs. ago at age 18

When I applied for admission to F. College, I was questioned by a panel of faculty members. About 60% of my 2 hour interview dealt with my experience at SVS. Reaction was mixed but I received all their votes for admission.

enrolled 2 yrs., left 5 yrs. ago at age 19

Attitude of Others Toward SVS

If any factor positive or negative, it would be on the positive side because of the weight of the decision to attend and the fact that it seems to others that it was a learning experience (also some social prestige because "that sounds cool")

enrolled 2 yrs., left 4 yrs. ago at age 18

People very interested ... students, teachers, and others: "she's from SVS; let's find out what her views are and about her school."

enrolled 2 yrs., left 1 yr. ago at age 15

People are always asking me what it is like at SVS.

enrolled 1 yr., left 3 yrs. ago at age 16

Kids did look down on me when I first went there ... thought it was weird. It doesn't really have any effect on my friends now.

enrolled 3 yrs., left 4 yrs. ago at age 16

When I came here everyone thought I was trying to be a freak and they used to cut me down ... my friends at traditional high school. Now when I tell people that I went to a "free" school, it's very impressive. People love to have me talk about it ... can't believe there's a school like it.

enrolled 1 yrs., left 4 yrs. ago at age 15

My personal friends were not impressed. It is my idea that in my town they had really no idea of how things really were at SVS, and many of my friends thought I was wasting my time. This just confirmed my reasons that going to SVS was right for me. My whole circle of friends has been so changed that many of my present companions are very much interested and together about their thoughts.

enrolled 1 yrs., left 1 yr. ago at age 16

Reactions mixed ... often asked questions about structure and motivation: "Did you really have motivation? I doubt I could do it ..." Wondered it they could perform in such a place ... looked upon with some scorn, perhaps jealousy from those in public schools.

enrolled 1 yr., left 5 yrs. ago at age 18

There is one reaction that still surprises me a little. A girl I hadn't really known in jr. high (I knew her by name only, actually) was in a local mental hospital. She saw my name in the SVS catalog and recognized it. She called me and said she needed a friend. She figured that someone who would go to a place like SVS would be "good people" and might help her.

enrolled 1 yr., left 5 yrs ago at age 17

People in job situations have always been very interested in the school. I think it gets very positive reaction from people ... they see me as being perhaps more mature and more motivated.

enrolled 1 yr., left 5 yrs. ago at age 17

The fact that I attended SVS did bring about many questions. People were interested in the philosophy behind a school like SVS and there were reactions from both sides; but students' eyes "sparkled" at the thought of a learning atmosphere such as that at SVS. I think things have changed since then and schools like SVS are becoming more accepted everywhere.

enrolled 1 yr., left 3 yrs. ago at age 18

People at college were fascinated with my schooling. They saw something in me not in other students ... enthusiasm in me for life.

enrolled 3 yrs., left 3 yrs. ago at age 18

I, as of date, am the only student accepted by S.F. University with no grades, etc. They were quite impressed with SVS. The company I work for thought the idea of the school was very good and have given me a very responsible position and have bonded me up to $50,000.

enrolled 4 yrs., left 1 yr. ago at age 21

Many people are very curious and ask about the school's philosophy.

enrolled 3 yrs., left 4 yrs. ago at age 18

Some people impressed that I didn't go to regular school but tried something different ... hard for a person who hasn't gone through it to understand.

enrolled 1 yrs., left 3 yrs. ago at age 18

All my friends were very impressed and envious of my experiences there.

enrolled 1 yr., left 1 yr. ago at age 18

My liberal friends find it interesting in passing, where conservative friends, family, etc. consider it "a phase."

enrolled 2 yrs., left 5 yrs. ago at age 19

Friends of mine with children enjoy asking me about SVS. I've never noticed a friend of mine having a reaction that seemed negative.

enrolled 2 yrs., left 5 yrs. ago at age 19

My friends are beginning to think about raising families, and they are talking about alternative ways of raising and educating their children.

enrolled 2.5 yrs., left 3 yrs. ago at age 18

People take to me because of my different approach.

enrolled 3 yrs., left 3 yrs. ago at age 18

Parents now notice all the good that came from it. Parents notice my responsibility.

enrolled 2 yrs., left 4 yrs. ago at age 18

Last job supervisor ... thought it was probably good experience that I hadn't had to suffer as others do.

enrolled 1 yr., left 4 yrs. ago at age 17

Attitudes Towards Life

Happy to see so much of the country ... able to sell ... get rid of ... lot of stuff ... meant to do for a long time ... feel freer ... easy to travel.
enrolled 3 yrs., left 3 yrs. ago at age 16

I'd like to travel some more ... will look for job to earn money, will continue same cycle again ... like changes ... never will be too settled ... get bored or disgusted. Better to change for bad or worse than be stagnant in one place.
enrolled 3 yrs., left 3 yrs. ago at age 16

I like going different places, meet people and see how others live.
enrolled 3 yrs., left 4 yrs. ago at age 16

(I like) to meet and know people of all kinds.
enrolled 2 yrs., left 2 yrs. ago at age 16

As long as living in world, might as well see what it looks like; enjoy meeting people, too.
enrolled 2 yrs., left 5 yrs. ago at age 16

Travelled ... met a lot of people, learned different ways people live all through Europe.
enrolled 2 yrs., left 1 yr. ago at age 17

I spent a summer working ... I met lots of people and got paid for having fun.
enrolled 1 yr., left 1 yr. ago at age 16

Travelling constantly presents new experiences and situations that can be both exciting and educational. Above all I enjoy the incredible diversity of people I meet from all walks of life.
enrolled 3 yrs., left 4 yrs. ago at age 18

Like meeting new people, seeing different life styles, and having new experiences.
enrolled 1 yr., left 4 yrs. ago at age 17

Travelling gives insight to rest of world first-hand; gives increased awareness and understanding of what fellow men are doing and experiencing.
enrolled 3 yrs., left 3 yrs. ago at age 18

I like to see how people live everywhere. Life styles differ among different parts of the world; I'd like to see why and how.
enrolled 1 yrs., left 3 yrs. ago at age 18

I have travelled, though do not now feel that it is as necessary ... I don't need to go anywhere in order to get perspective on my environment, or in order to learn things. I was drawn to France as a dream that life could be finer, somehow, lived at a more beautiful level. It can, but not necessarily in France any more than in the U.S.
enrolled 3 yrs., left 4 yrs. ago at age 19

I think I could write a book on life experience gained after leaving SVS. I have met many types of people and come into contact with as many lifestyles and ideas. I have learned from each what I could. I have experienced many changes and will continue to do so until I die. I feel that life is meant to learn what can be learned and to continually seek self-improvement. The main thing and most important thing I have learned is that the only person who can do anything for me is myself. Things just don't happen by themselves. If you want to achieve any goals you set for yourself, then you yourself will have to set out to make things happen.

enrolled 1 yr., left 3 yrs. ago at age 18

Have far better relationship with my parents ... I understand them more, which is weird. I thought I was going out of my way to be open to them and realized when everything clicked that I wasn't and they were.

enrolled 1 yr., left 1 yr. ago at age 18

Never think there's only one way that something should be, because if you do the only place you'll ever get is where you are right now.

enrolled 1 yr., left 1 yr. ago at age 17

Organizations don't appeal to me. Cliques form and they don't appeal to me either. My social life is quite active and I just enjoy being me and meeting all types of people.

enrolled 1 yr., left 3 yrs. ago at age 18

My personal involvement with people has been deepened ... i learn from other people. I don't regret anything I've ever done. I try hard.

enrolled 1 yr., left 6 yrs. ago at age 18

It changed me ... before here I hated educated people.

enrolled 3 yrs., left 2 yrs. ago at age 18

SVS got me to learn to trust people and to be a friend, not an enemy.

enrolled 1 yr., left 1 yr. ago at age 17

The (military) isn't the best situation, but everything depends on what you make it. I try to get out of it what I can and although I state my opinions, I know I can not change the system. I'd be fighting the whole federal government and I sure wouldn't be helping myself ... so I use my judgement in dealing with various issues.

enrolled 1 yr., left 3 yrs. ago at age 18

I'm starting to see if I'm every going to do anything, I have to do it on my own.

enrolled 1 yr., left 4 yrs. ago at age 17

When I quit school (preparatory) and came to Boston for SVS and music school, I encountered a lot of problems. I didn't know where they came from. This school helped to bring them out too. I didn't want to run away from them, wanted to face them and fight them ... Now I feel free to move around ... nothing unknown can mess me up. Handling problems doesn't upset me anymore.

enrolled 2 yrs., left 3 yrs. ago at age 18

I am seeking a more personally fulfilling job. It is a transition period, which is always difficult, but I have confidence that I will keep looking until I find something good.

enrolled 4 yrs., left 2 yrs. ago at age 19

I like what I'm doing because I'll probably like it better tomorrow; future doesn't look dim.

enrolled 1 yr., left 5 yrs. ago at age 18

My means of income is also very interesting, not just income.

enrolled 2 yrs., left 4 yrs. ago at age 18

I'm moving in a direction that pleases me.

enrolled 2 yrs., left 5 yrs. ago at age 19

(In answer to the question, "Do you belong to organizations?") Nothing more formal than friends ... friends and lovers ... no organization!
enrolled 1 yr., left 3 yrs. ago at age 21

I love my life. For a while I thought I'm doing music or I'm doing nothing or I'm doing reading ... I'm learning this or that; now I think I'm living and I love it.
enrolled 2 yrs., left 5 yrs. ago at age 19

I wouldn't change any part of the way life is unfolding itself ... good or bad ... for me. I see the world as a great testing ground for my attitude or philosophy. If I don't like an experience, or feel "poisoned" by something really negative, it usually can be used in a very positive sense (the poison). I learn that way, and the form of what I am doing (at the moment, positive!) is less important than the fact that I like myself, basically.
enrolled 3 yrs., left 4 yrs. ago at age 19

Chapter V. Comments on the Significance of Some of the Data in the Tables

Basically the Tables speak for themselves and each person can draw his own conclusions as to their significance. I would like to share my own thoughts as to the significance of at least some of the salient points of these tables. I will refer to the table numbers of those tables I want to make comments on and comment on them one by one.

If anyone wants to get a better feeling for the nature of the replies and the kind of things each person said when he did reply, he can always see the raw data. It is preserved in the files of the school. The material is all there for each person to draw his own conclusions.

What I'm going to do in this chapter is just give some of the thoughts that occurred to me as I studied the data in the tables. People may be interested, since I've been working with the material so long.

In many of the cases the conclusions I will draw are ones many people in the school have felt to be true intuitively, based on everyday experience. People associated with the school have expressed many opinions about the school that they feel are basically valid. What is interesting is to find out that now there is some data to support these opinions — and occasionally to refute them!

Table 1 outlines the overall range of the study. The total number of former students accumulated during the six years is rather impressive for a school our size. We average some 24 students leaving each year, roughly a third of our student body — and since our numbers have so far been fairly constant, this means we average about the same number of new students each year. An unexpected statistic is the high percentage of former students who did not stay for more than one year, as well as the fact that fully 82% of the total did not stay for more than two years. The study is thus dealing with a highly transient population, and it will be some time yet before we will be old enough to garner significant information about long-range enrollees.

Table 2 is notable for the extremely good response rate it shows for this study. I did not know what to expect, but I did not expect such a high degree of cooperation. Only 8 people enrolled more than one year did not respond, only one enrolled over two years! Most of the non-respondents were in the up-to-one-year category (as would be expected). Almost all those covered in the earlier study responded, thus making a longitudinal study possible (though this has not yet been undertaken with the data at hand). It is also interesting that very few people could not be located even with the large number who spent a short period at SVS.

Tables 3 and 4 indicate that the response rate was somewhat higher for older former students. This may reflect more of the parents' attitude than the students' attitude, since the parental role is greater with the younger students. However, not too much should be made of this difference, which is fairly small; the response rate is quite high for all ages.

Table 5 The main feature of this table is that the students who leave at a young age (before graduating or being ready to go on to life) are usually those who have been at the school for a short time. Over half of them leave after being enrolled no more than one year; another large group leaves by the end of two years. What this suggests very strongly is that there are a lot of parents who are trying out the school for a certain length of time. For one reason or another they feel their children should have a year away from the regular schools or they feel they want to try something different. They seem to be giving the school a test, and for the most part people who are trying out the school have made up their mind by the end of a year. By the end of two years, the overwhelming number of people who are testing the school have made up their minds.

Since the table is dealing with younger students, we are probably seeing an effect that is mostly caused by parents. Of course, this is hard to establish because, in many cases, parents are following the lead of their children. Anyway, this table shows that the decision to stay or leave is usually made within one year, and almost always within two years. To be sure, there is a certain background number of students who leave because life just takes them somewhere else. Such an external factor can be expected to operate in just the same fashion regardless of time enrolled, and so to lead to more or less the same number of students being forced to leave after any number of years of enrollment. The extreme imbalance in these numbers who leave after one or two years suggests very strongly that people coming for a short time are testing the school. Though a few of these may have left for external factors, the weight of the numbers suggests that most came to try out the school.

What's noteworthy is that I've had such a high return rate to my questionnaire, even from people who came for a short time. The returns seem to reflect a feeling that whether or not people who were satisfied with the school and got what they wanted out of it, a large number felt it played a significant role in their educational lives.

Table 6 adds perspective to Table 5 by showing that about half of the experimenting is done by teenage students and that the rest are divided pretty evenly between the other two age groups. This verifies the prevalent feeling around the school that the school is often tried as an alternative for problem students, those who have become problems by the time they're teen age.

Table 7 gives more insight into the results of Table 5 and Table 6. About half of those who tested us for up to a year were teenage. It appears that those who are trying out the school at a pre-school level are essentially all in the up-to-one year category. There seem to be people who are willing to look into the school while their children are very young, before there's any real danger of exposing the child to a possibly negative influence; then they find out that the school does not have a satisfactory elementary studies program. This apparently doesn't take more than one year to find out; essentially all of the testing out takes no more than one year for pre-school students. Those who try out a second year are fewer in number and are fairly equally divided between elementary age and teenage students. All in all, the school obviously comes in for a heavy amount of testing.

The first set of tables deals with students who left school under age 7, while still of "pre-school age."

Table 8 shows very clearly that students who leave here under age 7 are attuned to public school education. This suggests that when they were testing out the school they were toying with the idea of an alternative mode of education, and that they were not just looking for a private school for their children.

Table 9 indicates that certainly as far as the youngest former students are concerned the fact of attendance at SVS occasions very little external reaction. Most people don't care what pre-school, nursery, or kindergarten a child goes to. Neither friends nor schools nor others pay much attention to where a child is in school in the early years.

Table 10 shows that there is some continued interest in the school on the part of the former students, but what must be realized is that a child this age is dependent on parents for transportation to the school and to see friends who don't live nearby. Therefore, continued student interest must be accompanied by parent approval.

Table 11 Probably the most noteworthy thing about this table is the number who don't like what they are doing now — basically, they are not enjoying school. Also interesting is the high degree of mobility of this group. This tells us something about the type of people who try out the school — they travel!

Table 12 is not particularly significant for this age group.

Now I move to a set of tables for people who left SVS at primary school age.

Table 13 shows that out of a total of eight, four (really five, as the note shows) are attuned to public school education. Again we find that the majority of people who come to the school are basically public school oriented, and are at SVS to try something different. It would be a worthwhile study to determine what those who went on to private schools were looking for — whether they were still continuing to look for an alternative to traditional education after failing to find a satisfactory one at SVS.

Table 14 At this age, where SVS has a more visible impact on the child's education (it's not like pre-school, as I mentioned before, where SVS is not considered all that different from other pre-schools) the different external reactions are more significant to note. As it happens, the predominant reaction is still indifference, but you do begin to get a certain amount of negative reaction from other schools to prior attendance at SVS. However, as a social factor, attendance at SVS has no significant negative influence. On the contrary, attendance at SVS begins to show up as something friends react to positively as worthy of comment and as a noteworthy curiosity.

Table 15 In this case, continued contact with SVS is relatively meager. Again, whether or not they come back and visit or have any future contact is largely dependent on parents. Perhaps we are seeing in this table the results of some parents' disillusionment and dissatisfaction with SVS.

Table 16 indicates that this group shows a high degree of satisfaction with what they are doing now. One can only wonder whether the experience these students had at SVS enabled them to make a better adjustment to their subsequent environment. At any rate, the SVS experience certainly did not ruin the future for these students — which answers a question often asked of us, whether students who attended SVS find it distasteful to go elsewhere later.

Again, we find a rather high degree of mobility in this group.

Table 17 Considering the age of the students concerned, one expects that if they're going to be group oriented, it would begin to show up at this age. It's probably noteworthy that only a small number of these people belong to any group or organization — something we should keep in mind.

Table 18 Now we enter the group of people who left the school during their early teens. It is noteworthy that one of this group received an SVS diploma; that exceptional case probably belongs in the next older group but was included here because I adhered to a breakdown by age.

In this table there are several things worth noting. We find a significant number who continued at private school after leaving SVS. However, some of these private schools are institutions of higher education. For example, of those who are of high school age now (13-16), two are in public school now out of a total of seven. One is in private school and four are not in school. Of those who are presently over 16, two are presently in public schools, three are in private secondary school, and three are in private post high school programs. The totals are pretty evenly divided between private and public schools. Again, it is clear that the kind of people who try out SVS are not necessarily those looking primarily for a private school.

Furthermore, in this group a significant number have not received a high school diploma. It is noteworthy that out of those who left SVS under 17 and are presently 17 and over (a total of 11 persons) only four have received a diploma. This again suggests something I noted earlier — that at that age we are getting a number of people who are trying out the school because they have run into difficulties in their previous schooling. When these students didn't find what they were looking for even at SVS, they did not for the most part go on to get a high school diploma quickly even if they did continue some schooling. To be sure, they may still be in the process of working for it, or they may have come back to school later. What this table reflects is, at the very least, an interruption in the normal, traditional course of schooling and graduation for this age group. It tends to confirm that for many of these students their SVS experience was not just another episode in a smooth process of schooling, but that coming here probably represented an attempt to change directions in a way that would help them out of a bind. To the extent that it didn't work out for them at SVS, they didn't find their place very quickly elsewhere either.

Table 19 picks up again what was picked up in the previous group: a certain amount of negative reaction from other schools. Actually percentage-wise the negative response is not very high; only three out of eighteen reported a negative reaction. What is even more interesting is that obviously quite a number of schools considered it noteworthy that the students tried out something different. SVS attendance again seems to exert no negative influence on social relationships and no measurable influence one way or another on employer relationships, which really begin to come into play for the first time with this age group.

Table 20 By now we are probably into the age group of persons who can make their own arrangements to visit school. About half of them do come back to visit — not much different from the younger group.

Table 21 reflects a rise in the number of people who are not satisfied with what they are doing now. It probably tends to confirm what I noted on the other tables, that we are dealing with a group in which a significant proportion are working their way out of problems, and they are still not satisfied with their situation now.

Again, a strikingly high mobility is revealed in this table. On the other hand, in the table as in others only a very small number are unstable as far as where they live is concerned. Just a small number plan to move.

Table 22 shows that a very high proportion of former students work or have worked. Obviously, these people do not have a negative attitude towards employment. Also, we see again (as in the younger group) that only a very small number are politically active or belong to groups or organizations.

Now we move to tables which summarize the data for the entire group of those who left under age 17. Although the results are merely the sums of earlier tables, it is illuminating to note some of the highlights that emerge for the group as a whole.

Table 23 makes it quite clear that a large majority of those who left SVS went to public school. Basically, when we take into account the notes, we see about 2/3 of the people involved at SVS going to public schools. It establishes quite clearly that the majority are people who would obviously like to fit into the public schools and were looking here for an acceptable alternative. I believe this is one of the significant findings of the study.

Table 24 emphasizes the fact that attendance at SVS has no significant effect on employment, on social relations with friends, or even on schooling. There is a certain small negative reaction of some schools to people who attended SVS, but there's a counterbalancing positive reaction of other schools; SVS attendance may be something of a handicap for a few people, and it may be something of a benefit for a few others. For the overwhelming majority it doesn't seem to make any difference. The same goes for social reactions, except that SVS attendance is even more of a positive factor, not a negative factor at all.

Table 25 points out that throughout the age group, about half of the people who tried out the school and left because they found it wanting (for one reason or another) feel — or their parents feel — enough of a relationship with the school to come back and see others associated with the school.

Table 26 shows that about a quarter of those who left are not satisfied with what they're doing now, and a little more than that are planning a change in their lives. Some two-thirds are satisfied with where they're at now.

A strikingly high percentage in the entire group are highly mobile and travel. Somehow I've come to feel that this fact is related to their attending this school. It just seems to fit that people who are looking for new horizons in education look for new horizons in where to be, look for new people, new experiences, etc. and tend to travel more. What direct implications this finding has for the school is hard to tell.

Finally, only a very small number, less than a quarter, show any lack of stability as far as their home location goes. They are not a particularly unstable group in that respect. That again tends to substantiate what we said much earlier, that the overwhelming majority of people who left didn't leave because they had to move, but because SVS wasn't what they were looking for.

Table 27 is interesting because of the stark way in which it verifies what an apolitical and non-group-oriented type the SVS student seems to be. The individualism that one would probably hypothetically associate with the school tends to bear itself out in former students' behavior in groups and organizations and in politics.

Now we move on to the tables in Chapter III that have to do with students who left at age 17 and up. This group is harder to characterize. Many of these students came to the school, got what they wanted, and left because they were moving on to other things in life — what is usually called "graduation." Other people came, were looking for something, didn't get it, and went elsewhere — to other schools, to jobs, etc. All these people of different circumstances are lumped together here, and it is quite difficult, if not impossible, to sort them out.

Table 28 points this out. About a third of the group stayed at the school no more than one year. About two-thirds of the group didn't stay more than two years. Now, it's not possible to say all of these two-thirds just came to try out a new school and left dissatisfied. That was very likely to be the case in the majority of cases in the earlier, younger groups. It wasn't uniformly true there either, but here it's not necessarily even generally the case. Many came here just to be here to do one or two years of schooling and then move on; it was what they wanted to do, and they got what they wanted. Nevertheless, we can see one thing from the table without any question: that in this age group many people who come don't stay very long. Either because of dissatisfaction or by design, most leave within one or two years. The group that comes in at teenage is not by and large a highly stable or lengthily continuous group in the school. Rather, this group provides a kind of leavening to the school. It provides new faces, new outlooks, new personalities, but with a high rate of turnover. Only a third of them seem to stay any considerable length of time. This has been the experience in the past. Whether this pattern will change with time, we will have to see.

Table 29 points up some of the general comments I was making earlier. About half of the entire group received an SVS diploma. It is not unreasonable to assume that most of that half came for something and got it — at least they got a diploma. In addition, it is reasonable to assume that many of those who went on to life without a diploma also got what they wanted out of the school.

Table 30 gives a more detailed breakdown of the material summarized in Tables 28 and 29. This actually puts into sharper focus a lot of my specific comments and deserves being looked at rather closely. If you work your way up from the bottom, you see that all of the students who left SVS age 17 and up who had been enrolled for 4-5 years or 3-4 years — every single one of those — received an SVS diploma. Again, it is safe to assume that virtually all of these students left after achieving a large part of their aims at the school. Even when you go to the group enrolled 2-3 years, eleven out of twelve received their diploma, and the other one didn't go to another school but went on to life. He was accepted at a post-graduate institution of learning and is presently enrolled full-time without having received a high school diploma of any kind. The point is that if you look at people enrolled for over 2 years, you see that essentially all of the 20 people probably got what they wanted out of the school. It's only when you get into the 1-2 year group that you begin to have some doubts about that. Two-thirds of the group received diplomas, the remainder went on to life. It is hard to tell how many of those didn't get what they wanted out of the school. On the other hand, the table shows very clearly that of those who came for up to one year, a very large number were experimenting. Only two out of 23 received an SVS diploma. At least half a dozen went right on to another school. One can postulate that they didn't get what they wanted here, and perhaps those who went on to life didn't get what they wanted either. I must stress that in all instances where I speculate on whether people got what they wanted out of the school, I am referring to their perception of their aims. It is of course true that many people received some degree of benefit from attendance at SVS (and perhaps some people received a degree of harm) regardless of whether or not they got what they were looking for overall.

Table 31 is rich in its implications. Many things that the school often says in its interviews and its speeches are obviously substantiated in the table. For example, many students have gone on from SVS to colleges and other post-graduate types of education. In fact, we have no record from the responses, or from any other source, of persons who tried to get a post-graduate education and were unable to. This table shows that a very large number obviously tried and succeeded. The list in Note 4 reveals a very wide spectrum of schools which former students have attended. We also find in this table that a sizeable number of students tried more than one school after leaving SVS, so that they seem to be ready to look around for what they want. Over half the total number had some formal post-graduate instruction somewhere.

A word of warning is in order about the kind of interpretations put on this table, which refers specifically to formal schooling. Allowance has to be made for people who have been doing all kinds of interesting things with their lives and consider them to be learning experiences. These experiences don't show up under formal schooling, nor does the table reflect people who are planning to go to school and have not yet done so.

One thing I learned form this is that we will have to wait a longer time, because I found that many people, after being out of school for a while, went to schools when they zeroed in on some idea of what they wanted to do. They then went to school later or they indicated some plans to go to school later. It's probably only in a study to be made in another 5-10 years that we'll get a deeper insight into how many people ultimately decided to get more formal schooling because they felt the need for it. It's probably also worthwhile in future studies (whereas it wasn't now, because the school is as yet too young) to start finding out if there were people who felt they wanted to get formal schooling but couldn't either because life had frustrated them, or events had frustrated them, or specifically if there were people who felt that their studies at SVS had acted as a detriment to further schooling, something which has not appeared as a factor in any interviews or feedback to date. This question should be looked into in the future.

Table 32 is the breakdown of one detail of Table 31 and is interesting simply because it shows that the percentage of students who seek full time education after leaving SVS (or any formal education after SVS) increases as the length of time enrolled at SVS increases. The table appears to indicate that longer exposure to SVS does not discourage, and indeed seems to encourage, people to continue with their education.

Remember that due to the length of time that has elapsed since the school was founded, we're not dealing with people who left SVS at age 17 and up who have been here all their school lives. The school is still too young to show its influence on lifelong attendees. What we are looking at for the most part is people who came here at teen age, and we find that the longer they stay here the more positive is their attitude toward education. I find this an encouraging fact, because the school often wonders what effect it has on people who come here at teen age and have had problems elsewhere. We are going to have to be careful in future studies to somehow distinguish between people who came here when they were teenage and left and people who came when they were young and spent more and more years here.

Table 33 It is not clear how many of those who have not received a diploma may go on to receive one in the future. Also three students who did not receive a diploma went on to post graduate schooling without a diploma. The diploma in itself is not always a significant factor. Note 1 should be read together with data of this table. What it comes down to is, regardless of how long students stayed at SVS, the majority either got a diploma sooner or later or went on to get what schooling they wanted or whatever they needed. For the remainder, the final results are still not in, and probably won't be for several years.

Table 34 points out again that in future studies we're going to have to look more deeply into people who came to SVS for just up to 1 year. This need emerges more and more clearly for all the age groups. It might be possible to institute an immediate follow-up study through an appropriate School Meeting Clerk of people who enroll up to 1 year and don't return. It might be worthwhile, as a regular feature of the school's record keeping, to try to find out from those who stay a short time why they leave the school. Such records would help us in judging what the results of these studies mean. Similar records for students who leave after any number of years might also be valuable. It seems to be the kind of information that is valuable to have, if we can get it and if people will volunteer it, as an additional tool to help sort out the data we get. I don't think it would be as valuable to go back and try to get this data from the early students, because the intervening time and life experience will certainly color the replies and render them less accurate and hence less useful.

Table 35 indicates that what we already saw traces of in the earlier age group is overwhelmingly obvious now, that people who have attended SVS are not only highly employable and work-oriented but in fact go out and work when they feel the need to. They don't seem to have any trouble getting work. The second part of the table shows that many are skilled. The rest of the table shows that a not insignificant number of them shop around until they find what they like. They're not afraid to look for something better when they're not satisfied. They're both highly employable and yet seem to be rather selective. This is very interesting since we're in the midst of a period that is highly unfavorable toward young people seeking employment.

Table 36 shows results that are pretty much similar to what was found in the younger age group. There is a rather small but significant negative reaction from other schools to prior SVS attendance, a higher number of positive reactions from other schools, and mostly indifference. Again, SVS seems to play very little role in a negative way socially or from employers. It seems to have a significant positive role socially and an occasional positive role from employers.

Table 37 shows that of this age group, a much higher percentage maintain contact with the school. The significance of this reaction is even larger because a considerable number in this age group move away from this area, so that the number who did maintain contact with SVS is somewhat over two-thirds of those who were physically able to do so. By and large, there seems to be an attitude of positive feelings toward the school after leaving. This is worth noting, because the school has not officially noted or methodically made use of this fact. Perhaps the school will now begin to find ways to make sure that continued contact with former students is nurtured and maintained. I already noted in Chapter I how willing the respondents were to cooperate. We see here that many former students continued to maintain contact on their own, thus indicating a reservoir of good will the school should cultivate.

Table 38 accentuates the results of Table 37 and shows quite clearly that again the longer people are here the closer are their ties to the school. Even though the comments made on Table 37 apply across the board, it seems to be sheer folly not to maintain close contacts with people who have been enrolled over a year.

Table 39 is really striking. A very high percentage of former students like what they are doing. Only 10% are not satisfied. Fully half of them are planning to make a change, and with most of those it's a calculated change. This doesn't necessarily reflect dissatisfaction with their way of life but rather progress of life.

Virtually all of them travelled. Their mobility is simply phenomenal. It's interesting to note how many travel because they want to see things, for pleasure.

In this group a high number plan to move, but one must realize we're dealing with persons at an age when they usually leave their parents' homes and begin to strike out on their own and build their own homes.

Table 40 again shows the individualistic nature of those who go to SVS. Only one-third are politically active at all. Just a very small number belong to groups and organizations.

In conclusion, I'd like to add from my own experience that it was often interesting to distinguish between people who had been here for different lengths of time. It does seem that as the school gets older and we have more former students, the complexity of separating out these strands is going to get greater. In future studies we will have to take into account the differing effects the school has on people who were here different lengths of time and who arrived at different stages of their lives and left for different reasons. Even if the questionnaires are kept fairly simple, they should be prepared in such a way as to take these factors into account.

I wish to express my gratitude to Dan Greenberg for his assistance.

Appendix H

Article Derived from the 1981-82 Study of Former Students

Reprinted from *The Sudbury Valley School Newsletter*, Vol. 11, No. 6 (April 1982)

* * * * * *

GOING TO COLLEGE: SIX FORMER STUDENTS

David Chanoff

In the December [ed.: 1981] issue of the Newsletter, a list was published of Sudbury Valley students who had gone to college or professional school. In a way there was nothing remarkable about the list; former students have gone on to a variety of schools, from professional institutions (chef's school, music school, art school) to community colleges, four year liberal arts schools, and universities. Some had dropped out to pursue careers, others were deep into graduate studies. It was the kind of list one would almost expect, conspicuous mainly for its inconspicuousness.

But the apparent ordinariness of this group of people is entirely misleading. In fact, they are very special, special in ways that make them interesting not just to families and friends, but to educators and developmentalists as well. Not one of the people on this list had anything like a standard high school education, and many didn't have standard junior high or elementary schools educations either. They have lived their early lives in a way that almost no other people have. In many essentials, their formative experiences have been different from those of both their parents and peers.

One question always asked about a group that differs from the norm is how they manage the business of integrating themselves into a society that has so many standardized expectations of what people at given stages of life should be like. In this regard, one area of special interest to many parents and older students is college admissions. It's comforting to know that Sudbury Valley students who want to attend college do go (often to the school of their first choice) and that they succeed once they are in. But just how does this happen? How do they manage it, without the transcripts, and more importantly, without the years and years of sitting behind desks and learning in the prescribed fashion. Recently, Peter Gray and I had the opportunity to talk with six former students who had gone on to college or professional studies. What follows is a description of why they decided on further education, how they prepared for it, how they gained admission, and how they managed once in school.

The first former student we talked to was L.B. who had come to Sudbury Valley from a Catholic girls' school at age sixteen and stayed for two and a half years before graduating. She had been an A student at her former school, but had left because she felt there was not enough of a challenge and that she was wasting her time.

During her enrollment at Sudbury Valley, L. focussed in on three areas that became increasingly more absorbing to her: singing, writing, and "helping people." She thinks that each of these three interests came in one way or another from her family, but she had not been aware of them before coming to Sudbury Valley. While at school though, she had the time to think a good deal about the directions she wanted to take, and these three gradually came into rather sharp focus. Music and writing in particular figured prominently in the full schedule of study and work she arranged for herself.

College, however, did not seem the best place to continue these pursuits, and after graduating, she went to work in a hospital for a year. At the end of that time, L. had saved enough money to move to Europe where she felt she would have the opportunity to write and sing, as well as learn a foreign language. Once in Europe she joined a folk rock group and spent the year singing professionally and writing, as well as studying.

By the end of the year, L. had learned enough about singing to realize she didn't want to make a career out of it. Moving back to the U.S., she held several jobs before deciding that, to achieve a satisfactory level of participation in public service, she needed a degree. Accordingly, she applied to an experience-oriented program at a state university and was accepted on the basis of letters of reference and her employment background. Admissions people were, she reported, quite interested in her Sudbury Valley experiences; the school was, if anything, an advantage.

Though L. had taken courses at SVS and had done a great deal of "academic work" on her own — reading, writing, and music — she had not specifically prepared for college in any way. Yet she found she could handle college level work successfully; in fact, she found that the state university, though beneficial, was hardly demanding.

After two years, L. again moved, this time to Australia, where she got enrolled at a traditional European-style university. She got in, not by going through standard admission procedures, but by managing an interview with the university president who was favorably impressed (no doubt by her perseverance, as much as anything) and recommended her to the chairman of the social science faculty. L. found the university work quite a bit more rigorous than she was used to and fiercely competitive in a way that her old state school had not been. Nevertheless, she responded to the demands and she did well. After a year, she returned to the U.S. and found work with a refugee resettlement agency while finishing up her degree at the state university.

At this point, L. is raising her family and looking forward to graduate work that will further her career goals in the helping profession. Singing and writing, she says, continue to be a large part of her life.

C.B. came to Sudbury Valley from public school at age 12. He too had been a good student with no particular school-related problems, but Sudbury Valley seemed to Both C. and his parents an exciting alternative and they decided to try it. The following year C. returned to public school for a brief time before re-enrolling at Sudbury Valley, where he stayed until graduating at age 18.

At SVS, C. spent almost all of his time socializing. He had a large group of friends with whom he shared the days in a relatively unplanned, spontaneous way. Whatever plans there were definitely did not include taking courses or working with staff members. "I;m glad I didn't," he said, "I simply had no interest at the time, none at all."

After graduating, C. worked at various jobs — cook, painter, insurance salesman, warehouseman, but none of them sustained his interest for long. He would learn everything there was to know quickly, and after that it was just a matter of time before he moved on. It was with the thought of finding something that would present a continuous opportunity to learn that, at age 23, he applied to college.

Choosing a local community college, C. experienced no trouble in getting accepted on the basis of interviews and letters of recommendation. Since he had taken no formal academic coursework during his five years at Sudbury Valley, he did have some initial anxieties about how he would do. He found, though, that with the exception of math, he was more than adequately prepared in each area. The math he made up in a remedial course. For the rest, "I can't think of one course where I lacked the facts that everybody else had." This preparation C. attributed mainly to reading extensively, one of the things he did at Sudbury Valley and continued to do afterward. "What the school did," he said, "was free my time so that I could use it to read." Beyond that, C. found himself with a distinct learning advantage: "I was," he commented, "interested in what I was doing. I had had the time to develop an interest and that made it a lot easier for me to retain what I learned. It was fun, and a lot of people right out of high school don't think it's fun. They think it's a chore."

From the community college, C. transferred to a state university where he is finishing his B.S. in earth sciences. He has already accepted a job and intends to go to graduate work once he has had sufficient field experience. Looking back, he believes that his love for the outdoors was fostered at Sudbury Valley where so much of his time was spent with friends, walking, hiking, skiing and exploring. The school allowed him to do exactly what he felt he needed to do between the ages of 13 and 18. "It was," he says, "the best thing that ever happened to me."

M.A. came to Sudbury Valley from public school at age 11 and graduated when he was 18. Like C., he did almost nothing in the way of formal coursework during his time at school. Very early on, though, he discovered an interest in piano (he had taken violin lessons from ages 6 to 10 and clearly had musical ability) and found himself regularly playing around on the school's two instruments, both by himself and in pickup groups with other musicians. Over a period of time, playing became a major activity, at home as well as at school. Formal lessons, however, never entered into what became an increasingly deeper, more mature involvement with music. "I got," he says, " a really good feel for the instrument simply by having it around. Whenever I had an idea, I could just play."

Sometime during his seventeenth year, M. realized that he was seriously committed to the piano, that he wanted to make a profession out of it. In our talk, it wasn't possible for him to articulate just how he came to this decision; it was the kind of decision perhaps that can never be fully understood. There was simply the recognition that the circumstances of his life had changed, and that he was ready to move, almost that he needed to move, in a more focussed, planned, future-oriented direction.

Applying to a leading school of contemporary music was one step in this direction. M. auditioned for several professional musicians from whom he got recommendations, and these, together with letters of reference from the SVS staff, proved sufficient. Although he had never studied piano formally, M. found that he had more than an adequate background: "I had been preparing myself all along, just by playing. Especially in composition. When I got to play around on the piano, I ended up playing my own music. It turned out that had discovered the structure of chords and many scales that are used in modern theory. And so, when I went to school, I was already prepared. The first year was especially easy because they were just giving me names for things that I already knew, that I had discovered myself."

An interesting sidenote to this is that while M. was at Sudbury Valley, we had on our staff an accomplished musician who worked closely with a number of students who subsequently went into professional careers. He and M. talked together occasionally, but M. felt that the teacher's understanding of classical theory was not what he needed at that time. Years later, when he was already in the middle of his career, M. did study the theory that had been available to him at school. "But at that time, I simply wasn't ready for it."

Moving into the high structured curriculum of the music school from the freedom at Sudbury Valley presented no special difficulties for M. "All the courses at music school were the things I wanted to learn ... the reason I was there was to get things they knew, that I wanted to know. So I didn't find people (faculty) at all threatening." M. stayed at the music school for two years before setting out on his own. Even now he still takes courses from time to time as part of his evolving career as a pianist, songwriter and composer.

J.W. came to Sudbury Valley at age seven after spending what she remembers as an uneventful first grade in public school. She graduated at age 19.

Unlike M., whose thoughts about the future did no coalesce until he was 17, a sense of focus, of planning, marked J.'s activities from very early on. She was always aware of thinking far ahead; it was, she said, almost a character trait of hers. Consequently, a good deal of what she did at school was colored by thoughts about how it might fit into some sort of overall life plan. She didn't have, at the age of nine, a well-defined idea of what she wanted her future to be, "but it was something I was working towards." Reflecting on how she went about this process, J. felt that "It's hard to say. At school you might be playing for half a year. But you were always, at least I was always, thinking about what I should be doing and how I should go about doing it. I was trying things out randomly, but I was thinking about them ... actually everybody does, even if they don't know they're doing it."

Over the years, J.'s activities became more centered and she experimented in some depth with several career possibilities. One interest that had developed long before Sudbury Valley and that continued to exert a strong attraction was art. Eventually, her ability in this area, together with a talent for making clothes, suggested costume and theatrical design as an avenue she wanted to explore. In preparing for applying to college, J. worked on her portfolio, adding material appropriate to theater design and eventually chose a state university with an outstanding reputation in fine and performing arts. Her portfolio, together with an interview and letters of recommendation, led to immediate acceptance. But as she looked around the school and talked to faculty on the day of her interview, J. was less than impressed. In particular, she was unhappy about the sequential course structure that would have made it impossible to do advanced work for two to three years. As she put it, "That was not really my idea of what I was going to do."

In reviewing her portfolio, J. realized that her work was mostly painting and so she began thinking seriously about finding an art school. Selecting several, she read their catalogues, visited, talked to students, and finally settled on one that seemed right. It also happened to be a prestigious and highly competitive school, but she sent in her portfolio and was accepted.

This school J. found enormously stimulating and she spent a productive and happy year there. At the same time, however, there were other areas she was still interested in trying out, including outdoor education and related subjects, and the professional school allowed her no time for anything other than art. While at SVS, a large chunk of J.'s life had been spent outdoors, skiing, hiking, camping, and she wanted to see if a career centered around the natural environment, something she loved as much as art, made sense. Consequently, she located a university that offered the courses and setting that she was looking for, applied, and was again accepted.

At the university, J. was faced with all of the standard liberal arts requirements. Her attitude towards these was quite similar to those of other Sudbury Valley graduates that we've talked to. She regarded college as something she had chosen freely, and in so doing had entered into a contractual arrangement, part of which included taking prescribed courses. She didn't regard them as a burden to be disposed of, but as opportunities to learn, which she had in a sense arranged for herself. An illustration of this attitude was J.'s approach to freshman writing, to which most freshmen would prefer a regimen of electric shock treatment.

("Accommodating myself to the traditional structure) was easy. It was amazing how easily it went. In writing, for example, the class had to hand in a paper a week. But I was interested in what I was doing, and interested in writing, and so I asked it I could hand in three papers a week. So I ended up writing a lot more than other students. I figured the more papers I wrote, the more feedback I'd get."

Other courses were also handled with confidence; but more, with an approach to learning based on a need to satisfy the demands of curiosity. "Whenever I don't understand something, or why the instructor is doing what he is doing, I go and talk to him ... I'm pretty forceful in what I want."

After two years at the university and what J. considered an adequate exploration of outdoors education and nature studies, she found that she remained deeply involved in fine arts. Again in line with the continued development of her interests, she has now transferred to another university which combines an excellent art department with substantial academic offerings in other areas she is anxious to investigate.

D. G. came to school at age six, graduating when she was 18. She was not aware of having consciously decided at some point to go to college; she always just assumed she would. There seemed, she said, two available options: either to develop a particular skill or talent or else to acquire sufficient education to do something interesting in life. The second of these led naturally to thoughts if college and (one might infer) to special consideration of a liberal arts program.

Although D. had, for a long time, seen college as a way of continuing and broadening her education, it wasn't until she was 16 that she began to prepare for it in a systematic way. At that point, her work became more focussed. For many years she had used the school in a way that had given her a general background. "I had done a lot of reading and had studied a language. I had gotten a general education in the humanities just by being with people at the school, always involved in conversations that were stimulating. I learned a great deal without even knowing it, about history and about what was going on in the world."

Her background in mathematics, however, was insufficient, and she began preparing herself in this subject and others specifically for the College Boards. At the same time she started sifting through college handbooks and catalogues and applied to several that she felt would suit her needs. It addition to taking both College Board aptitude and achievement tests, D. also had grades from a college level summer course she had taken. Recommendations from staff members rounded out her resume.

D. recalls the application process clearly:

> I wrote an essay on the school. It gave me a chance to describe Sudbury Valley and also gave me a good topic to write about. Perhaps it would be harder for large colleges to deal with my sort of application, but at small higher level schools, anything different will at least make them look. They are looking for people who can do their level of work and add something interesting to their student body. And so they're more apt to look at you than if you're just from a regular high school. At least that's my supposition. It's not enough to get you in, but it certainly opens the door.

In any event, D. was admitted to her first choice school, a highly regarded liberal arts college. Once there, the perceptions she had about the adequacy of her preparation proved accurate. In the humanities, she was able to immediately settle in to courses that looked interesting; but in math and science she was uncomfortable; she simply did not have the necessary background.

D. felt strongly that it is difficult to attain access to math and science at Sudbury Valley — in contrast to what she saw as the easy and natural availability of humanistic knowledge. Her explanation for this was that a great deal of the learning that goes on at the school is informal and incidental. It happens in the ordinary course of interacting with people who bring a variety of perspectives to bear on problems and among whom there is in-depth knowledge of different areas. Topics of discussion at school are just what they are in many informal situations. Talk tends to revolve around personal experiences, social problems, current events and the history behind them, films seen and concerts attended. It was much rarer, D. said, that conversations would center on scientific or mathematical ideas.

To remedy her lack in those areas, D. has enrolled in several basic level non-credit courses, although there are no requirements that she do so. Asked why, she replied, "I don't think everyone has to have a liberal arts education. But for myself, I feel I would have a more informed opinion on other things if I had a scientific background."

Her attitude toward learning in these areas is characteristic of her general approach: "I think I have a good attitude towards learning. I'm much more apt to go up to a teacher and say, 'look, I have a problem ... I don't know this and I want to know it. What can I do about it.' Teachers don't intimidate me whatsoever."

Adjusting to the structure and workload at her college after twelve years at Sudbury Valley has not proved problematic. For D., the actual class time is about the same as it was at SVS and, although a lot more work is required, it seems to her that "It is almost easier."

> The work I'm doing is harder academically, but it's as if the responsibility has been taken away from you. Everything is taken care of for you — your housing, what you're going to eat, what you're going to do with your time. I realize that this is not reality, but I Think some of the kids don't realize that. But, in a way, it's kind of nice. For me, it's the easiest way to learn a large amount of material.

At this point, D. has no definite professional plans. She seems instead to be following the idea that she's had for years, of achieving a broad general level of education. One area, though, that has interested her is service work. "I think one of the things I've gotten from school," she said, "is the idea that you can't do things for people. You can help them, but you can't do things for them. And that's the kind of attitude that I would bring to service-oriented work. And that is a different attitude than a lot of people have."

S.G. came to Sudbury Valley when he was eight, spent a year and a half back in public school and then reenrolled, graduating at age 18.

Although he had immersed himself in academic pursuits as well as other activities from his earliest years, at the time of his graduation, S. was not convinced that he wanted to go to college. After working for a year and a half, though, he made up his mind that college was the place to follow through on his interests, that it would be "more or less an extension of the way I had been thinking."

One interest was music. S. had taken piano lessons for a time when he was six, then dropped them until age 13 when he decided he wanted to improve his efficiency. It was through his formal lessons that he became interested in classical music, an interest that has developed greater intensity over the years.

It was more difficult for S. to trace the origin of this attraction to physics and math. Somewhere between the ages of 11 and 13 he began to take notice of physics, possibly through the extensive science fiction reading that he was doing (C.B., the earth science student, had also noted a large early consumption of science fiction). In mentioning this connection, though, S. noted its tenuousness, and commented on the complex role that reading can play in exposure and motivation:

> It's amazing the little bits of information you pick up when you're reading that have nothing whatsoever to do with what you're reading. You'll read a novel and it will have pieces of factual information in it ... if you see a reference in a book you're enjoying, it always makes you want to see what the reference is like.

In working on physics, S. would get together informally with a staff member who could answer his questions and he began going through textbooks. "I would," he said, "read textbooks and just try to work things out. It seems to stick better that way, at least for me. Because you have to go through the effort to follow the argument the writer is presenting, and you have to justify every step in your mind."

S.'s work on physics eventually evolved into a pattern: reading on his own, then periodically meeting with a staff member to clear up difficulties. Learning math was a necessary concomitant to understanding physics and S. used the same technique as he became knowledgeable on topics such as calculus and vectors. Along the way, there were several sources of assistance he could turn to, at home as well as at school. "But really," he said, "I tended to work on my own."

The school's major role, he felt, was that "it allowed me to do what I wanted to do, as opposed to making me take up my time with things other people thoughtI should do." Beyond that, S. considered the school's social environment to be of special importance, in much the same way as D.G. had: "It was just being around people who had different interests and who would talk about them. If you're around a lot of different people and you're exposed to a large variety of ideas, you reenforce each other."

S.'s only formal preparation for college admissions was a review of the SAT practice books, not as much to familiarize himself with the material, as to get an idea of the test format. His application included recommendations, test scores, and the personal essays that tend to be standard requirements. Accepted at his first choice school, a large Eastern university that offered both first rate math and science and conservatory music training, S. had what appears to be the universal experience among SVS students. The formal structure simply was not difficult to adjust to. Having been at Sudbury Valley, he felt, seemed "to make me more directed than others generally, more directed and more capable of concentration. And these features enabled me to pretty much take everything in stride."

Attitude, S. felt, was crucial in the ability to master college level work. In most areas he found that his academic preparation was quite adequate, but his approach to work was what he found set him apart from many of his friends.

> My attitude is that I'm going to college for fun, and I fully intend to enjoy myself by taking advantage of whatever it has to offer. The attitude of many people here is that they were corralled. The difference seems to allow me to catch up very quickly in areas where others may have more experience.

S. described the essence of learning in a way that each of the former students we spoke with had noted, each in his or her own way. "Attitude," he said, "is more important than substantive learning in every way. The substantive things are trivial to acquire."

In reflecting on these interviews, I found that my overall impression was one of confidence, of ability to get things done, of maturity. Moreover, these character traits had clearly been present while the former students were enrolled at the school. I found myself being drawn back to remarks like C.B.'s, that he was simply not ready for academic work at that time of his life (that is, from his thirteenth through his eighteenth birthdays); M.A.'s, that formal study of piano or music theory was not what he needed then; S.G.'s, that the school allowed him to use his time the way he felt it should be used. It had been surprising to hear that J.W. was thinking in terms of something like a life plan at the age of nine, and that C.B. wasn't, even at 18, but that he was sure he was doing what was right for him anyway.

These statements all suggested that the people who made them had felt very much in touch with themselves. At an early age, they had been making decisions that were important to their futures, decisions that at times were quite different from the advice they would have gotten (and were probably getting) from every side. Doing so seemed to have helped them gain the strength and confidence that were so evident in their adult personalities. In fact, perhaps what we were seeing was nothing more than the maturation of a sense of self that had been theirs all along. And perhaps the school's most important role was that it had enabled them to become aware of their own inner organization and had allowed them to begin patterning their lives accordingly.

On another level, there are several educational myths that the stories of these people should help put to a deserved rest. One is the myth that if certain things aren't learned at optimal times, then they will not be learned at all, or only with the greatest difficulty (this is the rationale behind the standard sequential curriculum). We find instead that the formal concepts required for algebra, for example, may be learned far earlier than is considered normal and that they may be equally well-learned far later. From these interviews, in fact, there doesn't appear to be any magic moment or age for any type of learning. Rather, the crucial factor seems to be ENGAGEMENT — the recognition by the individual that now he or she wants to have, or needs to have, a particular kind of knowledge, a special sort of mastery. And engagement, why it happens, when it happens, and where it happens, is a process that appears to be quite unpredictable.

Other myths too fall by the wayside: that without formal structure, students will not learn discipline, that they will lack motivation, that they will be unable to plan ahead, that they will look always to the shortest route to gratification than to distant more substantial goals.

These are myths that, of course, die hard. Coincidentally, as I write this, a copy of today's paper is on my desk headlining the discovery that grades are by far the most important factor in gaining admission to college. Myths do die hard. But as increasing numbers of former students make places for themselves in the worlds of education and work, the challenge that Sudbury Valley poses to standard educational thinking will become increasingly more substantial.

Appendix J

List of Materials Available from Sudbury Valley School Press

Following are some of the items offered by Sudbury Valley School Press. For a complete list and for information on prices and ordering, write Sudbury Valley School Press, 2 Winch Street, Framingham, MA 01701, or call (508) 877-3030.

THE SUDBURY VALLEY SCHOOL EXPERIENCE, 2nd ed.
A collection of essays, articles and vignettes describing the philosophy of Sudbury Valley School, its organization, and its atmosphere. An excellent introduction to the life and style of the school.

FREE AT LAST: THE SUDBURY VALLEY SCHOOL, 2nd ed.
By Daniel Greenberg
The spirit and flavor of daily life at Sudbury Valley School come alive in this book, written in a light anecdotal style. Illustrated with photographs by Michael Greenberg, Carol Palmer and Andy Brilliant.

A NEW LOOK AT SCHOOLS
By Daniel Greenberg
The continuing difficulties that schools are having in fulfilling their mission is analyzed against a broad background of cultural and socio-economic theory. An analysis is presented of the type of schooling appropriate to the future in the United States. Illustrated by Nancy Hann.

THE CRISIS IN AMERICAN EDUCATION: AN ANALYSIS AND A PROPOSAL
An educational classic written in 1970, this book discusses several central features of Sudbury Valley School's philosophy, set against the background of American social and political traditions and the current educational scene.

"ANNOUNCING A NEW SCHOOL . . .": A PERSONAL ACCOUNT OF THE BEGINNINGS OF THE SUDBURY VALLEY SCHOOL
By Daniel Greenberg
A history of the early planning for the school, and of the first year of the school's operation (1968-69) written by a member of the founding group.

OUTLINE OF A NEW PHILOSOPHY
By Daniel Greenberg
A presentation of the author's general philosophy, including an exposition on the philosophy of education. Limited Edition.

CHILD REARING
By Daniel Greenberg
Issues of parenting and child development presented in a philosophical framework harmonious with the principles underlying the Sudbury Valley School. Illustrated by Raphael Bouganim.

"AND NOW FOR SOMETHING COMPLETELY DIFFERENT": AN INTRODUCTION TO SUDBURY VALLEY SCHOOL
A twenty two page booklet summarizing the philosophy and practice of the school, designed for use by study groups and university classes.

ABOUT THE SUDBURY VALLEY SCHOOL
A booklet enumerating some of the key concepts that underlay the school when it was founded in 1968.

SUDBURY VALLEY SCHOOL HANDBOOK
A compilation of the school's corporate by-laws, corporate policies, the School Meeting Lawbook, and the current budget.

THE SUDBURY VALLEY SCHOOL NEWSLETTER
A periodical containing articles on educational and philosophical questions of current concern to the school. Free to students and parents.

A PARADIGM SHIFT IN EDUCATION (Audiotape)
Presentation by Daniel Greenberg to the Portland Democratic School Community describing the philosophy underlying the Sudbury Valley School.

RESPECT FOR STUDENTS (Audiotape)
A seminar on a key concept in self-directed education presented by Daniel Greenberg at Fresno Pacific College.

ORDER IN THE SCHOOL (Audiotape)
A seminar on setting up a fair judicial system presented by Daniel Greenberg at Fresno Pacific College.

WHAT SUDBURY VALLEY SCHOOL IS ABOUT (Videotape)
An interview with Daniel Greenberg for the State University of New York exploring many facets of the theory and practice of the school.

TELEVISED PROGRAMS FEATURING SUDBURY VALLEY SCHOOL (Videotape)
A compilation.

INTRODUCTION TO SUDBURY VALLEY SCHOOL
A ten minute video expressing the mood and atmosphere of Sudbury Valley.

NEW SCHOOL STARTER KIT
Designed to help individuals and groups who are considering starting new schools similar in approach to the Sudbury Valley School.